SACRED JOURNEYS

PATHS FOR THE NEW PILGRIM

SACRED JOURNEYS

PATHS FOR THE NEW PILGRIM

JENNIFER WESTWOOD

Gaia Books Limited

A GAIA ORIGINAL

*Books from Gaia celebrate the vision of Gaia,
the self-sustaining living Earth, and seek to help readers
live in greater personal and planetary harmony.*

Managing Editor	Pip Morgan
Project Editor	Katherine Pate
Project Designer	Lucy Guenot
Project Researcher	Helena Petre
Illustrators	Ann Savage and James Mealing
Picture Researcher	Elly Beintema
Production	Susan Walby and Lyn Kirby
Direction	Joss Pearson and Patrick Nugent

Spelling differences between the UK and USA pose
problems for publishers. The UK spellings of *colour,
honour,* and *favour* have been selected for use throughout this book. However, we have used the following US
spellings: *airplane, organize, medieval, fulfill,* and *center.*

First published in the United Kingdom in 1997 by
Gaia Books Ltd, 66 Charlotte Street, London W1P 1LR
and 20 High Street, Stroud, Gloucestershire GL5 1AS

ISBN 1-85675-004-3

A catalogue record of this book is available from the British Library.

Printed and Bound by LEGO SpA, Italy

10 9 8 7 6 5 4 3 2 1

The publishers have tried to trace the copyright holders of the
extracts in the text and apologize to anyone who has not been
acknowledged.

Author's acknowledgements
Thanks are due for the exceptional
support I have received from Gaia
Books in the persons of Pip Morgan,
Lucy Guenot, Katherine Pate, and
Helena Petre. They have been kind,
patient, forbearing, intuitive, and
efficient – more than an author should
ask or expect.

Our feature writers have been an
inspiration: I thank them for agreeing to
contribute. Particular thanks are due to
Marion Bowman and Tristan Gray
Hulse, both of whom have been
generous with their time. Others to
whom I am indebted are David
Benham, the Rev Phillip MacFadyen,
Roger Shaljean, and Mrs Jean Tsushima.
On the home front, Barbara Littlewood
gallantly came on pilgrimage as friend
and interpreter; Jonathan Westwood
Chandler, Stephen Brearley, Sharon
Fulcher, and Sophia Kingshill kept my
life running, and my husband Brian
Chandler contributed both material
support and constructive criticism.
They know what this book owes them.

✠

*This book is dedicated to
my fellow countywomen
Margery Kempe (b. 1364) and
Mother Julian (1342– c.1416),
one who went and one who stayed.*

✠

Publishers' acknowledgements
The publishers would like to thank:
Patrick Harpur, for helping us find our
bearings; Hazel Bell for the index; Anne
Brabyn; Centre Christian Bookshop,
Stroud; Jenny and Owen Dixon for
design assistance; Pomme Van Drie;
Ingrid Evjen; Gloucestershire Libraries;
Claire Hutchings; Mother Meera UK
Network; Dana Mynárová; National
Poetry Library London; Erik Ness;
Francesca Ovington; Deborah Pate;
Ben Petre; Stroud Bookshop; Václav
Tíchávsky; and for contributions to Part
Two: George Ballentyne; Beryl Dhanjal;
Fiona Eadie; Joanna Godfrey-Wood; Sue
Harper; Tara Holmes of the *Universe
Catholic Weekly*; Chris Hooker; Steve
Hurrell; Louise Jones; Kajetan Kasinski;
Sophia Kingshill; Graeme Lang; Jola
Malin; Keith Mitchell; Richard Newton;
Veronica Ross; Matt Wallis.

Contributors

Part I features illustrated personal accounts of pilgrimages and sacred journeys from the following people:

GŸLNAR BALTANOVA lectures in Philosophy at Kazan University in Russia. In 1991 she was among the first pilgrims from the former USSR permitted to go to Mecca.
Mecca pages 22–3

MARION BOWMAN lectures in the Study of Religions at Bath College of Higher Education, England.
Glastonbury pages 42–3
Sainte Anne de Beaupré pages 142–3

PROFESSOR DONALD COSENTINO is Professor of African and Caribbean Folklore at the University of California, Los Angeles, and editor of *African Arts* magazine.
Sodo pages 130–1
Plaine du Nord pages 196–7

CHARLES FLETCHER is a community health educator. He co-ordinates Wilderness Spirit Adventures, which leads treks to remote and sacred regions of the USA.
Chaco Canyon pages 118–19

TRISTAN GRAY HULSE is the Editor of *Source – the Holy Wells journal*, and is an authority on holy wells.
Saint Winifred's Well pages 186–7
Noyal-Pontivy page 209
Lourdes pages 210–11

JAMES HARPUR is a writer and poet. He is the author of *The Atlas of Sacred Places, A Vision of Comets* and *The Monk's Dream*.
Croagh Patrick pages 90–1

ROGER HOUSDEN is the author of *Sacred India* and *Retreat*. He is a director of Open Gate Journeys, which leads groups on sacred journeys to spiritual sites.
Benares pages 34–5
Mount Athos pages 62–3
Saint Catherine's Monastery pages 122–3
The Western Wall pages 162–3
Arunachala pages 178–9

SATISH KUMAR is editor of *Resurgence,* an international magazine which promotes ecological and spiritual thinking. He is the author of *No Destination.*
Canterbury pages 26–7

WALTER LOMBAERT lives and works at the Oikoten community in Belgium, which aims to provide alternatives for young people in special care.
Santiago de Compostela pages 70–1

NICHOLAS MANN is the author of *The Isle of Avalon* and co-author of *Giants of Gaia*. He lives in New Mexico.
Home dance of the Hopi pages 196–7

ALMUT MARTINI is an acupuncturist, homeopath, and medical doctor. She leads the Haus der Begegnung seminar centre in Bad Pyrmont, Germany.
The Externsteine pages 154–5

COLIN MCINTYRE is a journalist, former Company Commander of the Lovat Scouts, and author of *Monuments of War.*
War graves of the Somme pages 174–5

PAMELA MEIDELL directs the Atomic Mirror from her home in California, working with writers, artists, and film makers to create a nuclear-free world.
Atomic Mirror pages 98–9

MIKE NICHOLSON is an illustrator. He has contributed to several British newspapers including *The Times* and *The Guardian.*
Assisi pages 146–7

DR JAMES PRESTON is Professor of Anthropology and Chair of the Religious Studies Program at the State University of New York, specializing in Catholic devotions and shrines.
Blessed Kateri Tekakwitha pages 54–5

DR IAN READER is a researcher at the Nordic Institue for Asian Studies in Denmark. He is an authority on Japanese pilgrimage.
Shikoku pages 82–3

DR MAYA SUTTON lives in New Mexico. She co-ordinates Sacred and Megalithic Sacred Journeys, helping people to plan their own pilgrimages.
Our Lady of Guadalupe pages 134–5
Rocamadour page 210
Chimayó page 214

PATRICIA STOAT works as an information consultant and has studied Japanese and Oriental history.
Mount Kailash pages 78–9

NIGEL WATTS is a prize-winning British novelist and teacher of creative writing. His books include *Life Game, Billy Bayswater,* and *Twenty Twenty.*
Mother Meera pages 110–11

Contents

Foreword
by Martin Palmer

To undertake a pilgrimage is to place yourself at risk. Not just some of the physical risks, of which Part I of this unique book speaks, but a deeper risk. The risk that you might not return as the same person who set out. The risk that all that you had thought that you knew, understood, had perhaps carefully constructed in your mind, might be blown apart. In some of the pilgrimage accounts in this book you can hear so clearly how this has affected the writers.

But there is a second risk. The risk that you will be surprised by joy. That in entering into the physical and metaphysical world of the pilgrimage, you will encounter people, places, thoughts, feelings, visions, and happenings which take you beyond anything you might have imagined.

I say all this because you might start your journey as a tourist or sightseer, but only when you are prepared to chance the deepest dangers of risk or joy do you become a true pilgrim. And this relies upon a basic state of mind, beautifully described by T S Eliot in his poem "Little Gidding":

"You are not here to verify
Instruct yourself, or inform curiosity
Or carry report. You are here to kneel
Where prayer has been valid. ... "

I have been on many pilgrimages to many places of the world and in many different religious traditions, yet I can count on the fingers of one hand how many of these became true pilgrimages. They are the transforming ones. For example, I used to go regularly to Assisi in Italy when preparing for the pilgrimages and events of 1986 which launched the involvement of the world's major faiths in ecological action. But only once did it become a pilgrimage. My life then was in a state of great emotional turmoil and I wanted to go and pray before the shrine of St Francis himself. However upon entering the great basilica, I saw an altar cloth bearing the words: "You who sin, sin no more for me." I never made it to the saint's shrine. I didn't need to. And although I fought those words hard, they changed my life.

More recently I walked the old Celtic saints' path to Nevern in South Wales. I had been told to look out for one of the few remaining pilgrims' crosses, carved into a small rock face beside the path. When I reached the spot I eagerly, as an antiquarian, sought this cross, but to no avail. I walked up and down looking, searching, but saw nothing. As I was about to leave I found a kneeling stone, set close to the rock face, with two grooves worn into it by untold thousands of pilgrims having knelt here to pray. I knelt to join them and looked up to Heaven. That is when I saw the cross, carved into the living rock, as clear as could be!

Surprised by joy: this is how I would describe the effect of this quite outstanding book. I have read and looked at many books on the subject of journeys and pilgrimages but have never found one as excellent as this. For it combines wisdom with experience; it brings intimacy to vast issues and brings alive the lived reality of the sacred journey. It reminds us all that the actual environment through which we move, is sacred, sacred land in its truest sense. And it knows that making such journeys is costly, risky, and unpredictable.

True pilgrimage changes lives. At some point in the late Middle Ages, an ancestor of mine undertook a pilgrimage to the Holy Land of Palestine and came back bearing a palm leaf as witness to his exploits. It so changed his life that he became known as a palmer – one who bore the palm leaf as testimony to pilgrimage. This is where my surname comes from. That one journey still echoes through time to this day.

But I had one worry about this book. Page after page reveals places of extraordinary power and awe. Places where Heaven and Earth touch and in touching change reality. Places that draw you close to the face of God, whoever and whatever you believe that to be. Yet few of us will be able to visit more than a handful of these places in a life time. Most will never make one of these sacred journeys. Does this mean pilgrimage is impossible? The answer is no. Pilgrimage, the sacred journey, is possible without walking the road to Benares, Taishan, Jerusalem, or Mecca. Let an old Muslim story illustrate this.

There once was a man, Fazlun, who had saved and saved all his life in order to go on pilgrimage to Mecca with his friends. At last the great day came. But the night before, his neighbours' house burnt down. Fazlun had to look after them so he told his friends to go on and he would see them in Mecca. He was almost ready the next day when a stranger was attacked in the town and left penniless and naked and in distress. Fazlun took him in and cared for him. Then an old lady in his street fell ill and having no family, turned to Fazlun for help. Soon his money was all spent and the time had passed so he was unable to get to Mecca on time.

When his friends returned, Fazlun asked them how it had been and what they had seen. His friends were amused, and told him "It was wonderful. But you know this. You were there, being given the places of highest honour!" God had honoured Fazlun's journey of compassion and generosity. Fazlun had made the pilgrimage of love and faith.

This inner journey – so often spoken of in this book – is perhaps, when all is said and done, the true sacred journey. For many years I have had a special devotion to the Chinese goddess of compassion Kuan Yin. I have frequently visited China and have tried on a number of occasions to visit her sacred mountain, Pu To, an island set in the eastern seas off China. Yet I have never made it. Now I realize that I probably never will. Just as we will probably never visit, you and I, most of the wonderful and awe-ful places described in this book. How do we make sense of this? For me the answer comes from a sixteenth century Chinese Buddhist master, Han Shan Te Ch'ing. To appreciate what he means, simply substitute the manifestation of the Divine most important to you and the destination of the sacred journey you most desire to undertake. Then go into the world with a new understanding.

"You don't have to go to the East Sea to meet Kuan Yin. Pu To is in your mind."

A journey of faith
Bangladeshi pilgrims cheerfully tolerate danger as they return from a Muslim prayer festival.

Martin Palmer is Director of the International Consultancy on Religion, Education and Culture (ICOREC), Manchester, UK, religious adviser to WWF–UK, and head of the Sacred Land project – rehallowing the environment of Britain.

Introduction

When I was first asked to write Part I of this book, I hesitated. Accustomed to writing about ancient places from the point of view of the myths and legends attached to them, rather than any sacred use today, I thought I had nothing to say about pilgrimage. The only thing in my favour seemed to be that I had spent a lot of time on the business of getting to sacred places – temples, shrines, churches, stone circles, standing stones, tombs.

Also, because of the nature of pilgrimage, there was not much possibility of following the normal procedure in writing about folklore: stand back from the material, keep your commentary on what you see as free of subjective interpretation as possible. Writing any other way seemed exposing. But, as some of the other contributors found, pilgrimage only becomes a truly revelatory experience once you start looking from inside out and not from outside in.

In the end it came down to trust. I had worked with Pip Morgan, Managing Editor of Gaia Books, before, and learned to trust him absolutely. Between us we decided that I would treat the entire writing process as a pilgrimage. Although the research began much earlier, I started writing in May during a pilgrimage to Les Saintes-Maries-de-la-Mer in the Camargue, France, and finished within days of returning there for the October Grand Pélérinage des Saintes Maries Jacobé et Salomé.

There were other pilgrimages in between, including a magical one to the cave at Sainte-Baume in Provence, France, in silent, primeval forest, where Mary Magdalene is said to have lived as a hermit for thirty years, clothed only in her hair. For me, participating in pilgrimage, and watching and reading about other people's participation, stirred up many issues. Much of the documentation made painful reading from the humanitarian point of view, and there was necessarily some rummaging around in my own belief-system. I am not a practising member of any faith, and was surprised at how upset I was at uncovering some of my own beliefs.

> Every man and woman has two journeys to make through life. There is the outer journey, with its various incidents, and the milestones of youth, marriage, middle age, and senility. There is also an inner journey, a spiritual Odyssey, with a secret history of its own.
>
> W R Inge,
> More Lay Thoughts of a Dean (1931)

Jewish legend says that the Rock of Jerusalem (now under the Dome of the Rock) is the foundation stone of the world. King David came upon it when building the Temple and the rock warned him not to move it. It said that the world had once started slipping through the hole that lay beneath it into the waters under the earth – the chaos of pre-existence. Only the rock's action in plugging the hole prevented the whole world sliding into this chaos.

This legend has manifold meanings: at one level it seems to be speaking of religion itself, at another of Judaism, at another of the operations of the human mind. Certainly, the turbulence that uncovering hidden beliefs creates is like chaos welling up when the rock has been lifted. My pilgrim road has not been smooth, and I don't expect yours to be: I see this as a major benefit.

AIMS AND METHODS

Pilgrimage exists in a multitude of variations. For all the work religious historians, anthropologists, sociologists, and geographers have devoted to it in recent decades, there seems as yet no clear picture of the nature and extent of the wood. For my part, I am content to show you the beauty and individuality of some of the trees.

Part I discusses issues raised by pilgrimage generally. The material is drawn from anthropologists and others writing over the past forty years, mainly from the world religions, within most of which there is a long tradition of individual pilgrims testifying to their experiences. Not

The spiritual quest
By renouncing the material world,
Buddhist monks free themselves
to confront the spiritual world.
The Buddha prescribed pilgrimage
as an important act of the
Buddhist's life – a first step on
the path to enlightenment.

all the pilgrimage places I mention are necessarily open to those who do not share the religion practised at the shrine. Having said that, I have used examples mainly from world religions which have some pilgrimage shrines open to those of other faiths, rather than from tribal and ecstatic religions, whose rites are normally closed.

If you wish to observe or join in a pilgrimage outside your own locality, remember that pilgrimages to local shrines are often private community events. For example, a Portuguese *romaria* may involve only a single village in celebrating its patron saint who symbolizes the community and is the focus of its sense of identity. To put it bluntly, local people may not want you there.

On a more general note, visitors *en masse* physically damage sites. Minor ancient monuments and small-scale landscape features such as holy wells and wayside crosses and tombs often cannot sustain the annual descent of even moderate numbers of people. However, I do not subscribe to the elitist view that the "public" should be denied access. We must compromise, so I ask you to treat every sacred landscape (however humdrum) with the reverence that the Japanese poet Issa (1763–1827) accorded Mount Kamji, the Shinto holy hill in the inner precincts of the Ise Shrine:

> "Kamji Yama.
> My head bent
> Of itself."

Because it is the very nature of pilgrimage to stand slightly to one side of organized religion, some of the practices I describe in Part I and the quotations I have chosen to illustrate its themes may displease orthodox practitioners. Nothing is intended to offend.

ATTITUDES AND DISCOVERIES

In 1994, the body of a fifteenth-century pilgrim, with rough robe and staff, was found buried in Worcester Cathedral, England. To me, the discovery of his remains is more touching than are some real-life pilgrims, in the same way as souvenirs of medieval Christian pilgrimage – amulets, holy water flasks, and pilgrim badges – seem more attractive than most modern pilgrim souvenirs. This is partly because I am conditioned by my British background, which places emphasis on traditional and conservative values, to see them in an approving way.

It is easy to patronize pilgrimage. Holy places the world over are often artistically more mediocre and

gaudier than Western aesthetics can accommodate. Saint Bernadette, seeing the statue of the Blessed Virgin made for the grotto at Lourdes, exclaimed, "My God, how you deface her!" But, really, what is "taste" in this context? The Lourdes statue may not be great art, but how could human hands represent the transcendental beauty of Bernadette's vision? The creators of the greatest religious art in the world cannot give us more than the faintest foreshadowing of divinity – not even the cave painters of Lascaux in France and Altamira in Spain, nor the carvers of the Cycladic deities of ancient Greece with their "archaic smiles". As an aid to focussing the mind on God, for the right person the most sentimental statue of the Sacred Heart may be as effective as a Michelangelo sculpture.

When we see the souvenir shops that line the streets leading to the shrine at Lourdes, we need to see the rosaries, medals, T-shirts, statues, and pictures in the light of the function they will serve: as gifts of love, as badges of religious devotion and affiliation. Often the objects pilgrims buy become the focus of shrines in the family home, reminders of the sacred journey and in some cases (as with water from the spring at Lourdes) representing the transfer into the home of the power of the holy place visited.

Patronage extends to too easily dismissing others' beliefs. You may have read of the "miraculous aubergine" discovered by Zahid and Farida Kassam, which brought

Sacred journeyers

The Japanese pilgrim to Shikoku (left), the three women making the rocky ascent of the Irish holy mountain, Croagh Patrick (above), and the Tibetan pilgrim with his begging bowl (p. 14), are all engaged in a physical journey, which at a deeper level leads them to spiritual awareness.

thousands of Muslims to what the British newspaper, *The Guardian,* of 28 March 1990 described as "a terrace house in the back streets of Leicester". (The journalist seems to be implying that these people live in humble circumstances, so what can you expect?) The story behind this is that, when the aubergine was sliced, the Kassams saw that the seed pattern read in Arabic "*Yah-Allah*", "Allah is everywhere". Though there is a tradition dating at least from ancient Greek times of the names of deities appearing in plants, to my mind it is missing the point to read this as "superstition". What is important is Mrs Kassam's description: "It is a miracle. This has happened to an ordinary family, that is why I am very proud of it. Allah never forgets anybody."

This devout and human remark echoes the belief at the center of every pilgrimage: that there can be direct communication between the individual and God.

We have to learn to accommodate the fact that the sanctity of pilgrimage shrines is often underpinned by a chain of reasoning that we would not accept in any other context. You may have read that images depicting the Virgin of Loreto have been carried on historic flights, including Lindbergh's crossing of the Atlantic in the "Spirit of St Louis" in 1927, and the 1969 Apollo 9 space mission. This is because in 1920, Pope Benedict XIV proclaimed the Virgin of Loreto the patron saint of air

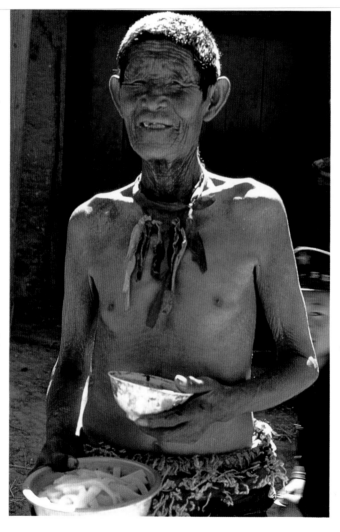

travellers. You may not know that the connection between the Virgin of Loreto and aviators arises from the original reason for Loreto's existence as a pilgrimage place: the Sancta Casa (Holy House), now encased in marble within the basilica. According to tradition, the Sancta Casa was the Virgin Mary's house at Nazareth, which on 10 May 1291 was carried by angels first to Tersatto near Fiume (Rijeka, in the former Yugoslavia), and finally, on 2 December 1295, to the Italian town of Loreto. Miracles took place there, and in 1507 Pope Julius II approved the Holy House as an object of pilgrimage.

This story of the Holy House's coming to Loreto, first recorded in Italian around 1472, received the caveat from Pope Julius "*ut pie creditur et fama*" – "as is piously and traditionally believed". In other words, he left it an open question as to whether or not the story was a pious fiction. This does not alter the fact that the association of the Virgin of Loreto with aviation rests on the story of the flying angels, and on the magical principle that "like produces like". We no longer think like this, so should we say (as many do) that the Holy House is just a symbol, that it is the Virgin and not the Holy House that is potent? But then why come to Loreto? Why don't aviators carry holy medals from Guadalupe or Lourdes?

Pilgrimage shrines worldwide raise similar questions: we have each of us to accommodate the meanings attached to pilgrimage sites to our own belief systems.

SIGNS ON THE HORIZONS

You will have noticed that I usually say "pilgrimage" rather than "sacred journey". To me, they mean the same thing, and I see no reason to use two words where one would do. On the same grounds I say "God" rather than using some circumlocution such as "the divine principle". These are the words for sacred journey and deity in my culture: brought up in a Christian country, I naturally use the vocabulary of Christianity to describe religion.

This implies nothing about my personal beliefs, and you, the reader, should substitute words that you are comfortable with. Anyone worried that the word "God" necessarily implies a male figure, should read Mother Julian of Norwich's *Revelations of Divine Love* (c. 1393) where this medieval mystic uses the word "mother" in addressing Christ.

If I hold any belief with conviction, it is roughly this. Muslim writers have seen one category of seekers after God as *salik* or wayfarers, whom God guides on the active way through asceticism and prayer. Their journey begins with learning to read the "signs on the horizon" – developing an awareness of the effects of God's actions in the world. "O God," wrote the ninth-century Egyptian mystic Dhu 'l-Nun "I never hearken to the voices of the beasts or the rustle of the trees, the splashing of waters or the song of birds, the whistling of the wind or the rumble of thunder, but I sense in them a testimony to Thy unity ... O God I acknowledge thee in the proof of thy handiwork and the evidence of thy acts ..."

I once experienced a literal "sign on the horizon". It was in the Finger Lakes district of New York State, US, and I was heading north. Suddenly I noticed a great

> I am not of this world nor of the next ...
> I have seen that the two worlds are one:
> One I seek, One I know, One I see, One I call ...
> If once in this world I win a moment with thee,
> I will trample on both worlds,
> I will dance in triumph forever.
>
> *Jala al-din Rumi (d. 1273),*
> Divani Shamsi Tabiz *trans R A Nicholson*

black scribble that began as a black dot and gradually sprawled across the sky as if someone were writing his signature: God's handwriting. It was like being at Belshazzar's Feast (The Bible, Daniel 5), and I was very apprehensive. Of course, it was only wild geese flying south for the winter. I'd never before witnessed their migration. But now that I have seen and pondered it, I know what Dhu 'l-Nun meant by "evidence of thy acts".

There is rather more to this than the simple thought that "Nature" is a wonderful thing and someone must have made it. While theologians through the ages have been troubled by the question of whether God is immanent (implicit in the universe) or transcendent (totally separated), the folk experience of divinity is not far removed from that of the solitary Hindu mystic who experiences oneness by reaching into the inner core, the *atman*, that he believes exists identically in all creation.

There is in myth and folklore a running theme of "Universal Sympathy" – that all things resonate together, and a pang that is experienced in one part of the universe will be experienced in the rest. It often takes the form of universal lamentation at the death of a god – the Greek Pan, the Norse Balder, even Christ. The orthodox Christian tradition that at the Crucifixion "the sun was darkened, and the veil of the temple was rent" (The Bible, Luke 23: 45) was matched in folk tradition with the belief that the whole world wept. And to balance the tears, the sun dances on Easter Morning with joy at the Resurrection; and at midnight on Christmas Eve, cattle kneel reverentially in their stalls, the bees hum in their hives, and the Holy Thorn blooms at Glastonbury.

What these traditions are saying is affect the part and you affect the whole. All things are one. It is almost a commonplace today that physicists have arrived at much the same conclusion: all creation is inter-connected. I stand with them.

PART I

The Pilgrim's Path

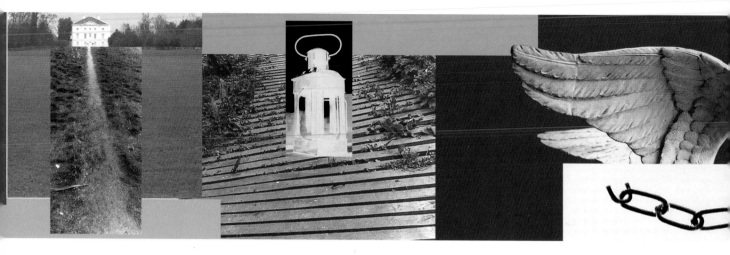

Longing

CHAPTER 1

The greatest regular assemblies of human beings on earth are those of pilgrims. They arrive in their tens of thousands for Holy Week in Rome, Passover in Jerusalem, and at Mecca there gathers annually over a million of the faithful from every part of the Islamic world. The Kumbha Mela, celebrated every twelve years at the river confluence at Allahabad in India, draws over ten million people.

Why do they come in such numbers? What is it that they seek? Why in all ages and all over the

world have people felt this same desire to set
out, launch themselves as it were from a spring-
board out of their normal lives and familiar places
on a journey into the unknown? The answer
seems to be that, to whatever faith they belong,
wherever their footsteps are directed, and
whichever immediate reasons they give for going,
at bottom all pilgrimages spring from an inborn
yearning for an encounter with the divine. This
yearning is compounded of the desire to reverence deity in its own special place and the hope
of persuading it to pay heed to individual prayer.

Sharing the common lot of people the world over and throughout recorded history – conflict, suffering, and death – all spiritual seekers ask, and all religions try to answer the same fundamental, impossible question: Why? We are all, from the moment we are born until the moment that we die, engaged in this search for meaning. Pilgrimage to a special place, where the divine pierces through the mundane, holds out the promise of help and comfort in this world, and of a living encounter with deity.

THE PLACE

First, the place. For Hindu mystics and for Sufis, this sacred place is within themselves: their pilgrimage is a journey with no physical movement, but a personal seeking within mind and body. For others, the sacred place may have a physical existence but the journey there be symbolic, as when medieval Christian pilgrims trod the foot mazes on the floors of cathedrals known as the "Path to Jerusalem".

Not even all real journeys had a geographic goal. The word "pilgrim" comes from the Latin *peregrinus*, meaning a wanderer or stranger, and early Christians saw pilgrimage as the search for a place of exile. On his landing in Cornwall, England, in the sixth century, the hermit St Meriasek exclaimed: "Jesus be thanked, to a foreign country here have I come ... " Detaching themselves from their roots, they chose to live as in every place a stranger, trading the fleeting companionship of this world in exchange for the everlasting company of the blessed in Heaven.

The idea of pilgrimage as a journey with no fixed goal is illustrated in the ninth-century *Voyage of St Bréanainn* (Brendan). This fantastical account describes a sea voyage by the sixth-century Irish saint who, with fourteen of his monks, embarked in a boat covered with oxhides and sailed westward, entrusting their fate to God. After seven years, they finally came to a marvellous island called the Land of Promise, after which they sailed home. Not all St Bréanainn's monks survived the adventure: his *Voyage* is partly based on mythic voyages to the Otherworld by Irish heroes such as Maol Dúin (Maeldun), and the journey to the Land of Promise is a metaphor for death.

Though Bréanainn's voyage is mainly fantasy, it also echoes the real-life practice of Irish monks such as the three – Dubslane, Machbethu, and Maelinmun – who in 891 landed in Cornwall and went to the court of King Alfred the Great, having cast themselves off from Ireland in a coracle without any oars "because they wished for the love of God to be in foreign lands, they cared not where". Similarly the European palmers of the Middle Ages roamed from place to place, and the Japanese beggar pilgrims of Edo wander from shrine to shrine on a pilgrimage that lasts the whole of their lives. Pilgrimage has become a metaphor for life itself, the journey we set out on the moment we are born, the road to the Otherworld, the Celestial City.

But most pilgrims make real, purposeful journeys, temporarily abandoning their normal lives to travel, often in great hardship, to a particular place. Though these places may have acquired their reputations for sanctity for different reasons, all seem to pilgrims to offer the possibility of closer contact with the divine. Often this springs from the deep-seated belief that a deity or saint is eternally accessible at the point where he or she lived or visited or appeared. Though the faithful can pray to the Blessed Virgin for help in any church, they believe that she is most likely to answer their prayers where she has manifested herself on earth, in such places as Fátima, Lourdes, and Guadalupe.

Particularly holy in pilgrims' eyes are places that prophets and saints knew in their lifetimes. The earliest Christian pilgrims sought out the Holy Land and the scenes of Christ's life and Passion. In the same way Hindu pilgrims are drawn to places where human saints or *avataras* (deities who have descended to earth) have dwelt, and the four most sacred Buddhist pilgrimage sites in India are places that have direct associations with the life of the Buddha.

Especially potent is the place where the saint or deity trod and left a permanent footprint. At the church in Rome that medieval pilgrims knew as the Palmalle, they could see the mark of Christ's foot, which was impressed on the marble when He appeared to St Peter before his execution. Another sacred footprint has made Sri Pada in Sri Lanka a more universal pilgrimage center even than Jerusalem. The footprint on the peak is said by Buddhists to be that of Buddha, by Hindus to be that of Shiva, by Christians St Thomas, Apostle of the Indians, and by Muslims Adam, the first man.

Pilgrims also eagerly seek the shrines of dead holy people and saints. The Jewish *Lives of the Prophets* from around AD50 gives the location of numerous tombs of Jewish saints. The Pilgrim of Bordeaux, whose *Itinerary*, from AD333, is the earliest description of a pilgrimage

"Alone in my little hut without a human being in my company, dear has been the pilgrimage before going to meet death".

IRISH HERMIT, 8TH/9TH CENTURY

to the Holy Land to have come down to us, visited more sites connected with the Old Testament of the Bible than with the New. Probably Christian pilgrimage grew out of the Jewish practice of visiting the tombs of prophets and saints. The Jewish followers of Jesus, who regarded him as "a prophet mighty in deed and word", would have found it natural to preserve his tomb as a site to which they could come as pilgrims. Islam also preserves the shrine–tombs of its saints, where miracles are asked of them.

To medieval Christian pilgrims, and still to some Christians today, the tombs of saints and the relics they contained were so nearly identical with the saints' living presence that spiritual benefit might be passed to the pilgrim by contact with them. The practice of sleeping

Holy area boundary
Secondary roads
Main arterial roads
Pedestrian route

Mosque
Car park

From Mecca to Arafat is
approximately 12 miles.

Uniting in a single belief

❰ I had read a lot about the Hajj, its rituals, obligations, and prohibitions. But because of the lack of information about the very few people who had journeyed to Mecca from the atheist USSR, I had some misconceptions. One of these was that it was forbidden for women. I never dreamed that I would be able to perform it twice: first, the Hajj proper, with my father in 1993, and then the Umrah ("little pilgrimage") with my mother in 1995.

This second pilgrimage was both the more interesting journey, and the more meritorious from the Muslim point of view. We performed it during Ramadan, the season of fasting, and were told by our Imam that Umrah during Ramadan is equivalent to the pilgrimage made with the prophet Mohammed. We travelled from Kazan by bus, a journey of more than nine days of non-stop driving and fasting. We crossed Western Russia, Ukraine, Romania, Bulgaria, Turkey, Syria, Jordan, and part of Saudi Arabia without the comforts of long stops, hotels, or hot meals.

The first group of pilgrims (men only) from Tartarstan had journeyed to Mecca in 1992. The following year my father and I joined a group of 170 pilgrims from Tartarstan and several other republics of the former USSR. Everything was new to us! We had been brought up under the banner of state atheism and lived in a secular society where no distinctions existed in any sphere of life between men and women. We were accustomed to having independence and the freedom to make our own decisions.

Thus, for most of us, the Hajj came as a culture shock. It was our first experience of the fully fledged Muslim way of life, and many of us were unprepared. To start with, though views differ on this question, most modern Islamic scholars insist that women participating in the Hajj must be accompanied by either their husbands or some close male relative – father, brother, or son. For Russian women this proved very difficult: many are single, and as the journey is expensive, few families can afford to send more than one member on the pilgrimage.

This rule is not without good reason: the Hajj is very strenuous physically. For instance, women are permitted to approach and kiss the black stone of the Ka'ba, but in the overcrowded mosque it is often physically impossible for a woman to do so. Moreover, some rituals can only be performed by men. For example, the Talbiya (sacred formula) has to be spoken out loud, but women are not permitted to speak in the presence of strange men.

When we first set out, given our preconceptions, we were surprised to find that nearly half of our group were women. We were even more surprised to discover that women constitute half of all pilgrims on the Hajj. We were amazed, too, to see how many young pilgrims there were, since the Hajj is traditionally performed by older people.

The Hajj begins with entering the state of *ihram* (ritual purity), which has both a spiritual and material aspect. For women, *ihram* means wearing a long white dress and veil covering the head. Nothing must emphasize the woman's figure: in fact, she must hide her age, beauty, and physical merits. Any man in the street is entitled to upbraid her if she infringes this rule.

Rituals of the Hajj

Before they arrive in Mecca pilgrims wash and dress in white to enter the state of *ihram* (purity). In Mecca they first visit the sacred Mosque, washing again before entering. There they circle the Ka'ba seven times anticlockwise and kiss the black stone. Then at the well of Zamzam they drink water before walking seven times between the hills of Safa and Marwa. At Arafat, where Mohammed preached his last sermon, they pray until sunset. The following day an animal sacrifice at Mina celebrates Eid-ul-Adha and pilgrims throw stones at pillars in a symbolic rejection of evil. Finally they return to Mecca to circle the Ka'ba again.

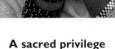

A sacred privilege

The Koran says that it is the duty of all Muslims to go to Mecca, provided that they can afford to do so. Pilgrims on the Hajj regard themselves as privileged, and pray for their less fortunate friends and relatives who have not be able to accompany them.

MUZDALIFAH

ARAFAT

Despite the difficulties and the patience needed to complete the rituals, the Hajj gave us a unique religious experience. Nothing in the world can compare with the atmosphere in Mecca, with its sea of people dressed in white, with tears in their eyes, all directing their thoughts to a common goal. Coming from a society where religion was synonymous with backwardness and ignorance, being part of the three million pilgrims in Mecca, seeing faces filled with passion, ecstasy, and exultation, meeting people from all over the world united in one belief, was a truly extraordinary experience.'

Gÿlnar R Baltanova lectures in Philosophy at Kazan University, Russia.

near the shrine (known as incubation), especially at healing shrines, presumed that the remains of the saint emitted a kind of radiation, which was more effective the longer the exposure to it. Relics are also treasured in other faiths. Though Buddha himself did not advocate pilgrimage, after his death his relics were distributed and placed in monuments known as *stupas* which became a goal for pilgrims. Outside India the best known is the Temple of the Tooth in Kandy, Sri Lanka, where in an inner chamber one of Buddha's teeth is preserved on a golden lotus flower inside nine golden caskets.

The goal of the pilgrimage is often described as a geographical location which attracts pilgrims because they deem it worthy of reverence as the scene of a divine manifestation or association with some holy person. In other words, human beings put the value of holiness on to the place. But is it possible that some places are holy per se, irrespective of their meaning for human beings? Some cultures have thought so. Places of pilgrimage are often places of great natural grandeur, possibly less in acknowledgement of a masterwork of the Creator than of a human propensity for investing certain kinds of geographical feature with symbolism. Certain places, particularly mountains, caves, rivers, and springs, have from ancient times been thought of as the dwelling places of the gods, or places where the world of the gods and the human world intersect. The place itself was (and often still is) regarded as holy, regardless of what human history has been enacted there through the ages.

This belief is sometimes formalized in mythology. According to ancient Hindu tradition, in the Himalaya lies Devabhumi, the country of the gods. The very mountain names proclaim this: Nanda Devi, "the Goddess Nanda", Chomo Lhari, "Goddess of the Holy

"... behold, I saw a man cloathed with rags, standing in a certain place, with his face from his own house ... and a great burden upon his back. I ... saw him ... burst out ... crying, What shall I do to be saved? I saw also that he looked this way and that way, as if he would run, yet he stood still, because ... he could not tell which way to go. I looked then, and saw a man named Evangelist coming to him, and asked ... Do you see yonder shining light? He said, I think I do. Then said Evangelist, Keep that light in your eye ... So I saw in my dream that the man began to run."

John Bunyan, The Pilgrim's Progress, Part I *(1678)*

Mountain", Chomo Lungma, "Mother Goddess of the Land" (the Tibetan name for Mount Everest). In both Hindu and Buddhist mythology, at the center of the earth stands a mountain around which sun, moon, and stars revolve. This mountain is Mount Meru, which Hindus believe is Mount Kailash in Tibet. Here is Svarga, Indra's Heaven, a paradise of the blessed who wait here until the time of their next rebirth on earth.

The belief in the holiness inherent in certain places caused Roman farmers to invoke the spirits of the countryside before encroaching on the wild to extend their cultivated land. Other Romans dedicated certain sites to the *genius loci*, or nameless spirit of the place, notifying passers-by of the fact in an inscription. In the Viking Era, Icelanders similarly venerated the *landvættir*, the spirits of the land, who were there guarding and cherishing the land before ever the first settlers arrived from Norway. Even today, it is hard not to believe that some places (particularly deserts) are of themselves filled with *numen*, a kind of overflowing of the divine that enfolds us when we visit.

Because of the worldwide belief in inherently sacred locations, some places remain a lodestone for pilgrims through changes of religion. At Mecca, which has the longest unbroken tradition of pilgrimage in the world, pilgrims were seeking that mysterious black stone enshrined in the Ka'ba well before Mohammed made pilgrimage to Mecca one of the Five Pillars of Islam.

The place is part of the desire.

The pilgrimage of the soul
This Oriental symbol is a representation of the soul's pilgrimage through life. It has to climb through the four worlds before being purified and passing from the darkness into the light.

THE PRAYER

Children in perplexity and trouble run to their parents: adults for the most part run to "god". Not for nothing does mythology use the language of parenthood: Alföðr (All-Father), Jaganmata (Mother of the World). We know that life is a hard road and uncertain, that we

CANTERBURY

A walk on the Pilgrim's Way

It is an Indian tradition that when you are fifty you should go on a pilgrimage. You have given enough attention to your family and your career; now is the time to pay attention to your soul, your spirit, your imagination, your divinity, and your creativity. From now on whatever you do should be in the service of the spirit. So, in 1986, I embarked on a journey to the holy places of Britain. I would walk from my home in Devon to Glastonbury, Canterbury, Walsingham, Lindisfarne, and Iona; I would take in many sacred places along the way and return home down the west side of the country.

I placed a small advertisement in the personal columns of *Resurgence*: could readers offer me a bed for the night along the way? The response was tremendous. When I set out I had an offer of hospitality in most of the places I was to visit. Each day I would try to walk 20 miles, starting at 9am and arriving at my host's house between 4 and 6pm. I started out with a small rucksack, one change of clothes, and the pair of Polish shoes I had on. I took no book, no diary, no camera, and no money.

On the twelfth day, starting from Salisbury Cathedral, following the old Roman road, I came to Winchester. As I walked the Pilgrim's Way to Canterbury, I was on the same path that many thousands of pilgrims had walked before. I had a sense that I was in the company of those people who had preceded me. As I stepped in their footprints, I felt I was in touch with their dedication, their purity, their sense of divinity.

The Pilgrim's Way

Pilgrims have followed this prehistoric route across southern England to the holy relics in Canterbury since the Cathedral was founded in the 6th century.

Iona

Lindisfarne/Holy Island

Walsingham

Glastonbury
Bideford

Winchester

Canterbury

Seale

Guildford

Box Hill

Bentley

Abinger Hammer

WINCHESTER

Bishop's Sutton

Practicalities

Traditional dates to make the pilgrimage to the tomb of St Thomas à Becket are the anniversary of his martyrdom (29 December) and the Feast of the Translation (7 July). Pilgrims enter the walled city by the medieval West Gate and walk through the narrow streets to the Cathedral.

The very beauty of the Pilgrim's Way is refreshing. In most parts it follows the ridge of the North Downs. Even though Surrey and Kent are riddled with motorways, conurbations, and built-up areas, in the woods of the North Downs I was able to escape the secular world. Now and then I had to cross the motorways and dual carriageways full of rushing lorries and speeding cars; I was amazed to see the madness of it all. The speed of my two legs and the speed of motorway traffic are worlds apart. Happily, I realized that for a pilgrim, slow is always beautiful.

In spite of our society's obsession with speed, I was impressed with the way this ancient pilgrim's path, over one hundred miles in length, is maintained. The Pilgrim's Way is not the same as it was in the Middle Ages, as in some places industrial growth has swallowed it; but, fortunately, a new footpath, the North Downs Way, has been created, which goes all the way to Canterbury. It is clearly marked and well defined, and I met a number of people walking it.

After thirty days of walking purification I entered the holy city of Canterbury. The first glimpse of the magnificent cathedral filled me with joy and delight. I felt the spirit of Canterbury enter into me. I rejoiced among the Christians without being a "Christian". On my arrival at the cathedral I went to an area designated for silent prayer and meditation where pilgrims light a candle. In this dark corner of the cathedral, lit only by the many candles, I too lit a candle and said the Prayer for Peace. After giving his blessings, Canon Brett led me to the chapel of Saint Thomas à Becket. A sword hanging above the altar spoke the language of power and pain. And the story Canon Brett told me of Becket's martyrdom caused my doubts and hesitations to vanish and my preoccupations with home and worldly responsibility to diminish.'

Satish Kumar is the editor of *Resurgence* magazine and the guiding spirit behind many ecological and spiritual ventures.

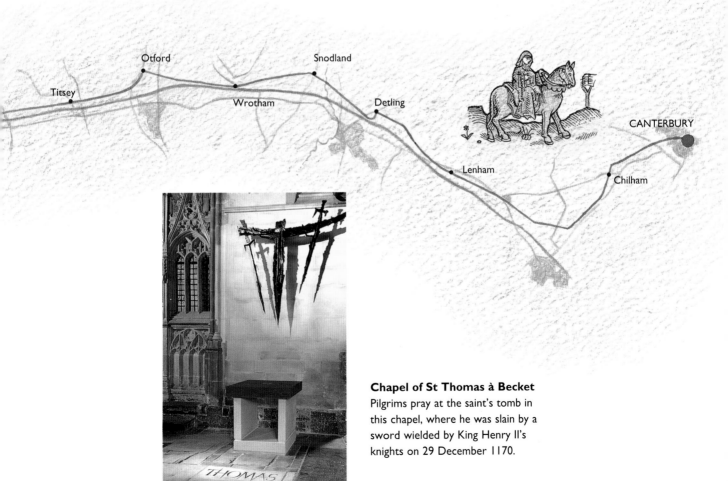

Titsey · Otford · Wrotham · Snodland · Detling · Lenham · Chilham · CANTERBURY

Chapel of St Thomas à Becket
Pilgrims pray at the saint's tomb in this chapel, where he was slain by a sword wielded by King Henry II's knights on 29 December 1170.

stumble, but that "he" or "she" is up ahead. Pilgrimage dramatizes the journey through life. In conventional pilgrimages a physical shrine or other holy place, having acquired a reputation for sanctity, exerts a spiritual magnetism that draws pilgrims to some fixed geographical location in the quest for the divine.

What we beg of our god may be something specific that is ardently desired – children, practical advantage, social status, even worldly gain. People yearn for personal miracles – what Shi'a Muslims in Iran call *kiramat* – modest miracles that solve a problem. At Iranian *imamzadeh*, shrine–tombs of the descendants of the Imams, one girl may ask specifically for her moustache to be removed, another more generally for a husband, a new wife will pray for a son, a pregnant woman for an easy delivery. Hindus in Bengal seek divine aid in curing baldness, passing an exam, saving a declining business. Haitian pilgrims to Sodo may want a particular job or to win promotion. King Henry VII of England went to the shrine at Walsingham in 1487 to pray to be preserved from the machinations of his enemies. In India, a Jain businessman may pay all the expenses of a communal pilgrimage to win both moral status (by eschewing the sin of satisfaction in possessions) and a sound financial reputation (by demonstrating that he has the ability to spend).

Chaucer's mixed bag of saints and sinners on the road to Canterbury is a lesson to all of us not to be too precious in our notions of who makes a sacred journey and why. There is seemingly no limit to the range of desires of the human heart laid bare before deity. In Culiacán, the narcotics capital of northern Mexico, the *narcotraficantes* or drug traffickers seek the shrine of a dead bandit named Jesús Malverde, hanged from a tree in 1909. Although unrecognized by the Church, he has his feast day, 3 May, when crowds gather at the shrine, illuminated by dozens of candles. The *narcotraficantes* are generous to the shrine (some say that they use it to launder money), but these multi-millionaire businessmen are at the same time devoutly religious, practising

the Catholicism of rural Mexico, with its folk-saints and visions and miracles. They wear Malverde scapulars and are said to ask him for a bountiful harvest for the cocaine and marijuana farmers in the Sierra Madre, and to bless their drugs for the journey to the USA. Their hitmen reputedly ask him to bless their bullets. Ordinary people are thankful not only for employment growing and transporting the crop, but for the benefits of hospitals, orphanages, and schools, endowed by the drug barons, not to mention the Jesús Malverde Funeral Service provided free for the Culiacán poor. They, too, come to thank Malverde, who, they say, like Robin Hood, robbed the rich to give to the poor. Who can say whose prayers God answers?

It is of course easier to empathize with the desperate longing for health that draws pilgrims to many shrines, in the hope that this will be accomplished by exposure to holiness, whether this resides in the general sanctity of the place, or in the specific virtues of healing waters, or in the *mana*, or life force, radiating from the relics of departed saints. Hindus resort to Baba Taraknath, the local deity of Tarakeshwar in West Bengal, in the belief that he can and does cure, among other things, coughs, dysentery, gonorrhoea, tuberculosis, and leprosy. The most active Christian shrines today are places that have reputations for miraculous cures: pilgrims come with a hope bolstered by the shrine's tradition of miracles to Lourdes in the Pyrénées, where in 1858 the Blessed Virgin reputedly appeared to a French peasant girl, Bernadette Soubirous. The characteristics of Lourdes – a manifestation of the divine, associated with a sacred spring at which miracles of healing subsequently take place – are repeated at other Christian pilgrimage places, including the important New World shrine of Sainte Anne de Beaupré, Quebec.

Among the poor and in poorer countries, this quest for wellbeing is perhaps pilgrimage's most urgent motive, and one which transcends the barriers of formal religion. In India, a land of many faiths, the desire for miracles of healing leads to shrines of one religion attracting supplicants from others, notably the shrines of the Hindu mother goddesses, of the *pirs* (Sufi "elders"), of the saints of Islam, places associated with the lives of Sikh gurus, and Roman Catholic shrines of the Blessed Virgin Mary. Hindus, Muslims, and Sikhs all ask for mental health in Badaun, at the shrine of two Muslim saints, Sayyed Hasan (Bare Sarkar) and Shah Vilayat (Chhote Sarkar). Ajmer, in Rajasthan, the

"The lovers of Brahman ask: What is the source of this universe? ... From where do we come? By what power do we live? Where do we find rest?"

THE UPANISHADS

Medina of Asia, is visited also by Hindus. Many seek cures for the incurable, irrespective of their religion, at the Roman Catholic shrine to Our Lady of Health at Velankanni in Tamil Nadu.

Like Christian in John Bunyan's *The Pilgrim's Progress*, some pilgrims are more concerned for their souls. Medieval Christians carried with them on the road the fear of Hell and a desperate hope that the pilgrimage, because the way was hard and long, would serve as an expiation of their sins. The medieval doctrine of Purgatory, as a staging post to Heaven where sins could be atoned for, and the belief that people's time there could be reduced by their own or their relatives' merit, led to the Church's practice of offering indulgences (essentially promises of time off in Purgatory) as a reward to pilgrims. A fourteenth-century pilgrim's guide to the Holy City, *The Stacions of Rome*, details the number of years' remission of suffering in Purgatory acquired at each "stacion" or shrine: at St Thomas of India's, 14,000 years; at St Lawrence's 7000 years; at the church of Holy Rood, 250 years pardon every Sunday and Wednesday, and 100 every other day. The Crusaders, essentially fighting pilgrims, were promised instant salvation if they were killed while liberating the sacred places of the Holy Land from the "Infidel".

Hindu pilgrims, too, regard the mortification and disciplining of the body as a way of acquiring merit. One of the hardest of all sacred journeys is the Ganga (Ganges) pilgrimage between the pilgrimage centers of Gangotri, Kedarnath, and Badrinath, at the sources of

Middle Ages, the Englishman Roger of Wansford left directions in his will for his executors to send someone on a pilgrimage to fulfill a vow he had made when in peril of his life he had "almost suffocated by the waves of the sea between Ireland and Norway".

For some, the sacred journey begins in the desire to participate in a ritual cycle concerned with the round of passing seasons, like the pilgrim festivals of Old Testament times – Weeks, Tabernacles, and Passover –

"The pilgrimage is like an ever flowing river ... at the banks of which Muslims may always wash from their faces the dusts of hardship and suffering, pollution and malaise ..."

AYATOLLAH AL-UDHMA KHAMENEI
ON THE OCCASION OF HAJJ 1416/1996

the Bhagirathi, the Mandakini, and the Alaknanda rivers, tributaries of the sacred Ganga. The pilgrimage, performed in May, June, and July each year, covers 600 miles, much of it on foot and in harsh conditions. Buddhist pilgrims, like their Hindu counterparts, believe that the merit gained on pilgrimage leads to higher status in the next life and eventually, if enough is accumulated, to freedom from the cycle of existence.

Sometimes the will to pilgrimage is a desire to fulfill an obligation. Islam enjoins all Muslims who are able to do so to visit Mecca once in their lives. Obligatory in a different way were the pilgrimages imposed by Church or State in medieval Europe as punishments or penance. Convicted criminals were sent on penitential journeys to Santiago de Compostela in northern Spain. Others were condemned to wander from shrine to shrine until their iron fetters were worn through by dragging along the road. Also involving obligation are pilgrimages undertaken in the fulfillment of a vow. In the late

when all Hebrew men would come to the temple at Jerusalem. Or it may have to do with the human life cycle, as among Hindus, for whom pilgrimage often serves as an initiation into a new stage of life. Children are fed their first solid food at pilgrimage shrines, or have their hair cut for the first time. The first act of newlyweds is often to make a pilgrimage. The elderly and the sick congregate at shrines in the belief that death at a pilgrimage center will free them from the cycle of rebirth. It is not unknown for the aged to commit

Shrine to Jesús Malverde
Candles burn at this shrine to the unofficial patron saint of drug traffickers in Culiacán, Mexico. The head of the plaster bust is painted blue in the Mexican folk art tradition.

ritual suicide at places such as Puri and Allahabad. The sacred space, filled with the immanence of the divine, is the blessed and the safe place for new beginnings.

This motive overlaps with the initiatory – the sacred journey undertaken from the desire to work some kind of transformation on the self. The Muslim who goes to Mecca comes home with both a new moral authority and a new social rank, and is henceforth distinguished by the title *hajji*. The reshaping of the self or its awakening to the divine is perhaps the main motive for New Age pilgrimage.

The world-famous musician Yehudi Menuhin has delivered this sad epitaph on the twentieth century: "I would say that it raised the greatest hopes ever conceived by humanity, and destroyed all illusions and ideals." Many would agree. As probably the most violent and destructive century on record, in the Western world it has also seen a weakening of organized religion, a growing cynicism concerning human responsibility and accountability, and the loosening of social and family bonds. Our traditional support systems are either weakened or gone. Perhaps at no time in history has the individual felt so truly alone.

We are also recoiling from the true cost of the technological explosion to the planet and our co-heirs in it (the rest of life). Where our ancestors perceived the inherent nobility in humankind and placed them at the center of creation, we have become ashamed of our species ("only man is vile").

But this modern Western malaise of alienation from ourselves, from each other, and from the rest of creation, is producing its own cure. Spiritual warriors are arising, learning from our past traditional strategies for dealing with despair and self-loathing (medieval monks suffered from it, too), and out of them evolving new ones. One of these old–new strategies is the sacred journey.

"... what he is who is in truth Maker, Keeper, and Lover I cannot tell, for until I am essentially united with him I can never have full rest ... He is true rest. It is his will that we should know him, and his pleasure that we should rest in him. Nothing less will satisfy us."

Mother Julian of Norwich
(1342–c.1416)

THE JOURNEY

Many seekers see their attempt to find an ideal to live by in terms of a journey. Some join the pilgrimages of the world religions to experience communitas, a spiritual solidarity. This is what brings tens of thousands of young adults of all Christian denominations and other faiths from all over the world on a "pilgrimage of trust" to Taizé in eastern France, to share in the worship of a Christian monastic community. When the Archbishop of Canterbury, George Carey, led a thousand young Anglicans there in 1992, he said: "I have come to Taizé on pilgrimage because it is a place of generosity and reconciliation."

Others devise their own sacred journeys: reconciliation was also the purpose of the multi-faith Atomic Mirror Pilgrimage of 1995 to Hiroshima and nuclear power sites in the USA. A journey to a place which has mainly personal meaning is as much a pilgrimage as a journey to a recognized sacred site if the desire to go there is strong and the experience spiritually uplifting. A journey of remembrance – the longed-for visit to a distant place where someone we love is buried or their ashes interred, whether in a churchyard or garden of rest in our own country or a war cemetery in some "foreign field" – is a pilgrimage. All these journeys represent the search for an ideal, something that the individual pilgrim values.

We are the heirs of a long and complex tradition, in which the sacred is entwined with the profane. Not the least impulse at the heart of many pilgrims has always been wanderlust, the desire for travel for its own sake. This was a strong motive in Europe in the Middle Ages when pilgrimage was the only opportunity for many to leave their towns and villages and see the wonders of the world outside, in the security of the company of other travellers, on a well-known route and with some prospect of accommodation in established pilgrim inns.

Organized pilgrimages to Santiago de Compostela or to St Thomas à Becket's tomb at Canterbury offered all the mental if not physical comforts of a packaged tour.

For women in particular this was the great escape, for they could travel on escorted pilgrimages without their menfolk, as did the religious ecstatic Margery Kempe, born in 1364, wife of a burgess of Lynn (now King's Lynn), in Norfolk, England, and mother of fourteen children. Her pilgrimages to Jerusalem and Germany allowed her to set aside her role as wife and mother and globetrot a little, whilst pursuing her own private journey into the divine. They are recorded with all their trials and tribulations in her spiritual biography, *The Book of Margery Kempe* – the first autobiography ever to be written in English.

We may find it difficult to perceive any inwardness in modern mass tourism and deplore the commercialization of holy places and of sacred journeying itself. But few world traditions of pilgrimage are free from an element of tourism: medieval pilgrims went to Rome to see the "sights"; not just the tombs of the apostles and the churches, but Roman antiquities, the traces of a great and vanished empire. They were drawn to Jerusalem not just because it acted as a spiritual powerhouse as a place important in the sacred history of Jews and Christians (they ignored its importance to Muslims), but also because the journey to Outremer, the "land across the sea", was the ultimate journey of travel and adventure.

In the Holy Land, pilgrims could engage directly with their sacred history by walking in the footsteps of Biblical characters. When the German pilgrim Theoderich made the pilgrimage between 1171 and 1173, he was shown, among other things, a grotto under the Church of Our Lady in Nazareth said to be the scene of the Annunciation by the Angel Gabriel, and in the same church the burial place of St Joseph and the very spot where Our Lady came forth from her mother's womb. In Nazareth, too, he saw a fountain spouting from the mouth of a marble lion's head, "from which the

The Pulley

When God at first made man,
Having a glass of blessings standing by,
'Let us', said he, 'pour on him all we can:
Let the world's riches which dispersèd lie,
        Contract into a span.'

So strength first made a way;
Then beauty flowed, then wisdom, honour, pleasure:
When almost all was out, God made a stay,
Perceiving that, alone of all his treasure,
        Rest in the bottom lay.

'For if I should', said he,
'Bestow this jewel also on my creature,
He would adore my gifts instead of me,
And rest in Nature, not the God of Nature:
        So both should losers be.

'Yet let him keep the rest,
But keep them with repining restlessness:
Let him be rich and weary, that at least,
If goodness lead him not, yet weariness
        May toss him to my breast.'

George Herbert (1593–1633)

BENARES

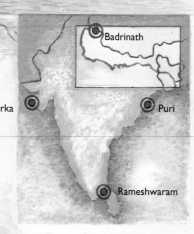

City of Light

 City of Light, City of the Dead, the Forest of Bliss, the Never-Forsaken, the City of Shiva – call it what you will (and it is known by all these names), Benares has to be one of the maddest, holiest, most entrancing cities on earth. Every trick in the book is used by the touts, the rickshaw wallahs, the boatmen, the hangers-on, to part another fool from his money. The assault is continuous, and only ceases when one flees to the Ganges in a boat of one's own.

Floating down the Ganges through the City of the Gods: then the light falls on the temples, the palaces, the water, in a shimmering haze. The whole river front takes on a dreamlike air – buffalo lounge in the water, a man meditates by the shore, a sadhu walks by with staff and water pot, children play chase among the funeral pyres. The ghats, colossal stone steps leading down to the water's edge, glow pink and gold in the afternoon sun. The washermen make use of them to dry their day's work – yards of sari, blue and bright yellow, stretch down to the water. Just by the washing a huddle of people, all dressed in white, gaze on as the body of one of their relatives crackles and dissolves in the flames of a great fire. Somewhere bells are ringing, firecrackers are being set off. Overhead, two vultures are circling.

The Four Dhamas

For many generations Hindus have undertaken a circular pilgrimage to the four *dhamas* (dwelling places of the gods). These are Rameshwaram in the south; Badrinath in the north; Puri in the east, and Dwarka in the west.

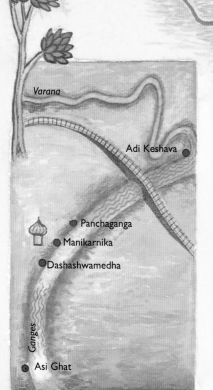

BENARES

The Panchatirthi Yatra

One of the most popular pilgrim routes along the Ganges waterfront at Benares takes in five (*pancha*) crossings (*tirthi*): Asi, Dashashwamedha, Adi Keshava, Panchaganga and Manikarnika. Despite a remarkable lack of hygiene, the waters of the river are regarded as the elixir of life: bathing, particularly at Dashashwamedha, brings purity to the living; while cremation, especially on the ghat at Manikarnika, brings salvation to the dead.

Practicalities

The best time to make a pilgrimage to Benares is October to November for the Ramlila Festival and Durga Goddess Festival. Bathing in the Ganges is particularly auspicious at this time. Be prepared to negotiate firmly if you want to rent a boat to catch the dawn. Pilgrims seeking the undiluted magic of Benares are recommended to rent accommodation in small lodges among the lanes of Vishwanatha near the ghats.

Hindus from all over the world come to Benares to die. It is their Holy of Holies, where the soul is guaranteed a speedy return to the celestial fields. Benares is "older than history," said Mark Twain after his visit there; "older than tradition, older even than legend." For more than three thousand years, this city has been at the heart of an unbroken spiritual tradition. I, a Christian by culture, came there not to die, as it turned out, but to reflect upon my own mortality. I have never forgotten the principle that the mystic philosopher G I Gurdjieff always emphasized to his pupils – that the awareness of our own inevitable end is the most powerful spiritual lesson that we can learn. Benares brings this home more than most places.

Half a dozen fires are burning day and night by the water, and a row of corpses, trussed in yellow and gold cloth on bamboo stretchers, await their turn nearby. The family members sit on the ghats up above, watching the proceedings in silence. I sit with them, in an almost casual atmosphere. No-one is shedding a tear, because mourning is considered bad luck for the dead, and everyone knows that the Hereafter is an easier place to be than the life we all share on earth.

One day I passed a procession of pipers and drummers leading a flower-covered bier down to the water. Just before the fire they stopped, and two young men leaped out in front of the body, which was still on the shoulders of the bearers, and threw themselves into a wild sexual dance, one with a stick in his trousers that seemed to give him a massive erection, the other gyrating his pelvis like a woman, with his arms and forefingers prodding the air. Round and round each other they turned, the musicians drumming them into an ecstatic frenzy. By now everyone was clapping and laughing, and the dancers motioned to me to come and join them. I had never been to a funeral like this before, and I backed away, embarrassed. Later, too late, I wished I had danced that cremation dance.'

Smoke rises from the funeral pyres on the cremation ghat. The fires are tended by the *doms*, the guardians of the ghat, while the relatives look on.

Roger Housden is a writer and photographer, the author of *Travels through Sacred India* and *Retreat*. He is a director of Open Gate Journeys, which leads groups on spiritual journeys to sacred sites.

Dhaka

Calcutta

child Jesus often used to draw water and take it to his mother". Such sites, some of them no doubt bogus, nevertheless added colour and immediacy to the visit through the exercise of the historical imagination, and served to reinforce faith (proving the Bible "true").

They also allowed the pilgrim to "fold" time, notably to share in Christ's passion by walking the Via Dolorosa, his journey to the Cross. Though raised to a higher power, such places functioned rather like the well-managed sites of Civil War battles in the USA, such as Bull Run, Virginia; or son et lumière performances in Europe and the Middle East – Karnak in Egypt, for example; or the re-enacting of ancient dramas in the open-air amphitheatres they were designed for, such as Epídhavros in Greece. By focussing the attention, and manipulating the emotions through sight and sound, they create an acute awareness, and allow the spectator or participant to "be there". Whilst saints and mystics might have empathized with the sufferings of Christ to the extent that they received the stigmata, others needed sensory aids. (For this reason the Via Dolorosa is still recreated symbolically at many Christian pilgrimage sites.)

Nowadays tourism is often marketed as pilgrimage. No longer a simple journey to visit the sights (and sites), the sightseeing tour has become a "pilgrimage" to the famous places of antiquity, a "pilgrimage" to great works of nature, a "pilgrimage" to the home of some famous writer or poet or painter or musician. And here the tour promoters have the truth of it: anthropologist Alan Morinis has written that the term "pilgrimage" can be put to use "wherever journeying and some embodiment of the ideal intersect". Often there is very little distance between sacred journeys to recognized holy places and shrines and "secular pilgrimages" to pay homage to some

"A man once wished to go to Jerusalem, and since he did not know the way, he called on another man ... and asked him for information. 'The way is long,' he said, 'and there is great danger ... Furthermore, there are many different roads which seem to lead towards it, but every day men are killed and robbed, and never reach their goal.' ... The pilgrim replied: 'I do not mind how much hardship I have to undergo on the road, so long as ... I reach my destination.' ... The other answered, 'I will set you on the right road. ... keep your mind constantly on Jerusalem. If you will keep to this road ... you will arrive at the place for which you long.'

Walter Hilton (d.1395)
The Ladder of Perfection

historical hero or modern icon, such as visits to Mount Vernon, the home of the first US president, George Washington, or to Graceland, virtually the "shrine" of the American musical phenomenon, Elvis Presley.

The diverse strands of pilgrimage give us something to work with when seeking the focus and intent of our own sacred journey. We do not need to be alone on our spiritual quest: we can engage in an historical process. Treading in the steps of revered ancestors is an act that unites and reconciles modern tourism, pilgrimage within living faiths, and orally transmitted sacred journeying, such as native Australian "travel" along the Songlines, where the journey is not a memorialization of times past but a mythic act.

Following in this ancient tradition, the pilgrim does not re-enact the myths of how things came to be but participates in the very act of Creation. And this participation in making a brave new spiritual world is perhaps in the end why, at a time when we are told that formal religion is losing ground, the impulse to undertake a pilgrimage seems to be gathering strength. In 1993, when the feast of St James fell on a Sunday and it was declared Compostellan Holy Year, 99,436 pilgrims walked the whole length of the 500-mile-long Camino de Santiago (Way of St James), the thousand-year-old pilgrim trail to Santiago de Compostela in Spain. Roughly another four and a half million arrived by coach or bus. Yet this pilgrimage had been all but abandoned by the late nineteenth century, the markers along the way and the pilgrim shelters vanished. It was only in the 1960s that the Camino was restored.

Essentially all pilgrims are seeking to access, by way of a significant site, a spiritual reservoir charged in the past and constantly refilled. For the pilgrim not only takes but gives, drawing spiritual sustenance and at the same time by an act of faith in the place of pilgrimage replenishing the never-failing spring. To be a pilgrim is not to perform an individual act of devotion, but to engage in humankind's dialogue with the divine: not in time, but eternity.

Ritual preparation

On a sacred journey secular time may be separated from sacred time by the wearing of special clothes or by following sacred rituals. For this Moroccan Muslim, having his head shaved is a part of his preparation for pilgrimage.

II *Getting ready*

CHAPTER 2

"The gods seemed to have possessed my soul and turned it inside out, and roadside images seemed to invite me from every corner, so that it was impossible for me to stay idle at home. Even while I was getting ready, mending my torn trousers, tying a new strap to my hat, and applying moxa to my legs to strengthen them, I was already dreaming of the full moon rising over the islands of Matsushima." So in the seventeenth century wrote the Japanese poet and pilgrim Matsuo Basho. Your pilgrimage, too, has begun. The place you want to be is in sight. You have embraced it in your mind: let your feet follow.

The practical preparations that you make for your sacred journey are as much a part of your pilgrimage as the travelling itself. Once you have decided on your goal, it is time to research the practical aspects of your journey: when to make the journey, whether to go alone or with others, how long the journey will take and how much it will cost. You may also wish to make spiritual preparation, perhaps as required by your religious faith, or as a personal preparation for your sacred journey. In this planning and preparation stage there are many questions to consider.

WHEN?

When will you set out? There are traditional seasons of pilgrimage, governed by the weather. Chaucer's pilgrims rode out on the road from London to Canterbury in April; Basho likewise felt the quickening of spring. Hindus still arrive at Badrinath, high in the Himalaya and snowbound for half the year, between May and October. Other considerations apart, like an ordinary holidaymaker you will probably choose to let good weather guide you.

But if you belong to one of the world's great faiths, you may want to attend some important festival in the religious calendar, when your community of belief gathers together not only in sacred space but in sacred time. For Sikhs, that space is the Golden Temple at

Catholic may choose 8 September, the feast of the Nativity of Mary, and the Catholic pilgrimage which begins with mass at the former Slipper Chapel.

Those of other faiths, or none, will probably also prefer to time their visit to the sacred place to coincide either with a festival or in accordance with some other traditional association. For example, local people and those who are historically minded may visit Walsingham in late January or early February, when snowdrops carpet the woods, mindful that these "Mary's Tapers" were traditionally used to decorate English churches on the feast of the Purification of the Blessed Virgin Mary, celebrated on 3 February.

The "when" of your sacred journey depends on more than flight availabilities.

HOW?

Then there's the "how". Down the centuries, pilgrims of all faiths have elected to go on an organized tour in company with others: a kind of spiritual Cook's Tour. When the Englishman Sir Richard Torkington set out for Jerusalem on 20 March 1517, he made his way to Venice, Italy, where he found a "patron", a courier who specialized in transporting pilgrims by sea to Palestine. Though the ship did not stick to the scheduled route, they eventually docked in Jaffa, from where the Warden of the Mount Sion Convent conducted them to

"Whan that Aprill with his shoures soote

Amritsar, and the time Baisakhi (the Punjabi New Year's Day, 13 April). For Hindus with devotion to Vithoba it is Pandharpur on Vithoba's special day, the *sukla ekadasi* or "bright eleventh". This is the eleventh lunar day of the waxing part of the month of Asadha. (As usual with festivals regulated according to the lunar calendar, the equivalent date in the Roman calendar varies.) Suppose you are Christian, wishing to make a pilgrimage to Walsingham, England. A Protestant may want to join the Anglican National Pilgrimage on 27 May, but a

Jerusalem. They were shown the sights – rather more than pilgrims nowadays: "We went to the house where the sins of Mary Magdalen were forgiven" – and on the last day of July, apparently all present and correct, set sail again for the return journey from Jaffa. This style of escorted tour was necessitated by the Turks and Saracens who controlled Jerusalem at this time and sometimes made trouble for visiting Christians. Even today some journeys will lead the pilgrim to parts of the world where it is unwise to travel alone.

As with ordinary travel abroad, there are sights and experiences you may miss without guidance. There are also religious observances you may fumble. This worries even pilgrims in their native country: in India, on arrival at their destination, Hindus often put themselves in the hands of *pandas* or *purohits*, guides who provide not only food and lodging but also ritual instruction.

Joining a guided tour may not be your idea of a sacred journey. But the meaning of what you do is in how you see it. Think of yourself as participating in an age-old tradition of companionship in spiritual adventure. You will be sharing good times and bad – excitement and boredom, ease and discomfort, revelation and doubt. Not the least of your sharing will be the act of eating together, which even in everyday life has a symbolic dimension and which in many religions is ritualized as the communal sacrificial feast. Seen in this light, the greasiest café becomes the Grail Castle.

The determined lone wolf's first step will be to consult a guidebook. Here, too, you are identifying yourself with a hallowed tradition: a pilgrim from Bordeaux, France, produced an itinerary of the road to Jerusalem for other travellers in AD333. *Information for Pilgrims unto the Holy Land* (c.1498) gives alternative routes and rates of exchange, hints on choosing a pilgrim ship out of Venice, and what herbs and spices, crockery and utensils to take. It advises the pilgrim on

"Don't wait to be ready.

Everything you need for this journey is available

to you right now."

K BRADFORD BROWN, POINT
COUNTER POINT (1988)

*The droghte of March hath perced to the roote,
... Thanne longen folk to goon on pilgrimages"*

GEOFFREY CHAUCER,
THE CANTERBURY TALES, 14TH CENTURY

how to hire a mule in Jaffa and what fresh foodstuffs to buy for a trip to Jericho. It also gives vocabularies in Greek and Turkish. No wonder it ran to more than one edition, exactly like its modern equivalents, volumes in classic guidebook series such as Fodor's Guides.

If you are travelling in a culture whose religion you do not share, look for a guidebook that gives precise information about visiting holy places. "When in Rome,

GLASTONBURY

A spiritual magnet

"Glastonbury – Ancient Isle of Avalon" reads the town sign, capturing the juxtaposition of location and legend, fact and faith, present and past, which pervades the place. As one woman told me, "There's a new myth created every day around Glastonbury." Described as a spiritual magnet, it is a "multiple choice" pilgrimage site, for a number of different Glastonburys coexist in time and space. People have been drawn here for centuries, bringing a variety of traditions and worldviews that currently interact. It is for individuals to discover which Glastonbury is "real" for them.

Christian Glastonbury is shaped by the traditions which have earned the town the title "cradle of English Christianity". According to legend, Joseph of Arimathea, provider of the tomb for Jesus and thought by some to be Jesus' uncle, landed at Glastonbury – 2000 years ago it was beside the sea – where he built a simple church dedicated to the Virgin Mary. Some claim that Joseph, a tin merchant, had already visited the area, and might have brought his nephew on such a trip. This idea continues to capture the imagination, expressed most eloquently by William Blake in his poem *Jerusalem*:

"And did those feet in ancient time
Walk upon England's mountains green?
And was the holy Lamb of God
On England's pleasant pastures seen?"

Joseph's staff, thrust into the ground on his arrival, flourished to become the famous Glastonbury Thorn, which flowers both in spring and at Christmas. He also reputedly carried with him another, more precious relic – the Grail. As the cult of Joseph developed and Arthurian romances proliferated, the Grail was variously described as the dish in which Joseph had collected Christ's blood after the crucifixion, two cruets filled with the blood and sweat of Jesus, or the chalice used at the Last Supper.

Inextricably linked with the Grail are tales of King Arthur and his Knights of the Round Table. After his last battle, according to legend, Arthur was taken for healing to Avalon, where some believe he remained, the once and future king, to return at some hour of great need. The twelfth-century "discovery" of the bodies of King Arthur and his queen in the Abbey grounds seemed to confirm the identification of Glastonbury with Avalon and Arthur in popular tradition.

The Abbey was built over the site of St Joseph's church, regarded in the words of one medieval poet as the "holyest erth of england". After the Benedictine monks were forced to leave it by the Dissolution of the Monasteries in the sixteenth century, it fell into disrepair. It is now administered as an historic site. But at the annual pilgrimage weekend in June, which has attracted crowds of around 14,000, some of the Abbey's original function and flavour – if not its magnificence – is recaptured.

Many contemporary pilgrims are attracted by Glastonbury's pre-Christian connections. Some claim that the Abbey lies on an ancient site of Goddess worship, and regard the banks around the sides of the Tor, perhaps created by prehistoric peoples, as a complex three-dimensional ritual maze. For others, Glastonbury's significance lies in its presumed association with ancient Druids: they maintain that it was a great center of Druidic learning – a sort of Druidic Oxbridge – attracting students from Europe and beyond.

Glastonbury is now also hailed as "the epicentre of the New Age in England", a center of converging ley lines and the "heart chakra" of planet Earth. People journey there to find themselves. Arthur is often invoked by people embarking on their own spiritual quest, symbolically rising again "to lead us into a New Age, a new cycle, a new beginning, a new phase in world evolution".

Marion Bowman lectures in the Study of Religions at Bath College of Higher Education, England.

GLASTONBURY

Glastonbury Abbey

Chalice Well

Glastonbury Tor

The Tor and Abbey

The Tor, with a 14th century church tower at its summit, rises dramatically out of a flat plain on the edge of the town. The site of the ruined Abbey (far left), in the town center, is considered sacred by pilgrims of many beliefs.

Practicalities

The small town of Glastonbury is in Somerset, southwest England. The annual pilgrimage to Glastonbury is in late June or early July, when thousands of Anglicans, Catholics, and Orthodox pilgrims flock to the Abbey for a service of prayer, devotion, and healing.

Non-Christian celebrations take place throughout the year, including the summer and winter solstices (21 June and 21 December) and the spring festival of Beltane (1 May).

do as the Romans do" may not get you by. You need to know how you as a foreigner are expected to behave. You may on arrival find locally published guidebooks that better answer your questions. Otherwise you may need a human guide. Again, this is not only a problem for non-believers. A British Hindu woman who wished to fulfill a vow to go to Varanasi (Benares) in India, enlisted her father's help in making the arrangements for her journey. "He wrote to relatives in India, who contacted a priest attached to one of the Varanasi temples. My son and daughter accompanied me and when we arrived, it was this priest who met us at the railway station and took us to our lodgings. He also acted as our guide around the city and made sure that the religious actions I carried out were correct so that my pilgrimage would be successful."

ORGANIZING YOUR TRIP

So, you have decided how you will travel. If you are joining a party, most of the logistics will be handled for you. If you are travelling independently, you will have more to think about, not least your own personality. Are you an anxious traveller (you may call it "organized"), making "To do" lists, practising packing, turning up at the airport too early? You might want to work on this – you will not be able to control a journey that is "sacred" so tightly. You are entering a different space and time, stepping into the unknown: this is the nature and the purpose of your journey.

Or are you at the other pole, forever unforewarned and unforearmed (you may see this as "spontaneous" – others might say "feckless"). On your voyage of the soul, choose to be the burden on no-one's back – neither your country's, nor someone else's. This entails being:

- legal (passport, perhaps visa)
- viable (money: foreign currency, travellers' cheques or credit cards; medical insurance)
- able (supplies of ongoing medication, up-to-date vaccinations: your doctor will have a list of which vaccinations are needed for which countries)

This is not the mundane, getting between you and your sacred journey – this is your journey. You are already (especially if you are not used to organizing such things) on your road.

"I had a desire to see the places where He [our Lord] was born ... and died ... And while I was feeling these desires, our Lord spoke in my mind and told me to go to Rome, Jerusalem and the shrine of St James. This was two years before I went, because I wanted to go but could not afford it." This is the illiterate English pilgrim Margery Kempe, dictating her story to a priest in the fifteenth century. You may feel that you have been as imperatively summoned on your pilgrimage as Margery, but can you afford to go? Muslims commonly wait to make the Hajj until they can do so without depriving their families. Pilgrims from other cultures defer their journeys to sacred places for the same reason. Journeys abroad in particular have a way of costing more than you think, and it is the essence of sacred journeys that they spring surprises, leading you down byways you had not expected to tread, offering challenges you had not expected to meet. Sad to be unable to respond and to take the chances offered to you because you have given no thought to your budget!

Margery again: "When the time came for me to visit the holy places ... I asked the parish priest ... to make an announcement from the pulpit for me: any man or woman with a claim for debt against myself or my husband was to come and have a word with me before I left and I would settle things to their satisfaction – which is what I did." Without going to the lengths of having your affairs announced from the pulpit, you might want to follow her example and settle outstanding business. This was more urgent for pilgrims of the Middle Ages whose travels might last a year or more, and whose chances of a safe return from almost anywhere were considerably less than ours. Still, you might regard this reckoning as they did, as being also a symbolic leave-taking, a letting go of worldly concerns, a marking of the division between secular and sacred time.

PACKING

For the pilgrims of many faiths, this separation of sacred from secular time was or is marked by the putting on of ritual garments. These are signs that proclaim a people temporarily set apart, treading the same roads as other travellers, but marching to a different drum. The staff and scrip (satchel) are no longer the marks of the Christian pilgrim but still today, to fulfill the requirement for an unstitched white cotton garment – symbolic of the equality of all Muslims – a British Muslim man going to Mecca will pack two white sheets, one to be wrapped round the lower half of his body, the other to be thrown over his shoulder. A woman will take a clean, plain, long dress with a white scarf to cover her head. At Gatwick Airport, before their flight, they will perform the ritual washing known as *wudu* and don their pilgrim's garments in specially provided rooms. They do this in case their flight passes over Mecca, because before they reach the goal of their sacred journey they must enter into the state of ritual purity known as *ihram*. (Pilgrims not already prepared are warned by the pilot so that they can wash and change on board the airplane.)

Common sense dictates that, like any other traveller, you will pack suitable garments of the right weight for the climate in the country you are visiting, comfortable and hardwearing footwear, enough but not too much. But if your journey is taking you to acknowledged holy places, be mindful that your dress should be respectful of the traditions of the faith and country.

A guided tour
This local guide shows pilgrims the route to the summit of Mount Kailash, as well as offering guidance on the observance of sacred religious rites.

Dress makes all sorts of statements and consequently is a touchy subject all round. It is a frequently observed phenomenon that people often become unreasonably truculent if asked to amend their dress, for example in restaurants. A pilgrim cannot afford to pack this attitude in his or her baggage. If you come from a liberal society where almost anything (or nothing) can be worn on the street, be prepared to abandon your own notions of suitability. Except for wilderness journeys, shorts won't see you through. Even on men, and especially when combined with bare chests, they are widely regarded as impolite in public.

In a number of religious faiths, including the more traditional branches of Christianity, displays of female flesh in holy places are particularly frowned on. Women going to Islamic countries should take clothes that are extremely discreet. In Iran, in particular, *hejab* (Islamic dress) must be worn by all women in public. When visiting certain Islamic shrines, women should also prepare themselves mentally to wear the *chador* (floor-length veil). You will normally be lent one at the entrance. You do not have a choice here: "will not comply" equals "cannot go".

Don't forget the head: the significance of a covered or uncovered head differs between cultures. Young American men may need reminding that, whereas at home baseball caps (and stetsons) are often left on the head indoors in public places, in Europe this is considered uncouth, and in churches and cathedrals irreverent. Conversely, in many Christian shrines worldwide it is

CAMARGUE

The Marys of the sea

☾ The paradox of a people always on the move going on pilgrimage brings us to Les Saintes-Maries-de-la-Mer in the Camargue, a region of lagoons and saltmarsh, white horses and black bulls, flamingoes and mosquitoes. The press call it the "Gypsy Pilgrimage". Certainly, gypsies arrive from all over Europe, defying expectations: mobile homes fill the parking lots, men carry mobile phones, girls wear orange day-glo leggings, singers working restaurants offer tapes.

But gypsies are only the half of it. The 25 May is the Feast of the Three Marys – Magdalene, Jacobé, and Salomé – first witnesses of the Resurrection and from whom the town is named. According to Provençal legend, these three faithful women were set adrift in a rudderless boat from Palestine in AD45, together with their black servant, Sara, and several other saints. Eventually their boat was washed ashore in the Camargue. Its cargo of saints, including Mary Magdalene, with her sister Martha and their brother Lazarus, dispersed to evangelicize Provence. The elderly Marys Salomé and Jacobé, with Sara, stayed and built themselves an oratory. Here they were buried, here pilgrims came, here was built the church.

On 24 May, the Eve of the Feast, we arrive in the church for the "Descente du chasses" at 3pm. These *chasses* are painted reliquaries containing the relics of the Marys, which

were discovered by "Good King René" of Provence in 1488. Soon the church is packed. A steady trickle of gypsies flows up the aisle and down into the crypt to pay respect to a diminutive statue with a nutbrown face – Sainte Sara, their adopted patron.

Before the reliquaries descend from an upper chapel – tantamount to the coming among us of the holy women themselves – the bishop asks us not to take photographs, but flashlights pop and TV cameras roll. The reliquaries are winched down in stages and at each halt bunches of florists' flowers, wrapped in cellophane, are tied to the ropes. Gypsies reach up with their candles and their hands to touch the wonder-working caskets. These will return to their eyrie tomorrow at 3pm. Now Sara is carried down to the sea.

Next day, a Missa Solemnis at 10am launches the Marys on the same journey. Charged with the energy of the Mass, we struggle out of the crowded church and hurry to the beach. We station ourselves beside a retired fishing boat. Presently, the bishop

The journey to the sea
The *gardians* on their white horses accompany Saints Mary Jacobé and Salomé in the procession.

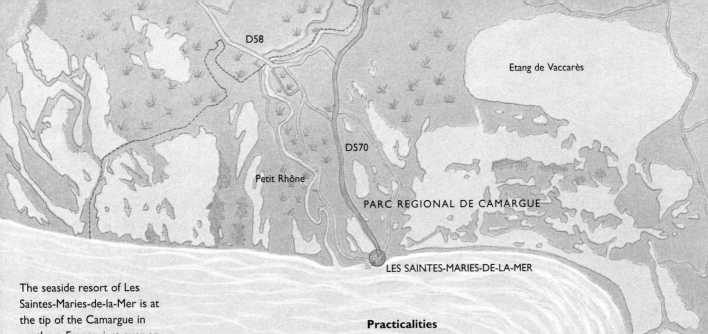

D58

Etang de Vaccarès

D570

Petit Rhône

PARC REGIONAL DE CAMARGUE

LES SAINTES-MARIES-DE-LA-MER

The seaside resort of Les Saintes-Maries-de-la-Mer is at the tip of the Camargue in southern France, just over an hour's drive from Marseille.

and parish priest climb aboard. "Will it be launched?" we ask fishermen. "Heavens no," they say. (Tourists!) Half a dozen *gardians* (herdsmen) on the famous horses of the Camargue mark the seaward limit of the procession.

Now come the Marys in the little blue boat, in which they normally sit in the church, amid votive plaques that thank them for prayers answered, miracles performed. Borne shoulder high, they are grave little persons, uncommonly like Queens Mary and Anne of England. We join the rush to touch them or their gauzy cloaks. Camarguais, gypsies, and – catching the infection – tourists transfer that touch to companions and bless themselves and each other with seawater made holy by the saints' presence.

We are in the surf, beside a horse who stamps as waves wash in behind him. His *gardian* watches out for our bare

Practicalities
There are two pilgrimages a year. *Le Pélérinage des Sainte Maries* on 24/25 May is followed by a civic celebration on 26 May in honour of the *gardians'* champion, the Marquis de Baroncelli. The *Grande Pélérinage des Saintes Maries Jacobé and Salomé,* on the penultimate Sunday in October, is also attended by gypsies but does not include a procession for their patron saint, Sara.

feet – everyone here looks out for pilgrims. I have heard that the saints' blessings are reserved for Provençals and gypsies. Perhaps other years, surely not this: for these people catch us up in their own open generous spirituality. It is as natural as breathing to reach up our arms in church and sing with them over and over: "*O Saintes de Provence, Nous vous tendons les bras, Venez ...*"

We may burst if we don't join their shouts in the church, in the streets: "*Vive les Saintes Maries, Vive Sainte Sara!*" They are why, contrary to expectation and in my go-to-church outfit, I stand here beside the horses up to my waist in the sea.'

Jennifer Westwood is an expert on sacred and spiritual places worldwide and English folklore, and the author of *Atlas of Mysterious Places* and *Albion*.

still considered respectful for women to cover their heads with a scarf, as it is in many other religions.

People may warn you if you are infringing their notions of propriety: but do you want it to come to that? Do you truly mean to give them the message that their spiritual tranquillity is less important than your search for the divine? If not, accept finding out about, buying, and wearing appropriate clothes as part of the disciplines of pilgrimage. (Don't go to the other extreme and play Lawrence of Arabia, by dressing up as a local – this is impertinent.)

TAKING THOUGHT FOR OTHERS

Amid the excitement of getting ready, take thought for those you leave behind. If your way lies somewhere that to them seems remote and alien, they may harbour unfounded fears. Try to allay these before you go by sharing information with them. Once embarked, send regular messages home, although this may not be easy (we all know about the wish-you-were-here postcard that does not arrive until three weeks after our return).

One way of staying in touch is to identify yourself with another old tradition, and keep a diary of your journey, like Nikulás, abbot of the monastery of Munkatherá, Iceland, who set out for the Holy Land in 1154 and recorded his impressions of sights and people en route. Every so often post a copy of your entries home. One of your family or friends may be willing to make photocopies and circulate them to others. That way you preserve your memories whilst they are fresh, and the people you love go with you on your journey, almost step by step.

Think, too, of all those unknown souls you may encounter. Among the more useful things to lug around the world are "trade goods" – small presents to express gratitude and love. In cultures where cameras are not

"Give me my Scallop shell of quiet,
My staffe of Faith to walke upon,
My Scrip of Joy, Immortall diet,
My bottle of salvation:
My Gowne of Glory, hopes true gage,
And thus Ile take my pilgrimage."

SIR WALTER RALEIGH,
THE PILGRIMAGE (1604)

commonplace people often appreciate an instant picture of themselves with the exotic stranger (you), from a polaroid camera. You will need to do some homework as to what gifts are likely to be acceptable (and importable) where you are going, and whether there are any reasons of belief for personal photographs to be taboo.

CARING FOR YOURSELF

You may not want to emulate Basho by burning the dried leaves of Artemisia moxa on your legs in order to strengthen them, but if you intend to walk any distance and are unaccustomed to exercise you might want to build up some stamina. If you are considering walking barefoot, like medieval pilgrims before you, remember that you may be walking on hot metalled roads, not the soft (albeit sometimes stony) dirt tracks of their time. Remember, too, that their feet were often already hardened and calloused from going barefoot or wearing ill-fitting shoes. Seek advice on foot care from long-distance walkers.

Finally, your inner self. Our religions will enjoin some of us to make spiritual preparation. This may entail ritual fasting or cleansing, or abstinence from sex, learning special prayers, or studying sacred texts. We may be required to treat the world around us better than usual. Among the rules Muslims must follow to maintain *ihram* throughout the Hajj is to do nothing dishonest or unkind, neither uproot nor damage any plant, neither kill nor harm any animal or insect.

Both followers of organized religions and other spiritual adventurers may prepare by spending time in meditation. From the Christian tradition comes this definition: "Meditation is the deliberate ... reflection on some truth or passage of Scripture. It has a threefold purpose: to instruct the mind, to move the will, and to warm the heart for prayer." To warm the heart for prayer – not bad preparation for any sacred journey.

"When you feel ... that he is calling you to this work ... lift your heart to God ... A naked intention directed to God ... is wholly sufficient. If you want this intention summed up in a word, to retain it more easily, take a short word ... to do so. The shorter ... the better ... A word like 'GOD' or 'LOVE'. ... And fix this word fast to your heart, so that it is always there ... It will be your shield and spear in peace and war alike. With this word you will hammer the cloud and the darkness above you."

Anonymous author of The Cloud of Unknowing, *14th century*

III Setting out

CHAPTER 3

The moment has arrived. You are physically and intellectually prepared, with bags packed, tickets booked, guidebooks studied.

But are you *really* ready? Western preachers and poets have for generations used "pilgrimage" as a metaphor for life's journey toward death and eternity. This is why Bunyan wrote in *The Pilgrim's Progress* of Christian: "Now he had not run far from his own door, but his wife and children ... began to cry after him to return; but the man put his fingers in his ears, and ran on, crying, Life! Life! Eternal life! So he looked not behind him ..."

No-one is suggesting that you apply this ruthless attitude to real life, or emulate the Roman matron Paula, who in AD382 embarked for the Holy Land ignoring her young son piteously stretching his arms out to her from the shore, and her older daughter, who "by her tears silently besought her mother to stay until she was married". Pilgrimage is a journey *to*, not an escape *from*.

However, this is the point at which the pilgrim must shed his or her security blanket, the web of everyday concerns and people that makes us feel safe and competent and on familiar ground.

Pilgrimage itself is a "rite of passage". All human life involves transitions ("passages") in space, time, and social condition. Some of these transitions – notably, marriage and death – are judged critical and marked by rites. This is as true of Judaism, Christianity, and Islam as of Greek and Roman paganism or the religions of tribal societies.

The anthropologist Arnold van Gennep divided "rites of passage" into three phases. In the first phase people become separated from their social condition; in the second phase they lead a marginal existence, separated from their normal lives; and in the third phase they either rejoin their former condition or join a new one.

This is a description of pilgrimage. The Muslim on the Hajj is separated from his previous life on entering *ihram* (a state of purity); he exists outside his normal life during the Hajj; and he returns to a new condition of improved status in his community, marked by the respectful title *hajji*.

CROSSING THE THRESHOLD

All sacred journeys, great and small, are rites of passage. The word "liminal", used to describe the second phase of such transitions, comes from Latin *limen*, the Roman word for a threshold: the slab or bar at the main door-way that prevents water or mud flowing into the house. It is the thing that separates outside from inside. Such a significant place was the threshold that it was sometimes taboo (forbidden). The worshippers of the Philistine god Dagon, so the Old Testament of the Bible tells us, took care not to step on the threshold of his temple, a practice echoed by pilgrims in Syria in the nineteenth century who still thought it unlucky to step on the threshold of a saint's shrine or of a mosque. According to the thirteenth-century traveller Marco Polo, visitors to the marvellous palace of Kublai Khan in Beijing,

"Here among the shadows in a lonely land,
With strangers we're a band of pilgrims on the move;
Thru dangers burdened down with sorrows,
And we're shunned on ev'ry hand,
But we are looking for a city built above."

*"Looking for a City", hymn by W Oliver Cooper
(1885–1963)*

China, were prevented from stepping on the threshold by guards stationed at every doorway for that purpose.

In ancient times the threshold was built with ritual, sometimes with sacrifice and the burial of the sacrificial victim beneath it to provide a ghostly protector for the house. Roman thresholds were presided over by a pair of deities, male and female, one each side, Limentius and Lima. In India the threshold is the seat of the goddess Lakshmi. Doorways all over the world in ancient times were guarded by statues of monsters: winged bulls in Mesopotamia, sphinxes in Egypt, dragons in China. Doorways all over the world today are still hung with sacred, protective objects. British people often fix a horseshoe over the main door to the outside world. Although they say it is "for luck", it began as an evil-averting magical practice to keep out witches. Orthodox Jews still fix the *mezuzah*, a small case of religious texts, to their doorways.

These beliefs externalize a psychological truth. The threshold of a house marks not only a place of physical movement, inside to outside, but also a transition from one world of experience to another – from the familiar (from Latin *familia*, family) to the unfamiliar, from the known to the unknown, from the safe grip on the hem of the mother's skirt to the hand timidly held out to a potentially hostile stranger. We make this transition every day without noticing it: but children notice it on their first day at play-group or school.

The mother who kisses her child goodbye at the door in the mornings is "noticing" it in another sense – marking it, by engaging in protective magic as old as time. The Western bride carried over the threshold of her new home by her husband, is sharing the experience of Roman brides, and that of brides in China today, where care is taken that her foot does not touch the threshold when she first goes to her husband's home.

When we cross the threshold on entering a temple, we are passing not only from known to unknown, but also from the profane (the realm of everyday) to the sacred (the realm of God). When we cross our own threshold to set out on our pilgrimage, we are making the same transition. In the words of van Gennep: "to cross the threshold is to unite oneself with a new world".

"NOTICING"

The step that takes us across the threshold on to the path of pilgrimage is momentous. We do not know where it will lead. We do not know who we will become on our sacred journey.

And so that first step demands "noticing". Most organized pilgrimages within the world religions begin with an opening ritual on the eve of the pilgrimage or on the day itself. This ritual formally marks the moment when we pass from secular to sacred time. A Roman Catholic pilgrimage may begin with High Mass, during which pilgrims fortify themselves spiritually by taking Holy Communion. Hindus – for whom sacred journeys involve austerities and are often physically extremely arduous – will before departing offer worship to Ganesh, the god of beginnings and of difficulties to be triumphed over. If your pilgrimage is short, involving not much of a journey, or no journey at all, there is all the more reason to mark its beginning.

The raw material for such "markers" lies all around. I opened my week of pilgrimage in May 1996 to Les Saintes-Maries-de-la-Mer in the Camargue, France, with a visit to Saint Walstan's Well at Bawburgh, Norfolk. Allegedly buried here in 1016 amid miraculous happenings, Walstan was once patron saint of farm labourers, and water from his well was used locally to cure sick animals until well into the nineteenth century. Usually I join the annual procession to the holy well on the Sunday nearest 30 May, Walstan's pre-Reformation feast day. This year I would be in the Camargue, but it seemed right not to neglect my own humble local saint, even if (as historians suspect) he is mostly mythical.

Pūsan on the Road

Traverse the ways, Pūsan, and keep away anguish,
O child of the unharnessing. Stay with us,
O god going before us ...

Lead us past our pursuers; make our paths pleasant
and easy to travel. Find for us here, Pūsan,
the power of understanding.

Lead us to pastures rich in grass; let there be no
sudden fever on the journey. Find for us here, Pūsan,
the power of understanding.

Use your powers, give fully and lavishly, give eagerly
and fill the belly. Find for us here, Pūsan,
the power of understanding.

We do not reproach Pūsan, but sing his praises with
well-worded hymns ...

From "Pūsan on the Road", a hymn to the solar charioteer Pūsan who presided over roads and journeys, from the Rig Veda (c.1200–900BC)

Three shrines of simplicity

C North America is not well-known for its pilgrimage shrines. Yet some of the most interesting and most popular pilgrimages in the world are found here. Millions travel each year to Our Lady of Guadalupe in Mexico City, to Sainte Anne de Beaupré near Quebec City, and to St Joseph's Oratory in Montreal. There are over a hundred pilgrimage shrines located throughout the United States, some of which attract several hundred thousand pilgrims each year. Many of these shrines are associated with ethnic devotions and particular religious orders, with only a few devoted to indigenous saints such as St John Neumann, Mother Cabrini, or the North American Martyrs. The three shrines associated with the life of the Blessed Kateri Tekakwitha are unique in North America because they span the border between the USA and Canada.

As I departed with a busload of pilgrims to visit the Kateri shrines, I was hoping to experience the unfolding history of this Native American maiden, a devout convert to the Catholic faith who is also known as the "Lily of the Mohawks". The first shrine we visited is in Auriesville, New York, where, in 1656, Blessed Kateri was born to a Mohawk father and an Algonquin mother.

When she was four years old a smallpox epidemic killed her parents and left her scarred with pock marks and nearly blind for the rest of her life. The Auriesville shrine stands on a hill overlooking the Mohawk River. Here, several Jesuits were killed during their missionary work. Nowadays the shrine attracts thousands of pilgrims like us, interested in both the Jesuit Martyrs and their famous convert, Blessed Kateri Tekakwitha.

We journeyed to the second site in this pilgrimage cycle, to Fonda, New York. It was here, a few miles further up the Mohawk River, that Blessed Kateri experienced her first deep encounter with Christianity. Resisting her uncle's attempts to force her into marriage, Tekakwitha (as she was then known) was baptized into the Christian Church and given the baptismal name Kateri (Catherine). The wooden shrine at Fonda is very much appreciated by the Mohawk people because of its unpretentious simplicity.

Pilgrims visit the Native American Museum under the church, climb the hill overlooking the Mohawk River, and view the excavations showing the outlines of the original village. There is a small stream which is believed to be where Blessed Kateri was baptized. Pilgrims may purchase holy water or take home sacred earth from this tranquil place.

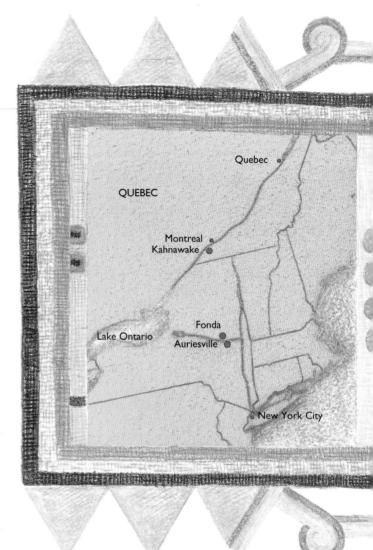

The journey to Kahnawake, the Mohawk reservation near Montreal, is one of the most moving parts of this pilgrimage cycle. In 1676 the Blessed Kateri fled here to the newly established Jesuit mission, to escape persecution by non-Christian Mohawks. Her remains are enshrined at the St Francis-Xavier Mission on the banks of the St Lawrence River. Pilgrims have a strong feeling that they have stepped back several hundred years into the past. This shrine is all the more remarkable because it is the only major place of pilgrimage situated in an Indian reservation.

Blessed Kateri lived a devout and pious life for three years in Kahnawake before she died at the tender age of

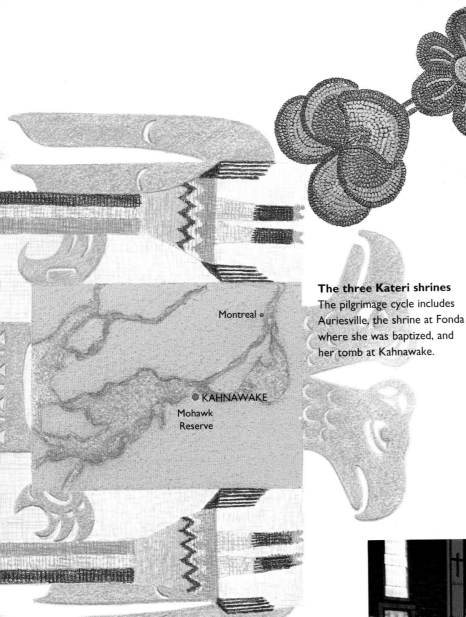

Practicalities

The winter months are extremely cold, with a lot of snow. The best months to visit the shrines are May and June, before it becomes too humid.

St Francis-Xavier's Mission is on the Kahnawake Mohawk Reserve, 6 miles southeast of Montreal. Pilgrims are welcome to attend the daily services at the Mission.

The three Kateri shrines

The pilgrimage cycle includes Auriesville, the shrine at Fonda where she was baptized, and her tomb at Kahnawake.

The Auriesville shrine

Thousands of pilgrims each year visit this shrine at the birthplace of the Blessed Kateri Tekakwitha.

twenty four. In the words of the Church, she lived an "exemplary life", engaging in severe penances, proposing to found a community of Indian nuns, and taking a private vow of perpetual virginity. It is said that at the time of her death her face became radiant and many miracles were reported. Today, pilgrims come in their thousands, and from all parts of the world, to pray at the site where Blessed Kateri lived during her final years.'

Dr James Preston is a Professor of Anthropology and chair of the Religious Studies Program at the State University of New York in Oneonta. He is a specialist on Catholic devotions and pilgrimage shrines.

Other markers to open my pilgrimage might have been a prayer at the shrine of the medieval anchoress Mother Julian in Norwich, England, or at the tomb of John Bunyan in the Nonconformist Cemetery in Bunhill Fields, London, both places that for me hold personal meaning. But neither shrines nor tombs, neither churches nor temples nor mosques are needed for this moment of dedication and leave-taking. In the quiet of your own home – or better still, your garden as an image of Paradise – a piece of music, a poem, a prayer, a minute or two's silent contemplation will serve. It is the act of "noticing" itself that opens the way.

LETTING GO AND TAKING HOLD

Formal openings to pilgrimages also help pilgrims to notice in the ordinary sense: they wake us up, make us alert to what is happening to us, change our mindset. The early Romans again provide illustration of this. Basically countrymen and farmers, they saw the world as charged with numen, an outpouring of the divine.

"God over me, God under me, God before me, God behind me,

(Numen literally means a nod – deities need only nod to get things done.) This numen was embodied in the nature spirits who inhabited the landscape – every spring, lake, hill, valley, rock, and tree had its caretaker – and the sometimes barely personified gods who presided over human life.

Central to early Roman life was the home, in which the *paterfamilias*, father of the family, also acted as priest, conducting the rites that kept household and farm in spiritual health. And central to the home was the hearth, for which the Latin word is *focus*. We speak of being focussed, as often as not unaware that the word carries a charge of historical and psychological meaning from archaic times, when the fire was literally in the middle of the hut. Before the days of the emperors, the hearth-rites were the center of Roman worship. It is no accident that the goddess of the hearth, Vesta, was one of the few old Roman deities to survive throughout the Roman period, holding her own against incomers from Greek mythology and eastern mystery cults.

The further from his hearth a Roman travelled, the greater the psychic exposure. His progress from the hearth outward took him gradually out of the guardianship not only of Vesta, but of Lares and Penates, the household spirits. Once past Limentius and Lima on the threshold, he was also beyond the protection of Janus, the two-faced god of the gate or door and also of the month of January, looking both in and out, behind and before. Last, he passed Terminus, the boundary god, symbolized by a great stone marking the limit of the property. Each year on 23 February (once the last or "terminal" day of the year) Roman neighbours would meet at the boundary stone between their properties. Together they would garland the stone with flowers and sprinkle it with the blood of sacrifice, recharging the numen that would safeguard their adjoining lands for another year, and reaffirming their own concord.

I on thy path, O God, Thou, O God, in my steps."

Carmina Gadelica
(Charms of the Gaels)
Collected in the 19th century

Once beyond Terminus the Roman was outside his familiar support system, in "liminal" territory, in a land he perceived as crowded with alien gods looking after other people's interests. He would attempt to establish friendly relations with these local deities by building them altars, even if, not knowing their names, he had to dedicate them vaguely to the *genius loci*, the "spirit of this place", or *si deus si dea*, "whether you be god or goddess". The further he travelled away from his hearth, the more "unfocussed" he became – but the more aware that the world was full both of dangers and manifold wonders.

WAKING UP

Detachment from the familiar, coupled with acute awareness, is exemplified by the travels of the Japanese poet Basho, especially those recorded in an account which has become a classic of Japanese literature, *The Narrow Road to the Deep North*. In the spring of 1689, accompanied by one friend, Basho set out on foot from Fukagawa, on the outskirts of Edo (old Tokyo), along the Oshukaido, the great road north through the eastern coastal plain up into the remote province of Oshu. Turning inland, he finally reached the sanctuary of the *yamabushi*, the hermit-priests of the northern mountains, and spent a week with them before walking south for two and a half months in the summer heat down the Hokurikudo, the highway leading back down the coast of western Japan to the town of Ogaki.

This was a pilgrimage in something of the Western sense, in that he had a physical goal – the hermits. But more than that it was a journey of self-exploration. Basho separated himself from the material world before he went, selling his house as if he did not expect to return, and this not only because of his own frailty or the physical dangers of the journey. The far north in the Japanese imagination of that time was the Other, mysterious and remote from the civilized world of Edo. For Basho it represented the unfathomable mystery of the universe. He travelled along The Narrow Road to the Deep North as he travelled through his life on earth – seeking a vision of eternity in the everyday.

The things Basho thought worthy of contemplation on his journey included sights that any ordinary tourist might have wanted to see. In his six months on the road (he reached Ogaki in the autumn), he visited not only

The pilgrim caravan sets out for Mecca
"It is their caravan prudence, that in the beginning of a long way, the first shall be a short journey ... Of a few sticks (gathered hastily by the way), of the desert bushes, cooking fires are soon kindled ... In the first evening hour there is some merrymaking of drum-beating and soft fluting, and the Arcadian sweetness of the Persians singing in the tents about us; in others they chant together some piece of their devotion. In all the pilgrims' lodgings are paper lanterns with candles burning; but the camp is weary and all soon is at rest. The hajjies lie down in their clothes the few night hours till the morrow gun-fire; then to rise suddenly for the march ... not knowing how early they may hear it ... At half past five o'clock was the warning shot for the second journey."

C M Doughty, Passages from Arabia Deserta *(1888)*

temples and shrines but also places which had inspired poets in the past, historical monuments and other local "wonders". In going out of his way to visit such famous landmarks, Basho might have seemed to be connecting himself to the Japanese past, defining his own cultural identity. But he sought the ancient monument of Tsubo-no-Ishibumi no more fervently than he sought the species of iris known as *katsumi* in the hills of Asaka. "I went from pool to pool, asking every soul I met on the way where I could possibly find it, but strangely enough

no one had ever heard of it, and the sun went down before I caught even a glimpse of it." Perhaps as a consolation prize, perhaps because he reached the city of Sendau on 4 May when it was the custom to throw fresh leaves of iris on the roof and pray for good health, the painter Kaemon whom he met there gave him two pairs of sandals with deep blue laces of which he wrote:

> "It looks as if
> Iris flowers had bloomed
> On my feet ..."

The Narrow Road to the Deep North is often said to be essential reading for pilgrims. But Basho's style of pilgrimage is different from the prevailing "great religion" models, with fixed goals and hopes of specific benefits, such as time off in Purgatory for Christians. Imam Reza promised Shi'ite pilgrims to Mashad, Iran: "Whoever makes the pilgrimage to my tomb will have my presence with him at three important times: first, when the good and bad are separated to the right and left; second, at the bridge of Sirát; and third, at the weighing of merits."

Hajj paintings
The record of the pilgrimage to Mecca painted on the walls of a Muslim house is a sign of the owners' new status as *hajji*. Traditionally a boat represents the journey, however the pilgrims actually travelled to Mecca. With no experience of boat travel to guide them the artists give their imagination full rein.

We can learn from Basho instead to look at the world with the unfocussed but all-seeing eye, making everything the matter of our pilgrimage. During his time in his little house in Fukagawa (given to him in 1680), Basho had practised Zen meditation. He often claimed to have one foot in the Otherworld, and one in this: in other words, he had not attained enlightenment. Nevertheless he arrived at a truth which he summed up as: "No matter what we may be doing at a given moment, we must not forget that it has a bearing upon our everlasting self which is poetry."

He sought his "everlasting self" through travelling. For other pilgrims, too, the journey may prove more insightful than the destination. Whether we are on the road to Compostela or on a tour of stone circles and standing stones, even with a fixed itinerary and a tight schedule we can lay down the agendas that we carry like burdens on our backs and simply be aware. We can open ourselves in readiness, waiting on our moment with the divine (enlightenment, whatever), which may come to us not on top of the mountain or in the cave where it has revealed itself to others but by the way, in the grain of a stone, the petal of a daisy. We too can have blue laces.

> "... upon the sliding doors, or immediately above the principal entrance of nearly every house, are pasted oblong white papers bearing ideographic inscriptions ... The white papers ... are ofuda, or holy texts and charms ... one ... can nearly always discern at a glance the formula of the great Nichiren sect ... all bristling with long sharp points and banneret zigzags, like an army; the famous text Namu-myo-ho-ren-ge-kyo ... Any pilgrim belonging to this sect has the right to call at whatever door bears the above formula and ask for alms or food."
>
> *Lafcadio Hearn,* Glimpses of Unfamiliar Japan *(1894)*

TAKING COURAGE

Basho's account is not all mystical insights: "my bony shoulders were sore because of the load I had carried"; an inn "was a filthy place ... A storm came upon us towards midnight, and between the noise of thunder and leaking rain and the raids of mosquitoes and fleas, I could not get a wink of sleep.

> Bitten by fleas and lice,
> I slept in a bed,
> A horse urinating all the time
> Close to my pillow."

"Who would true valour see, Let him come hither," begins Bunyan's well-known hymn "To be a pilgrim". Valour is certainly needed by anyone embarking on a physically hard journey or stepping into unfamiliar situations: loneliness for the normally gregarious, the harassment of large crowds for the normally solitary. From the early stages of the journey some pilgrims will encounter and have to adapt to physical discomfort and psychological uncertainty.

Those who have chosen the walkers' road will soon find out just how hard it can be. Satish Kumar writes of his walk to Canterbury across southern England: "Why, oh why are a pilgrim's legs lacking in strength? In India, walking was my birthright. From the age of five I walked every day with my mother to our smallholding. From the ages of nine to eighteen I was a wandering monk of the Jain order. And then I had walked almost around the world! However, since that long walk I had become a householder and lost touch with walking."

"... an 'opening of one's eyes', a revelation, can never be given directly in so many words. We see inner reality only through an 'aha!' experience, a sudden insight into our own being."

John Sanford, The Kingdom Within *(1987)*

But calling on both his own personal valour and his spiritual tradition he went on. "I knew that walking was not solely a means to get somewhere; it was an end in itself, a form of meditation, a way of being. Reflecting in this way, I gathered strength and kept going."

Pilgrims who walk to the shrine of Saint Giles, in a crypt below the half-ruined hill-top abbey of Saint-Gilles in Provence, France, leave their pilgrim staffs behind the rails of his tomb with a justifiable sense of achievement, as thank-offerings for having completed their journey. Sights such as these inspire others when the pain begins to bite.

Those who have elected to catch the bus to a local shrine, or to recreate a mythic journey from sacred site to sacred site from the comfort of a car, need valour of a different order. Even before they have crossed their own threshold, some will assuredly fall to doubting their own purposes, thinking that their journey is not "real" and

MOUNT ATHOS

SALONIKA

The garden of the Mother of God

Mount Athos forms the tip of a finger of land that juts into the sea east of Salonika in Northern Greece. For almost two millenia the peninsula has been revered as the sacred territory of the Virgin Mary, and twenty monasteries of the various Orthodox faiths – Greek, Russian, Serbian, and Bulgarian – are spread along its shores and among its wild mountains. Some 1500 monks live there now – women and "beardless boys" have been forbidden access to the Holy Mountain for centuries.

My papers in hand, I boarded the ferry from the tiny port on the border of Athos – the name which generally signifies the whole peninsula. We chugged for an hour or more along the Athos coast, passing monasteries with onion towers and massive stone ramparts along the way. The boat, filled with Greek pilgrims, finally anchored in Daphni. We made our way to Karies, the administrative center for the Holy Mountain, and then we were on our own.

The only transport on the peninsula is an ancient bus which rattles over the hills from Karies to Iviron monastery, on the northern coast. The best way to travel on Athos is on foot, along the pilgrim paths which thread their way from one monastery to the next. This is what I had come for, to set my body in motion in the rarefied air and the natural elements of the Holy Mountain; to join the countless pilgrims who had travelled these paths down through the centuries, and made of their walking an active communion with the world about them.

I was given permission to stay for two weeks. I would walk all day and arrive in the late afternoon at the gates of a monastery, usually to be greeted by the guestmaster with the traditional glass of ouzo. I often walked, or scrambled, over the cliff paths hanging precariously over steep drops of shale that plunged into the dazzling water below; through forests where the paths would peter out and leave me turning in circles; up steep crags and rocky bluffs where everything was sky, a vast canopy of blue; and through sheaves of white and silver light.

When I reached a monastery in the evening, I was always surprised to notice how little food I wanted. A bowl of thin soup and a slice of bread filled me up till morning, when I would take another slice of bread with thin black coffee. I would never have lunch, and yet my body was humming with a living energy that I have only rarely known again since.

Suddenly, one morning on the path above the ocean, I realized what it was: I was being fed, literally filled up, with the wind, the water, the hard earth, the slant of Greek light, and the vibrations of tens of thousands of monks who had lived out their lives on this land in an intensity of prayer.'

Roger Housden is a writer and photographer, the author of *Travels through Sacred India* and *Retreat*. He is a director of Open Gate Journeys, which leads groups on spiritual journeys to sacred sites.

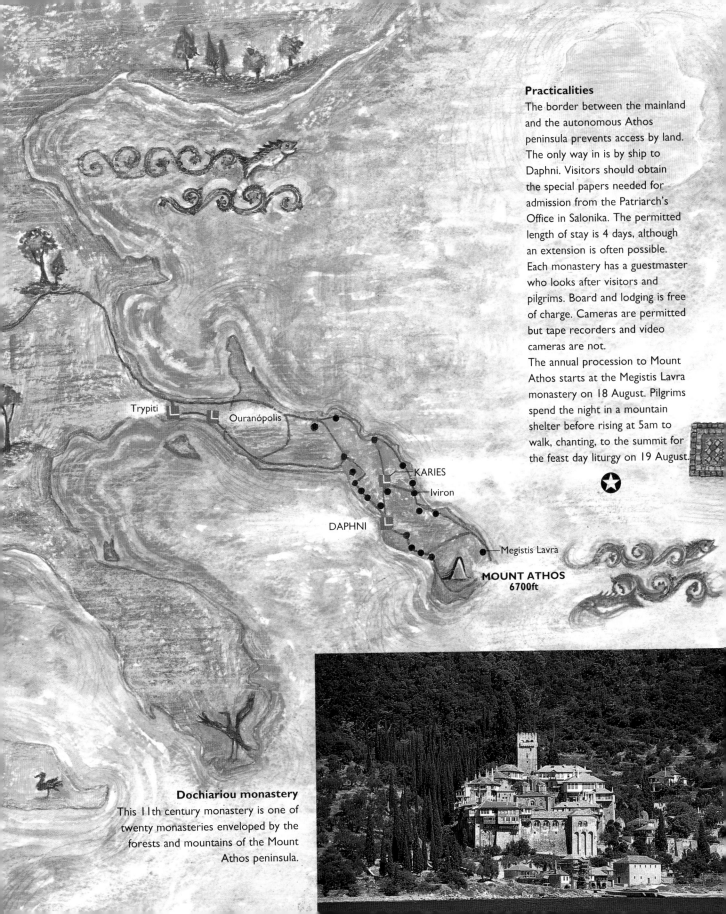

Trypiti

Ouranópolis

KARIES

Iviron

DAPHNI

Megistis Lavra

MOUNT ATHOS
6700ft

Practicalities

The border between the mainland and the autonomous Athos peninsula prevents access by land. The only way in is by ship to Daphni. Visitors should obtain the special papers needed for admission from the Patriarch's Office in Salonika. The permitted length of stay is 4 days, although an extension is often possible. Each monastery has a guestmaster who looks after visitors and pilgrims. Board and lodging is free of charge. Cameras are permitted but tape recorders and video cameras are not.

The annual procession to Mount Athos starts at the Megistis Lavra monastery on 18 August. Pilgrims spend the night in a mountain shelter before rising at 5am to walk, chanting, to the summit for the feast day liturgy on 19 August.

Dochiariou monastery

This 11th century monastery is one of twenty monasteries enveloped by the forests and mountains of the Mount Athos peninsula.

that in the world of pilgrimages they are second-class citizens. They may receive little support from others, who have fixed ideas of what constitutes spiritual endeavour. However, this is one cross that they do not have to bear.

Though pain and hardship are historically associated with pilgrimage, the idea that a sacred journey must be one long slog – "no pain, no gain" – is a cultural value that we put on it and a part only of some religious traditions, particularly Christianity, that equate suffering with redemption. Outside these, reaching back to rites of separation and initiation from very ancient times, are philosophies which accept that physical hardships, including hunger and lack of sleep, may have to be endured, but which do not ascribe to them any redemptive purpose or result. These hardships are used (as in intensive military training, for example by the French Légion Etrangère) to jolt the mind out of a rut and into awareness.

So long as the pilgrim becomes and remains aware (and this takes practice), sacred journeys do not have to be all misery and mosquitoes. Basho, already infirm when he embarked on his journey, did indeed suffer, but not for any virtue in the pain (he took the chance to soak his aching bones in hot springs and when things got too bad he borrowed a horse). His walk up the Narrow Road was not penance but a waking up to his everlasting self.

If self-doubt creeps in, we can take support from the good historical precedent for symbolic pilgrimage. In China before Communism there existed "mountain societies" for making the journey to the Great Mountain, T'ai Shan. The societies were of two sorts: "travelling" and "stationary". Both collected a fixed amount of money per month from members. Soon after New Year, members of "travelling" societies went to the Great Mountain, while members of the "stationary"

> "Three young clerics, of the men of Ireland, went on their pilgrimage ... there was no provision taken to sea save three cakes. 'I will bring the little cat,' says one of them. Now when they reached the shoulders of the main, 'In Christ's name,' say they, 'let us cast away our oars into the sea, and throw ourselves on the mercy of our Lord!' This was done. Not long afterwards they came ... to a beautiful island ... The little cat goes from them. It draws to them a veritable salmon ... 'O God,' say they, 'our pilgrimage is no pilgrimage now! ...'
> Thereafter they abode for six watches without food, until a message came from Christ that some was on the altar ... half a cake of wheat for each man, and a piece of fish."

The Book of Lismore *(1890)*
trans Whitley Stokes

societies celebrated a festival involving worship at a paper "mountain", for all religious purposes held to be identical with the real T'ai Shan.

Though the "stationary" societies were sometimes referred to disparagingly as "squatting and fattening societies" because of the feasts entailed, such symbolic pilgrimages prevented people who could not make a "real" pilgrimage from suffering spiritual deprivation. This may also have been the main purpose of the medieval pavement labyrinths in European cathedrals sometimes known as *Chemins de Jérusalem*, "Paths to Jerusalem". They provided a stage for the pilgrim to act out his soul's voyage.

If we are too solemn about pilgrimage, we may miss the spiritual insights that may arrive in the midst of fun. The turf mazes that were once plentiful in Britain are often claimed gloomily to have been traversed by people on their knees as a penance. But their names – Shepherd's Race, Trojaburg, Troy Town – and their frequent association with sites of fairs and gatherings, suggest that they may have been used to play a game linked to an ancient Roman sport. However they were used originally, "maze-running" today can generate something of the euphoria that, as athletes know, often carries with it moments of startling clarity. Jeff Saward, the founder in 1980 of the Caerdroia Project in Essex, England, dedicated to labyrinth research, speaks of "the intense concentration required to keep from straying from the path and the momentary flash of revelation as one reaches the sudden centre".

What happens to a pilgrim's feet is important: more important is what happens to the head and the heart. Pilgrimage is about willingness and trust: willingness to open ourselves up however briefly to the divine in the world around us, trust that the "flash of revelation" will come. We do not know what form it will take, or when it will arrive. In the film *Mermaids*, the actress Winona Ryder says something like: "Whoever heard of anyone hearing the Voice of God doing 70 miles per hour down the freeway?" She couldn't be more wrong.

IV Sacred way

CHAPTER 4

You are on your road, literally or metaphorically, your body and mind adjusting to your journey in this marvellous time and space outside normality. Hopefully you are wide awake and aware, even if you are sitting comfortably. If you travel by air, put your consciousness into take-off and landing, not letting yourself be distracted by the strategies employed by cabin crew and other passengers to "take your mind off" these most hazardous moments in any flight. This is your life: live it.

Pilgrimage is about receiving what is there, all of it, as part of the liminal experience. Even on a day-trip, there will be some stretching of the mind and spirit so that a new person goes back home. If you are on a journey in a strange land you are missing something if at times you are not half-drunk with seeing, smelling, hearing, tasting, feeling, as well as spiritual exaltation. It is not suffering that keeps the true pilgrim going, but expectation and joy.

In the summer of 1983 for the third time in five years a Westerner made the entire pilgrimage on foot from Alandi to Pandharpur in India. Hindu Varkaris (devotees of this pilgrimage) when asked about this said that they were very pleased that others were experiencing the pilgrimage, but were anxious that in focussing on the laboriousness of the journey Westerners were missing its essential joy.

People have different expectations of pilgrimage. Largely this is a matter of culture. The Latin word for pilgrimage, *peregrinatio*, comes from *per ager*, "through the fields". The idea of a journey is uppermost and because of the laboriousness of that journey in historical times the word "pilgrimage" often implies hardship or discomfort. The Greek word for pilgrimage, however, *proskynesis*, means prostration or veneration: focussing on the goal, it relates to what you do when you arrive at your pilgrimage destination, rather than how you get there. It contains no implication of suffering.

But both words contain the idea of movement: movement toward deity, or in its presence. As we shall see in a later chapter, on closer approach to the godhead walking may be replaced by dance, crawling on the knees, or prostrations. This movement creates a kind of sacred choreography. All pilgrimages have shapes which may be functional but which also assume a symbolic dimension. The contemplation of the shape of your pilgrimage gives you a framework for reflection and strengthens your imagination to grasp what it is you will do, are doing, or have done.

SACRED CHOREOGRAPHY:
PATTERNS THROUGH SPACE

Pilgrimages the world over make the same patterns through space. The principal pattern is the linear one. In pilgrimages where there is no intention of returning, such as the pilgrim-voyages of early Irish monks, or the wanderings of medieval palmers, the line extends up to the moment of death. More usual is the linear journey from A to B with a return by the same route, as along the Pilgrim's Way through southern England to Canterbury. Linear pilgrimages often take the form of processions, transforming the movement from an act of locomotion into a performance. The celebration of the Eleusinian Mysteries in Ancient Greece was preceded by a day-long procession offering local produce at shrines along the way, each of which reflected some aspect of the story of the Corn Goddess, Demeter.

A variation on this is the massing pilgrimage. After leaving home from various starting points over a "catchment area" people converge on an assembly point and then proceed en masse to the shrine. One of the most striking examples of this is the pilgrimage to Pandharpur on the banks of the Bhima river, in Maharashtra, India. Myth and legend relate how Krishna, in the form of Vithoba, came to be at Pandharpur, and how Pundalik, the mythological first saint or holy man of Vithoba's cult, also came there. Poet-saints from Pandharpur and other places expressed their devotion to Vithoba by coming to visit his shrine and the tomb of Pundalik, singing on their way devotional songs composed as offerings.

The most famous among these devotees is Jnanesvar, a poet-saint of the thirteenth century from Alandi, where he voluntarily entered a living tomb. His tomb became a focus for pilgrimage, but also, soon after his death, his followers began venerating replicas of his feet called *padukas* and carrying them to Pandharpur, recreating his own pilgrimage there. Today, the tombs of the saints of Vithoba's cult are starting points for thirty or forty groups of pilgrims called *palkhis*, from the Marathi word for the palanquin in which they carry to Pandharpur the *padukas* of their particular saint. These *padukas* were once stone and quite small, and were worn round the necks of individual pilgrims. However, since the early nineteenth century these have been replaced by life-size silver replicas, borne on a palanquin by particular members of each *palkhi*.

Plotted on a map, the traditional routes of the *palkhis* run like tributaries of a stream to join at the tiny village of Wakri on the outskirts of Pandharpur for the great procession into the holy city. Rituals of joining are performed at the point where two *palkhis* meet: in one popular ritual, members from each group approach one another, and, with arms crossed right over left, clasp hands and swing each other round in a circle.

Some pilgrimages themselves take a circular form, from the practical desire not to return by the same route (in tourist parlance the "round trip") and also from the deep satisfaction that the circle as a geometric shape gives the human mind. The thirteenth-century Christian theologian Thomas Aquinas said that the circle was the perfect whole, as a return is made to the beginning. The Ancient Greek philosophers likewise held that the circle was the perfect figure and circular motion the perfect motion. It is an appropriate figure for pilgrimage.

At the level of imagery rather than metaphysics and geometry, the circle is connected with the sun: the sun's shape, and the shape of its course through the day and the year. Clock faces are circular because they chart the round of hours through day (sun's presence) and night (sun's absence). The zodiac is the circle of the sun's apparent progress through the stars. Not only do Hindu pilgrims to sacred cities often follow a traditional circular pilgrim route round the city, the following of which in its entirety brings especial merit, but they also move from one holy place to another in a rough circle, always moving around to the right, their right shoulders pointing inward toward some invisible center. It is a common practice, too, to circle individual shrines, keeping the shrine on one's right (*pradaksina*). This ritual movement is probably in imitation of the passage of the sun.

People worldwide assign a beneficent influence to sunwise (clockwise) movement, but maleficent to movement counter to the sun (anti-clockwise). In British folk practice these are the directions called *deiseil* or the "sunwise turn", and widdershins. The first is used in rites and charms of blessing, the second in cursings and

"... the universe is a sacramental kind of place in which the material elements and bodily actions can speak of God."

J G Davies, Pilgrimage Yesterday and Today (1988)

SANTIAGO DE COMPOSTELA

Walter Lombaert (right) cooking over an open fire. Coping with the rigours of the walk developed the boys' resourcefulness and sense of self worth.

When the festival of St James (25 July) falls on a Sunday, as many as two million pilgrims come to Santiago to see the dance of the giants and the fireworks at the Cathedral.

A saint, a star, and a shell
Legend has it that St James the apostle fled persecution in the Holy Land and came to northern Spain. There he preached the gospel until his return to Jerusalem, where he was martyred in AD44. His remains were brought back and buried in Spain, where in the 9th century they were rediscovered in a field indicated by a bright star. Santiago de Compostela means literally "St James of the star field".

Pilgrims and penitents have made the pilgrimage to Santiago, the most arduous in Europe, since medieval times, when they would gather at monasteries to travel in groups for safety. Four routes through France meet at the Spanish border. Pilgrims carry a shell, the symbol of St James, since it is said that an early pilgrim who fled to the sea to escape vagabonds returned to land covered in shells.

SANTIAGO DE COMPOSTELA 26 June

Piedrafita 20 June
Villafranca del Bierzo 19 June
León 12 June
Astorga 15 June
Carrión de los Condes 11 June
Santo Domingo de la Calza 1 June
Estella 27 May
Lourdes 11 M
Burgos 4 June
Najera 30 May
Jaca 19 May

Version of the Bible. It is a tale of serendipity. Briefly, it tells how God answers two prayers, one offered up by Tobit in Nineveh (in modern Iraq), the other by Sara in Ecbatana (modern Hamadan in Iran). Both of them are so poor and wretched they want to die. Tobit suddenly remembers (why didn't he think of it before?) that he once lent some money to someone in Rages (Ray, just outside Tehran). His son Tobias must fetch it, but he doesn't know the way. "Seek thee a man which may go with thee, ... and I will give him wages ... Therefore when he went to seek a man, he found Raphael that was an angel. But he knew not; and he said unto him, Canst thou go with me to Rages?"

And so God's plan works itself out: Tobias and the angel, and Tobias' dog, set off for Rages via Ecbatana, where Tobias marries Sara (solving her problem), and brings back the money (solving Tobit's). They try to reward Tobias' guardian and guide with half the money. "Then he took them both apart, and said unto them, ... I am Raphael, one of the seven holy angels, which present the prayers of the saints, and which go in and out before the glory of the Holy One." It is a satisfying parable by a master storyteller, who even remembers to bring the dog home (Tobit 11:4) to join in the happy-ever-after.

Above all, it is a good parable for pilgrims. God, Providence, life has an uncanny way of delivering us what we need when we need it (although we don't always recognize salvation when we see it) and of placing people in our paths who make a difference. Even if you have never travelled much beyond your own town, much less to distant places, your own memory will provide examples.

"O every shower and dew, bless ye the Lord: praise and exalt him above all for ever. ...

O ye fire and heat, bless ye the Lord: praise and exalt him above all for ever. ...

O ye frost and snow, bless ye the Lord: praise and exalt him above all for ever.

O ye lightnings and clouds, bless ye the Lord: praise and exalt him above all for ever.

O let the earth bless the Lord: praise and exalt him above all for ever."

Apocrypha, *The Song of the Three Holy Children* verses 42, 44, 50–2

BUILDING BRIDGES

When you follow the pilgrim road, there will be people who, if you let them, will enrich your physical journey with their travellers' tales of other days and other places, and their observations of things seen along the route. Landscape historians and naturalists make wonderful travelling companions, but so does anyone with a keen eye for the beautiful and the odd. Others will enhance your intellectual journey as a human being, deepening your understanding of your own life and enlarging your horizons with their own experience.

Sometimes this will be the shared experience of the like-situated, such as on the International Military Pilgrimage to Lourdes, which takes place every June. This carefully orchestrated three-day event – days of instruction, initiation (baptisms, confirmations, first Masses), and praising God – brings together around 20,000 soldiers from twenty or so nations, to share their hopes and aspirations for their family and military lives, and also for the future, in a spirit of reconciliation.

Sometimes it will be a matter of contrast. Irawati Karve made her Maharashtrian pilgrimage in an organized party of Brahmins and Marathi. Although they were all approaching the same goal, on their journey toward it they led more or less separate lives: cooking, eating, sleeping apart. "All of the people were clean, and ate their food only after taking a bath. Then why this separateness? Was all this walking together, singing together, and reciting the poetry of the saints together directed only towards union in the other world while retaining separateness in this ... ?" The question was in her mind the whole time, and she joined first one

ATOMIC MIRROR

Banishing the nuclear chain

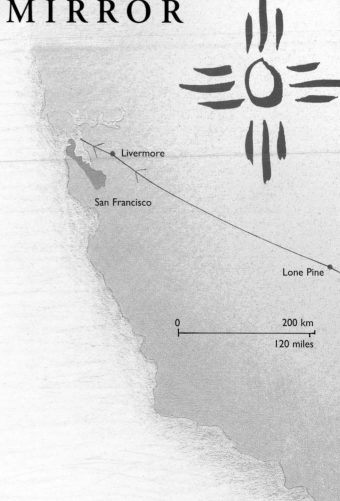

Inspired by a Franciscan priest, who for ten years brought healing earth from Chimayó, New Mexico, to the Los Alamos National Laboratory 20 miles away, an international group of pilgrims carried the earth over the route of the first atomic bombs, 50 years after the birth of the Nuclear Age. Our intention was to retrace this destructive route with creativity and compassion, to focus awareness on the nuclear chain by making it tangible, and to encourage people to reflect and take action at every phase of it.

The Atomic Mirror Pilgrimage began on 14 July 1995, at the Santuario de Chimayó, with an opening ceremony in the outdoor chapel, led by Rabbi Lynn Gottlieb. Setting out were 26 pilgrims of various backgrounds, nationalities, and beliefs, who share the conviction that nuclear weapons should be declared illegal and abolished, and that nuclear power should be phased out, thereby liberating human and natural resources to support genuine human needs.

At Los Alamos National Laboratory, Yoshi Tsukishita, a Hiroshima survivor, returned the fire of the atomic bomb to its origins by presenting the flame he had carried from the Peace Park in Hiroshima to the Deputy Program Director for Public Affairs. At nearby White Sands Missile Range, we walked into the Trinity Site at 5:29am on 16 July, joining over 1000 people who had come to mark the 50th anniversary of the world's first atomic explosion. We held a small ceremony near the obelisk that marks ground zero, and left gifts of healing earth and paper cranes at its base.

After this first weekend our numbers stabilized at twelve and our pilgrimage continued until 9 August, visiting sites representing every part of the nuclear chain: nuclear design laboratories in Livermore, California; uranium mining areas in Navajo country, Arizona and New Mexico; nuclear test sites in Nevada; nuclear waste dump sites in Western Shoshone Country and on Mescalero Apache land; and the atomic-bombed cities of Hiroshima and Nagasaki.

We carried the four elements – earth, water, air, fire – that had been dedicated in the opening ceremony. Healing earth from Chimayó; water from Mount Shasta, California, a sacred white mountain and sister to Mount Fuji in Japan; air, represented by a fan of owl feathers, a gift from the Umatilla people in Washington State; and fire lit from the eternal flame in the Hiroshima Peace Park. To the people of Hiroshima and Nagasaki we brought gifts from the people and communities of the nuclear chain and from Hanford, Washington and Oak Ridge, Tennessee, the source of the plutonium and uranium for the first two atomic bombs.

In the main Zendo of the Green Gulch Zen Center in Marin County, California, and at the World Cathedral for Peace in Hiroshima, we offered the ceremonial performance piece "Atomic Mirror: Reflecting Our Nuclear History". Mayumi Oda's larger than life-sized banners of wrathful, protective goddesses surrounded us and Edie Hartshorne's evocative music carried us. At Crane Harbour in Nagasaki we presented Mayor Iccho Ito with the healing gifts of the four elements that we had carried the length of our journey.

We began, and sometimes ended, each day with a circle of reflection, where each person could contribute their thoughts or feelings on our events or activities. We cooked together, ate together, camped out, discovered each other's skills, agreed and disagreed as we faced the nuclear shadow of the United States, still dark and alive, and our own more private shadows. In essence, we became a community. Together, we made public presentations calling for nuclear abolition, offered ceremonies, and gave gifts of healing to our host communities.

Eire, can go there at any time of year and perform the *turas*, praying at each sacred site at the shrine-complex of Saint Gobnat. But only on the feast-day, 11 February, can pilgrims buy a blue silk ribbon measured along and around the statue of the saint. This *tomha Gobnatan* ("Gobnat's Measure") is kept to use against illness, by "measuring" the ribbon around the affected part.

For everyone, the decision comes down to aligning action with fundamental purpose. In *A Jewish Pilgrimage*, Israel Cohen tells how, before setting off on a fund-raising tour in aid of the Jewish national cause in 1920, he decided to make a pilgimage to the Holy Land. But news reached him of the persecution of Jews in Budapest, Hungary, so he made a detour. Though he later continued his pilgrimage, his purpose – to strengthen his will to help found a Jewish homeland – had already been partly accomplished in Budapest.

By contrast, Mukul Dey, in *My Pilgrimages to Ajanta and Bagh*, speaks of his struggle as a young artist in Calcutta to see the Buddhist cave-paintings at Ajanta,

> ## *"The courage of his choice will honour those Who taught this pilgrim everything he knows"*
>
> FARID-UD-DIN ATTAR (C.1142–C.1220), THE CONFERENCE OF THE BIRDS (MANTEQ AT-TAIR)

in western India. Having endured poverty, ridicule, a 1000-mile train journey, and a carriage drive through country infested with tigers, snakes, and bandits, he arrived at the village near the caves just before sunset.

His driver advised him to find lodgings, officials told him it was too late to visit the caves that night, a party of pilgrims invited him to join them. Despite these well-meaning attempts to deflect him from his purpose, Dey went to the caves and was rewarded with something he would not have seen had he waited until the next day: as dusk fell the paintings became clearer, for as the sun set its light was reflected from the hills, so that briefly the caves became radiant with light.

Once action and purpose are aligned, flexibility and dogged persistence may bring unexpected rewards.

VII Doubt and hope

CHAPTER 7

You are past the turning point, moving closer toward your goal. You have set out in the hope that the journey itself or the holy place you are heading for will perhaps confirm your beliefs, or loose well-springs of faith hidden within you.

But on the road you will meet others heading the same way, either from different religions, or from nominally the same religion but with beliefs seemingly far removed from your own learned in churches or synagogues or mosques or temples.

Confronted with these different versions of "truth" you hit sudden turbulence: your mental baggage is turned upside-down as you react to the beliefs of others and question your own.

The more we learn, the more we doubt. Is your faith only fantasy – just a hope that there is something more to life than what we are stuck with? Pilgrimage tests like nothing else not only your physical endurance but the sturdiness of your spiritual roots.

Many pilgrims never question the basis on which the place they are going is supposed to be holy. We may be able to accommodate miracles provided that they are remote, performed long ago (such as Christ's turning of water into wine) or far away (such as the superhuman running powers sometimes attributed to Tibetan lamas). Our faith may wobble, however, the closer we get to our own society and modern times.

FAITH

" ... faith", said the sixteenth century religious reformer John Calvin, "cannot be acquired by any miracle ..." He taught that faith comes first: miracles are its confirmation. But on a sacred journey, faith can be sorely tried. Just as it takes us physically into the unknown, so pilgrimage often takes us beyond the teaching of our

France, when I saw pilgrims touch the statues of the Marys and Sara. Their faces were ardent with the belief that through that touch blessing was transmitted. With four hundred years of Puritan ancestors behind me, when I touched the saints it was purely symbolic.

Your sticking point may come when you least expect it. According to an apocryphal story, Martin Luther when in Rome crept up the structure known as "Pilate's Staircase" on his hands and knees, this being a penance for helping souls out of Purgatory. Luther was doing it for his dead grandfather but, when he got to the top, stood up and asked himself (roughly speaking): how can this be true? Especially if we have had an education that places emphasis on rationality, we shall see and hear things on our pilgrim road that challenge us: how can this be true?

> ## "My path is lost; my wandring steps do stray; I cannot safely go, nor safely stay; Whom should I see but Thee, my Path, my Way?"

> FRANCIS QUARLES (1592–1644)
> FROM "WHY DOST THOU SHADE THY LOVELY FACE?"

religious leaders into marginal territory. Out here we may witness practices that belong to folk religion rather than the mainstream. We may encounter beliefs that are survivals of archaic ways of thinking, an embarrassment to orthodox religion trying to remain valid in an ever-changing world. Hitherto we may have accepted the explanations of such things as anomalies or symbolic. Seeing faith in action on pilgrimage may be a shock.

Perhaps the most challenging pilgrimage to go on is not one of a totally different faith – where everything is new and exciting – but one of a different "brand" of our own religion. As a Protestant educated at a Catholic school, I am comfortable with holy water, genuflection, lighting candles, the Stations of the Cross. But I hit my own belief-boundary in Les Saintes-Maries-de-la-Mer,

In modern times many of us have been lulled into thinking that pilgrimage is all about healing. Some of the most famous Christian pilgrimages founded in the past two centuries have been for healing – among them Lourdes in France, Fátima in Portugal, and Beauraing in Belgium. In the past few decades, pilgrimages for the sick have been introduced even at sacred shrines with no previous reputation for cures. Familiar with the concept of "mind over matter", we can fit healing shrines into an acceptable psychological and scientific framework. The Western Church disarms critics further by placing less emphasis on miracles (though acknowledging that

Doubt
A sacred journey is a journey into the unknown, physically and spiritually. When faith falters, hope leads the pilgrim through doubt.

sudden and unpredicted cures do take place) than on the general therapeutic benefit pilgrimage confers on the sick and terminally ill.

But pilgrimage is an ancient strategy for coping with all sorts of life-hazards, not just sickness. Shrines have been founded in response to invading armies, environmental dangers, accidents, famine, bad harvests, and supernatural threats. Some are created from inspiration or eccentricity, depending on the point of view. In the 1960s a Yogi established himself in a hut inside the premises of the Government College of Chandigarh, India. Beside it he built a mud structure, which he claimed was the grave of his ancestral guru, marking an ancient sacred site. Officialdom attempted to evict him, but he serenely maintained that he had had a dream that someone "from abroad" would help him. It was not long before local residents were coming to the "grave" to pray.

I don't know what happened next – whether history judged the Yogi a madman, a charlatan, or a holy man. But, as S M Bhardwaj, reporting this in *Hindu Places of Pilgrimage in India*, remarks: if the Yogi found financial support from abroad, it is "entirely possible that there may one day be a shrine of allegedly ancient origin in the modern city of Chandigarh". The point this story illustrates is that a pilgrimage may hinge wholly on one person's credibility.

If we are heading for a reputedly miraculous shrine, now is a good time to ask: do we believe in miracles? Not just a vague hope that deity will answer our prayers, but an explicit belief in the possibility of overturning natural laws. Perhaps a million pilgrims every year visit Juazeiro do Norte, a poor city in north-east Brazil, on account of a Catholic priest, Padre Cicero Romao Batista (1844–1934). In his lifetime he was credited

CHACO CANYON

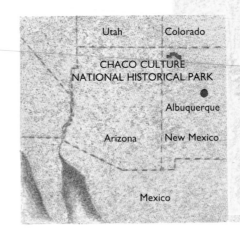

Peñasco Blanco

Reconnecting with the ancient ones

❝ Often it's the simple pleasures in which memories are embedded: leaning against the cool walls of impeccable stone masonry, seeking relief from the summer heat as the Anasazi had 1000 years ago. Alone in the *kiva*, I hear the prayers of the ancient ones, the predecessors of today's Pueblo Indians of the American Southwest.

At a time when Europe was emerging from the Dark Ages, a New World civilization was flourishing in what is now called the Four Corners region of New Mexico, at the state boundary with Arizona, Utah, and Colorado. Chaco Canyon was the political, economic, and spiritual center of the Anasazi culture, with an extensive network of long straight roads radiating like spokes to at least 70 regional settlements. The underground sanctum in which I sit is one of 40 such *kivas* within Pueblo Bonito. Covering three acres and originally containing over 600 rooms, this beautiful village is the largest excavated prehistoric ruin in North America. As many as 400 smaller villages are located in the canyon and the surrounding plateau.

It is a bittersweet journey. I have returned to the land where one year earlier my young family last vacationed, where my daughter took some of her first walking steps, where my wife and I held each other at night. In this past year I have lost my marriage to divorce, lost my father to lung cancer, and lost my grandmother to old age. I now come to Chaco Canyon on a spirit journey with a group of gay brothers, to seek an expanded sense of self and community.

It is a difficult journey. Chaco Canyon is in a remote area of northwestern New Mexico. Clay roads, impassable when wet, provide the only access. There are no services, meaning no gas, no food, no lodging. The discomfort of the searing heat is only amplified by the dry winds in a desert landscape that hardly seems suitable for lizards, let alone a once thriving center of 6000 people. Rainfall is marginal, the growing season short. Winters are long and cold. Yet there is something about this land that beckons the soul.

It is a blessed journey. As the moon rises full over the desert landscape, silhouettes of ancient faces gaze down upon our contemporary tribe. Emotions percolate within me as I open my heart to my fellow gay journeymen, as we attempt to understand the ephemeral connection with a lost civilization. We come from all walks of life, with individual stories that tell of our unique experiences. Yet we share a common thread, a wound that is understood without words. I sense the silent tears as we stand together, hand in hand,

under the brilliant night sky. I am in the company of a strong tribe, a tribe filled with constrained passion and talent, a communion of immortal souls with a vision that could heal our times.

At dawn's earliest light, soft drumming welcomes in a new day. Our circle is in Casa Rinconada, the largest ceremonial *kiva* in Chaco Canyon. A fleeting dust devil enlivens the vital breath of the ancient ones who drummed before us. In silent prayer, we listen carefully to the whispers of this land. We bestow homage on, and spiritually reconnect with, the legacy of the Anasazi. On this day, even as the earth's climate is reportedly changing, our tribe of gay men dedicates itself to persevere in the expression of our unique heritage. We do so with a sense of aliveness and freedom – and we sing with gratitude in our hearts for the gifts we have received from the ancient ones.❜

Charles Fletcher is a community health educator and leads outdoor programmes exploring sacred connection to wilderness and personal and spiritual growth.

CHACO CULTURE NATIONAL HISTORICAL PARK

Casa Chiquita

Pueblo Alto

Pueblo Bonito

Pueblo del Arroyo

Chetro Ketl

CASA RINCONADA

CHACO CANYON

Hungo Pavi

MOCKINGBIRD CANYON

Tsin Kletsi

The Anasazi settlements
One of the newest national parks in the USA runs along 12 miles of Chaco Canyon, inhabited by the Anasazi until the 12th century. Research has suggested that climate change may have forced these ancestors of the Pueblo Indians to leave the canyon, which is now arid desert.

Pueblo Bonito
This Great House (far left), contained 800 rooms in four stories and 37 *kivas* (large underground ceremonial chambers). The great *kiva* Casa Rinconada (left) is thought to have functioned as a community center.

with miraculous powers and stories of them abound. One tells how, when one man went to Juazeiro to see him, Padre Cicero greeted him warmly but said: "My son, why did you leave your dagger by the jua tree?" On the way home, the man found his golden dagger where Padre Cicero had said, lying under the tree where he had slept the previous night. Do we believe this? Or that Padre Pio (1887–1968) could bilocate? According to General Cadorna, the Italian Army Chief of Staff, the padre appeared in his tent after an Italian defeat in 1917 and saying "Don't be so stupid!" prevented his suicide.

Do we believe in the powers of relics? More than any other feature, the physical remains of martyrs and saints were the focus of early Christian pilgrimage. Though often explained today as a focus for piety only, a reminder of the person we are praying to, this is not how they were originally thought of nor what many present-day pilgrims believe. If you look at medieval shrines, such as the recently restored shrine of Saint Melangell at Pennant Melangell, Llandgynog in mid Wales, you will see that the reliquary containing the bones of the saint is supported on arches. Under these pilgrims would lie, to be as close to the saint as possible. At saints' tombs, pilgrims came into direct contact with the saint, simultaneously present here on earth and in Heaven. Watch pilgrims at the shrines of saints reaching out to touch their tombs or the reliquaries (caskets) holding their remains. Underlying what they are doing is belief in the physical presence of the holy.

A saint's potency was believed to be transmissible. This is why in Rome, at the shrine of Saint Peter, pilgrims thrust their heads through a small window above the tomb to address their prayers directly to Peter and lowered on to it little cloths, which they drew up charged with his sanctity. This is why pilgrims to Assisi today give the attendant nuns articles to touch to Saint Claire's preserved body.

Away from the tomb, small fragments of the saint's remains were thought still to contain their full potency. However Protestantism rejected relics and pilgrimages to places where they were enshrined, at the same time as it rejected wonder-working images and on much the same grounds. Thomas Hobbes wrote in *Leviathan* (1651) "to worship God as inanimating or inhabiting ... an image or place, that is to say an infinite substance in a finite place, is idolatry".

This belief is not confined to Christianity. Relics form part of a wider cult of "traces", which exists even within Buddhism, although according to orthodox Buddhism, the Buddha, having achieved *parinirvana*, is permanently gone from the world and cannot be accessed. By the time the Chinese pilgrim Hsü an Tsang went to India in AD629, a great range of objects had been preserved for the veneration of pilgrims: remnants of the Buddha's cremation; hair and nail clippings collected in his lifetime; his begging bowl, waterpot, and staff; bits of his robe. Also preserved were the sites of his birth, enlightenment, first sermon, and *parinirvana*, and physical traces, such as his footprints embedded in

"Martin in heaven

rock and trees supposedly rooted from sticks he had used to clean his teeth (much as Joseph of Arimathea's staff became the Holy Thorn at Glastonbury).

In Buddhist societies, the Buddha's footprint is revered as symbolizing his "setting forth" and temples, monasteries, and shrines in Thailand not infrequently include representations of it (*phra bat camlaung:* "holy footprint copy"). But in Thailand there are also several depressions in rocks venerated as "real" Buddha footprints. When the meditation master Luang Phau of the monastery of Wat Phra That Naung Sam Meun wanted to construct four "holy footprint copies", one each for Gautama Buddha and his successors Kokusandha, Konakomana, and Kassapa, he remembered that in northern Thailand he had once seen what local people believed were the genuine footprints of the four Buddhas. In May 1972, he led an arduous pilgrimage by bus, then truck, then on foot, to collect detritus from the surfaces of these footprints and chip off small flakes of rock. These were then incorporated, each under its appropriate "footprint copy".

For some pilgrims, the "footprint copies" are symbolic; for others, they are charged with the sanctity of the originals. Such transfers of sanctity worldwide have allowed sacred places to change location, and copies of places and buildings to function as if they were the "real" thing. At least 15 out of the 88 pilgrimage places on Shikoku in Japan have been moved. In western Japan, Imochigaura Lourdes on Goto Island is the outcome of a transference of sanctity from Lourdes. Loreto in Italy was created by a transference from the Holy Land.

"Now there was not far from the place where they lay, a castle called Doubting Castle, the owner whereof was Giant Despair, and it was in his grounds they now were sleeping: wherefore he, getting up in the morning early, and walking up and down in his fields, caught Christian and Hopeful asleep in his grounds. Then with a grim and surly voice he bid them awake, and asked them ... what they did in his grounds. They told him they were pilgrims, and that they had lost their way. ... The giant therefore drove them before him, and put them into his castle, into a very dark dungeon ..."

John Bunyan,
The Pilgrim's Progress, Part I *(1678)*

"Now a little before it was day, good Christian, as one half amazed, brake out in this passionate speech: What a fool, quoth he, am I, thus to lie in a stinking dungeon, when I may as well walk at liberty. For I have a key in my bosom called Promise, that will, I am persuaded, open any lock in Doubting Castle ... Then Christian pulled it out of his bosom, and began to try at the dungeon door, whose bolt (as he turned the key) gave back, and the door flew open with ease ..."

John Bunyan,
The Pilgrim's Progress, Part I *(1678)*

here shines forth in the tomb"

INSCRIPTION ON TOMB OF ST MARTIN OF TOURS

For many this is an unaccustomed way of thinking: in the West particularly, we set great store by the "genuine". When we arrive at our chosen sacred place, it matters to us to discover that it is no longer at the very spot where the irruption of the divine into the mundane (that we have come to celebrate) took place. It makes us uneasy to learn that the special blessing available at some holy place or shrine derives from something in which we simply cannot believe.

Whilst we labour under doubts that separate us from our fellow pilgrims, the way is blocked for the flow of synergy that comes from being at one with others. The struggle with our beliefs also inhibits the operation of synchronicity: that apparently random falling into place of the answer to our question, that vital but elusive piece of the jigsaw. Doubts stultify: the way through them is hope.

SAINT CATHERINE'S MONASTERY

A jewel in the desert

C I grew up in St Catherine's valley, a steep cleft in a Cotswold ridge on the edge of Bath. In my late teens I spent hours alone in the village churchyard, wondering each time I passed it at the medieval carving of the patron saint and her wheel that stood over the porch. I wondered how her fame could have spread even to this hidden valley in the depths of England from some remote desert far away; so that, even then, seven hundred years later, a boy should grow up there in the shadow of her name.

St Catherine's in the Sinai: bastion of old Byzantium, far-flung jewel of a once Imperial crown, survivor through fifteen centuries of changing fortunes, the coming and going of civilizations, religions, conquerors, and vanquished. I had always wanted to go there. I wanted the living truth behind a childhood dream.

Now here I was, one November morning thirty years later, in the Eastern Standard Bus station in Cairo. A sleek bus, with shiny aluminium flashes down the sides and video entertainment already beginning, was about to leave direct for St Catherine's. Sailing to Byzantium in a video bus: it just didn't fit. Another, shabbier bus stood alongside. Destination: Nuweiba, on the Sinai coast of the Aqaba Gulf. I would go to Nuweiba, and find a guide there to take me on the seven-day walk through the desert to the monastery. I wanted to arrive at the monastery gates in the way that travellers and pilgrims had done for centuries.

I spent much of those seven days on the back of a camel, dipping up and down over a vast and empty expanse of black stones and yellow dust, through coloured canyons and dun-coloured mountains. On the fourth day, though, I followed Sliman, my guide, clambering up precipitous rock faces while his assistant led the camels the long way round.

Cairo

Nile

Nuweiba

ST CATHERINE'S MONASTERY

St Catherine's Monastery, in a narrow valley below Mount Sinai, was founded in the 6th century as a fortification of the site where, according to the Old Testament of the Bible, Moses saw the Burning Bush.

St Catherine of Alexandria
The monastery holds the skull of St Catherine, a 4th-century martyr. She was persecuted for her Christianity and her refusal to marry the Emperor, since she considered herself a Bride of Christ. Her punishment for successfully arguing her case against anti-Christian philosophers was to be broken on a wheel and beheaded. In medieval Europe a cult developed from this legend and the monastery became a pilgrimage center.

I wished I had gone the long way. We eventually reached a broad, flat sandplain, 1500 feet up. It was bitterly cold, a strong wind in our faces suddenly; we trod on for hours beneath a sullen sky.

Was this what I wanted? My feet were sore, my legs were aching, the wind was whipping through me. I seemed to be plodding head down through this bare and featureless land for no other reason than for the sake of it. Fear hovered over me. I imagined St Catherine's suddenly, a jewel in the desert; and found myself moving towards it now – and me, not even a practising Christian – with the old Orthodox prayer "Lord have mercy" on my lips.

We pushed on for hours, until finally we reached the other side of the plain to find Selman, Sliman's assistant, crouched by a fire among some rocks below. We climbed down to join him, my legs barely holding. I threw all the clothes in my bag on to my back and lay down by the

flames like a child, teeth chattering, vital force gone. Sliman took his only blanket and covered me with it gently.

The next morning the world had righted itself again, and for three more days we trod on through the desert silence, until at last I stood before the tall fortress walls that still protect the monks, the relics of St Catherine, and the ever-flowering Burning Bush from which God spoke to Moses. I had arrived; yet those days in the desert had shown me that the way is as much the end in itself as the apparent destination. I returned home to England with two souvenirs of my journey, each as significant to me as the other: a copy of the Byzantine icon of Christ Pantocrator and a rock from the Sinai desert.'

Roger Housden is a writer and photographer, the author of *Travels through Sacred India* and *Retreat*. He is a director of Open Gate Journeys, which leads groups on spiritual journeys to sacred sites.

HOPE

We easily enter into and share the hope of those who long for bodily health and spiritual wholeness. We may not be so sympathetic, when we meet it in the flesh, to aspirations that cut across our views of what is spiritual and "right". What of those whose beliefs seem to us alien, primitive, superstitious, wrong, or even wicked?

If we are truthful about our reservations, we may find that deep down they are rooted in fear that other people's beliefs somehow threaten our own value-system. If you are a Christian or a Muslim reading these words, how do

I am a man
and account nothing human
alien to me.

TERENCE (C.195–159 BC)
HEAUTON TIMOROUMENOS

you feel about the arrival in Portugal of Iranian pilgrims who believe that the shrine of Our Lady of Fátima is a Christianization of one originally dedicated to Fatima, the daughter-in-law of Mohammed? Are you comfortable with syncretic religions in which your own faith has been merged with something else? What about the religion of the Macha of Ethiopia, in which Mohammed, the Virgin Mary, and a number of Islamic and Christian saints are all revered *asayanas*, subsidiary manifestations of the central deity Waka? Or Candomblé from Brazil or Vodou from Haiti, blendings of Catholicism and African native religions?

Consider the villagers of Chumpón in Mexico, who venerate a miraculous cross which communicates its wishes through signs. If disobeyed or offended it expresses its wrath by means of drought and epidemic. Can this be a Christian cross? The Maya Indians of Chumpón believe so. In 1850, after an unsuccessful revolt against Mexican rule, the Maya retreated into the largely uninhabited forests of what is now the state of Quintana Roo. From then until well into the twentieth century a series of such crosses spoke and issued written instructions governing the life of the Maya. For those who still perform the pilgrimage to it, The Holy Cross

of Chumpón – born of a fusion between Christianity and Mayan cosmology – still focusses their hope of preserving their cultural identity.

Consider also a pilgrimage in 1996 that brought Rastafarians to southern Ethiopia to celebrate the 105th birthday on 23 July of the former emperor, Haile Selassie. Dressed in red, yellow, and green – the Rastafarian and Ethiopian colours – with images of the emperor hanging round their necks, they gathered to consecrate the new tabernacle at Shashemane.

In 1937, in support of the American Back to Africa movement founded by Jamaican-born Marcus Garvey (1887–1940), the Ethiopian Emperor Haile Selassie donated land where people of African descent could be repatriated. Rastafarianism grew from this movement, the name coming from *ras*, meaning prince, and *tafari*, the Emperor's title before his coronation in 1930. Haile Selassie ruled Ethiopia until the Marxist revolution of 1974 and belonged to a royal dynasty that claimed direct descent from King Solomon in the Bible. It was this charismatic tradition that made my mother take me as a child on a long train journey to London to see him. For us, and thousands like us lining The Mall as he rode by in an open carriage to Buckingham Palace on his State Visit, he was a living legend.

To Rastafarians he is divine – the fulfillment of the Revelation of St John 5:5: the "Lion of the tribe of Juda". Though interpretations differ, many believe he is not dead but will return. The Welsh and the Bretons in the early Middle Ages believed this of Arthur, the Once and Future King. Oppressed peoples the world over yearn for a saviour.

Rastafarians generally have a bad press: the dreadlocks, smoking of *ganja* and sporadic violence provide better newspaper copy than the facts that strict Rastafarians do not eat meat or drink alcohol, and are mainly pacifist. Though Rastafarianism is commonly labelled a "cult", if we listen with pilgrims' ears to the songs of Bob Marley (1945–81), who articulated its hopes of a fairer world, we begin to understand why the Catholic Commission for Racial Justice in 1982 recommended that "Rastafarianism should be recognised as a valid religion".

Pilgrimage gives us a unique opportunity to try our faith, to push on our personal boundaries and to look through the differences that divide us to the hopes that unite. From here it is but a short step to that overflowing of compassion and respect that Christians used to call *caritas*, charity, but nowadays simply call love.

LOVE

Remember on our pilgrim road the Bible's supreme parable of the triumph of love over difference, "The Good Samaritan" (Luke 10: 29–37). As pilgrims we are required not necessarily to approve others' hopes, but only to recognize that all humankind is needy: not only sick people who long for health, but heretical Catholic devotees of a Wisconsin shrine who believe that only they will be saved from eternal damnation; Maoris, Maya, and Rastafarians who each see pilgrimage as a way of asserting themselves against an uncaring society; Sikhs and Hindus, Theravada Buddhists and Tamils, Muslims and Jews, all battling it out in different areas of the world to possess a square foot of sacred ground.

Pilgrimage gives us the chance to meet, at the very core of our beliefs, our own humanity. The road may be hard and painful. Find your way through the labyrinth of doubt by following the shaman Don Juan's advice to anthropologist Carlos Castaneda: "Look at every path closely ... Then ask yourself ... one question ... Does this path have a heart?"

"Peace and love are always at work in us, but we are not always in peace and love"

MOTHER JULIAN OF NORWICH
REVELATIONS OF DIVINE LOVE (C.1393)

125

VIII

Drawing near: anticipation

CHAPTER 8

You are drawing near. Although physical hardship possibly, and spiritual doubts almost certainly, are not entirely behind you, you are carried forward by a mounting suspense. The road that yesterday was just a road to a far place is now bringing you within the ambit of the sacred.

As you draw close, the landscape becomes dense with cosmological and symbolic meaning: clusters of shrines, holy wells, caves, trees, and other features of sacred topography that prepare you for the encounter which is the purpose of your journey.

There are still practicalities to consider – the most urgent at this point being whether your arrival will be at the appropriate moment in the religious timetable. If you are behindhand, and there is something you can do about it, then do it. As with much else with pilgrimage, you will not know what "missing" something means to you until after the event.

Now is the time to begin actively preparing for the climax of your journey, reminding yourself again of what it is you seek.

The road to the sacred
For these women arriving in the Indian city of Allahabad, the physical journey is almost complete. Their pilgrimage is to the Sangam, sacred to all Hindus, where the Yamuna and Ganga meet the mythical River of Enlightenment.

126

Now more keenly than ever you may feel yourself to be part of an historical process. You are a member of that community of seekers which, by making them their goal, has brought into being and activated many thousands of pilgrimage sites and shrines all over the world. During the Middle Ages there were a hundred and more well-attended pilgrimage destinations in England and Scotland alone.

You may develop strong feelings of the communitas we spoke of earlier, the spiritual "togetherness". In the 1970s the anthropologist Victor Turner suggested that

being brought together by a shared religious goal. The experience of oneness is perhaps sharpest at sacred sites where there is no appreciable tourist element, as at Fátima, in Portugal. The devotion to Our Lady of Fátima began at a time of crisis, when Europe was involved in World War I and Portugal itself was in a difficult social and political situation. Three shepherd children, Lucia Santos, and Francisco and Jacinta Marto, saw three apparitions of angels in the spring, summer, and autumn of 1916 in and around the village of Aljustrel. There followed six appearances of the

"How I long to see among dawn flowers,

this was the core experience of pilgrimage, the response of people used to a structured and unequal society who find themselves on pilgrimage in an unstructured community of equal persons. Turner writes: "Pilgrimages seem to be regarded by self-conscious pilgrims both as occasions on which communitas is experienced and journeys towards a sacred source of communitas, which is also seen as a source of healing and renewal."

Pilgrimage indeed may bring together the most diverse groups of people: between 13 and 31 January 1951, pilgrimages to Guadalupe, Mexico, were made by: parishioner groups from five different villages in Mexico State; personnel of the Ejidal bank, of a drug store, of a hotel, of the Bank of Mexico, of a printing and paper company, of a candy and chocolate factory; the Union of Fishermen; a neighbourhood group from Peralvillo in the Federal District; alumni of an engineering school; the Guild of the "children of America"; the Congress of Catholic Schools; coach workers; and pilgrim students back from 1950 Holy Year observances in Rome under the leadership of the Society of Jesus.

This is an impressive list of people with nothing much in common but their jobs or the place they live in,

Blessed Virgin Mary on 13 May, 13 June, 13 July, 19 August, 13 September, and 13 October 1917, all except for that of the 19 August taking place in a semi-circular hollow, the Cova da Iria, one mile west of Aljustrel, and near which the sanctuary is now situated. The second apparition of 1917 in the Cova da Iria was witnessed by about 50 people; the third by perhaps 4000; the fourth by 5000. No fewer than 25,000 people were present during the fifth apparition and at the last, in October 1917, 70,000 people were present. Not unsurprisingly in view of this mass witness, devotion to Our Lady of Fátima grew, and in 1929 the first foreign group of pilgrims arrived, from the German city of Munich. Nowadays organized parties come from many countries, their purpose not to "see the sights" but to participate in the miraculous nature of the place.

But on many pilgrimages cohesion is far less than you might expect. Theravada Buddhist pilgrimages in Thailand unite pilgrims spatially, but anthropologists have observed that there is no social mixing of one group of pilgrims with another, or between individual pilgrims of different regional and economic backgrounds. On the 1987 pilgrimage the Indian and Nepali pilgrims interviewed by Barbara Nimri Aziz maintained their accustomed social structures, pilgrims travelling with family and friends and not mixing with outsiders.

"Togetherness" is less than universal where some religious taboo also comes into play. As mentioned in the last chapter, in recent years Muslim pilgrims from Iran have also come to Fátima, although neither the Christian nor Muslim communities of Portugal give them support. Communitas clearly has limits.

Irawati Karve, whose Maharashtra pilgrimage was described in Chapter 5, was so moved by the experience of communitas within her *palkhi* group on the pilgrimage that she could not bear the subdivision into smaller

the face of God." HAIKU BY BASHO (1644–94)

groups by caste. After taking a meal with the Maratha women (there are strong taboos in Hinduism against eating with other castes) she found they were more friendly toward her, a Brahmin. "Towards the end, they called me 'Tai,' meaning 'sister.' A few of them said, 'Mark you, Tai, we shall visit you in Poona.' And then one young girl said, 'But will you behave with us then as you are behaving now?' It was a simple question, but it touched me to the quick. We have been living near each other for thousands of years, but they are still not of us, and we are not of them."

There is a dilemma here. Pilgrimages by their nature as convergences of human beings at a center would seem necessarily to engender feelings of unity, but they are constricted by the religious systems to which they belong. Division runs all the way down the scale. The Hajj to Mecca and Medina unites Muslims from all over the world but separates the Umma (nation of Islam) from all other faiths. The Maharashtra pilgrimage temporarily unites Hindus spatially but maintains the barriers between castes.

The complexity of the situation is epitomized by Malcolm X, the first Black Muslim to go on Hajj.

SODO

HAITI

* SAUT D'EAU
● Port-au-Prince

Gifts from a cool goddess

Sodo is the popular name for an annual pilgrimage to the Haitian village of Bonheur ("Happiness"), and its adjacent waterfalls, Saut d'Eau. At this mountainous site, sixty pot-holed and cork-screwed miles from the capital city of Port-au-Prince, the Miracle Virgin ("Vierj Mirak") is honoured each 17 July, feast day for Our Lady of Mount Carmel. She is said to have manifested herself there in the nineteenth century, and during the American military occupation from 1915–33. According to local tradition, the first sighting took place on 16 July 1841. A man named Fortuné, searching for a lost horse, came to a palm grove. He looked up and saw a beautiful woman in a palm tree. Soon afterward, pilgrimages to the site began.

Every year since Fortuné's vision, 20,000 or so pilgrims have set out by foot, donkey, or rickety public transport for Bonheur. Their immediate focus is the church built to commemorate his apparition. Roiling crowds of pilgrims now lend Sodo the look and feel of a Caribbean Brighton on a summer weekend. Ecstatics, beggars, vendors, nuns, gamblers, penitents, hookers, army officers, journalists, anthropologists ... here is God's plenty in Haiti. They have come with many purposes – to seek a cure, fulfill a vow, pick a pocket, escape the city heat, eat fresh fruit, take a cool bath. Bonheur wishes all its pilgrims well.

Holy waters
Pilgrims immerse themselves in the Saut d'Eau falls, sacred to the Vodou goddess Elizi and the Vierj Mirak, two aspects of the same divinity.

Few travellers remain for Mass. Most head for the waterfalls a mile or so away to immerse themselves in torrents sacred to Ezili, the Vodou goddess of love, and to her serpent lover Danbala, the patriarch of the Vodou pantheon. Water is a divine element, and many pilgrims become possessed by these aquatic deities while standing under the falls. Pilgrims feel no contradiction in their dual devotions to the Vierj Mirak and the Water Gods. For in their Vodou practice, Mary and Ezili are different aspects of the same divinity. Many clergy are not happy with this assimilation. One bishop complained, "We have not Christianized the people. They have made superstitions out of us."

I journeyed to Sodo in 1986, the year the parish priest decided to take the pilgrimage back. He stripped the church interior of the saints' images which were being revered as manifestations of the Vodou gods. For the same reason, he cancelled the procession through Bonheur of the plaster statue of Our Lady. He did however bless a group of his parishioners intent on carrying a wooden cross from the church to Sodo. Along the way they prayed the rosary, planning to confront Ezili with Christ, as St Paul had done to Diana in her own temple at Ephesus. But the confrontation never came off. The pilgrims with their cross simply vanished into the ecstatic spume and thunder of devotions at the falls.

Failure to vanquish these popular devotions is an old story. When the Miracle Virgin appeared again on top of her palm tree in 1915, the parish priest asked a captain from the occupying US Army to cut the tree down. As he did so, the vision moved from tree to tree, until the wood was destroyed. As the last of the palms fell, the vision changed into a pigeon. From what the townspeople say, the bird remained close to Bonheur for several days, and then flew to Sodo, where it disappeared into the iridescent mist. What a splendid metaphor both for the pilgrimage, and for Vodou as a religion of tolerance and endurance. The pigeon in the palm tree links Church and Falls into one holy site, sanctioned only by the devotion of the Haitian people. Miracles will no doubt continue to occur there, gifts from a cool goddess in a hot season.

Donald Cosentino is Professor of African and Caribbean Folklore at the University of California Los Angeles. He is the editor of *African Arts* magazine and curator of the travelling exhibition "The Sacred Arts of Haitian Vodou". He writes widely on African and Diaspora cultures.

Vodou
An amalgamation of several traditional African religions, Vodou has also borrowed freely from Roman Catholic and Freemasonic rites first introduced by 18th-century French slave masters. Although in Euroamerican folklore "Voodoo" is usually protrayed as a mixture of malign superstitions, it is the national religion of Haiti and a vital part of its Creole culture.

"... by this time the pilgrims were got over the Enchanted Ground, and entering into the country of Beulah whose air was very sweet and pleasant ..."

"... neither could they from this place so much as see Doubting Castle. Here they were within sight of the City they were going to ..."

John Bunyan, The Pilgrim's Progress, Part 1 *(1678)*

Recalling his experiences in Cairo, Jedda, and Mecca, he wrote: "Everything about the pilgrimage atmosphere accented the Oneness of Man under One God" and "Never have I witnessed such sincere hospitality and the overwhelming spirit of true brotherhood as is practised by people of all colors and races, here in this Ancient, Holy Land ..." But the truth is that if Malcolm X had been a Christian or a Jew, this "spirit of true brotherhood" would not have been extended to him. And his announcement in the United States that his revelation of brotherhood in Mecca extended also to white Muslims may well have led to his assassination by racists soon afterward.

Such considerations lead some to avoid structured pilgrimage. But within the limits of its religious framework, pilgrimage gives the individual pilgrim the choice, like any other traveller, of transcending the constraints on social behaviour that operate at home, and presents for him, however imperfect, a living model of human brotherhood. This is something to be going on with in a far from ideal world.

HOLIER THAN THOU

As you see other people going about their business as pilgrims, you may find yourself judging the way they are doing things. Though the classic way to perform the Shikoku pilgrimage is to begin with the Ryozen-ji temple and follow a circular route round the island, many Japanese pilgrims today begin their journey with other temples, visit the sacred sites out of the "right" sequence, or only visit one or two. You may see this as a falling short, a kind of lackadaisical approach to the spiritual. Ian Reader, in his personal account of the Shikoku pilgrimage on pages 82–3, records his first reaction to pilgrims arriving by bus: "I would be annoyed, for I had walked, and climbed mountain paths, and they had just sat on luxury buses. Was I not better, because of the arduous nature of my journey?"

The answer is, who knows? Pilgrimages were necessarily arduous in days when most were made on foot. Religion has justified that hardship by fostering the notion that the greater the difficulty, the more merit the pilgrim earns. Crusaders were told that if they perished on the Crusades (which were essentially military pilgrimages) all their sins would be forgiven. This belief was shared by Muslim pilgrims to Mecca who, if they died along the way, expected to go straight to heaven. Pilgrimages in many religions today are still considered particularly worthy if made the hard way.

But there are horses for courses. Pilgrimage as an austerity is bound to the ascetic tradition of the wandering Hindu or Buddhist sadhu, or Christian mendicant. Austerities practised today at Saint Patrick's shrine at Lough Derg in Eire, for example, are possibly an inheritance from ascetics in the days when it was a monastic center. However, in most pilgrimage traditions a distinction is maintained between ascetics who have renounced the world and spend their whole lives in pilgrimage, and lay people for whom pilgrimage is an exceptional happening.

In Japan, one of the most rigorous sacred journeys carried out by Buddhist priests in training is the ancient Kaihogyo pilgrimage of Mount Hiei, performed over one thousand days, broken down into ten terms of one hundred days each, spread over seven years. It includes a nine-day period without food, water, sleep, or even lying down, and, in the earlier years, a 25-mile circuit of the mountain each night. In the last two years of the training this is replaced by a 37-mile circuit. Very few complete it, but lay people can earn proportionate merit by performing a much shorter version.

If distance were all that counted, one of the greatest pilgrimages on record would be a journey made between 1935 and 1936 by Mary Augusta Mullikin and Anna Hotchkis, two artists who despite advancing years – Mary Mullikin was over 60 – the threat of political unrest, and the ubiquitous brigands, undertook a tour of China's nine sacred mountains. Travelling by horse, mule, train, and other means, painting and sketching as they went, they visited every one of the nine mountains, whereas Buddhist pilgrims rarely achieve more than two.

They covered vast distances – Heng-Shan in Northern Shansi is over 1000 miles from Heng-Shan in Southern Hunan Province. In the nature of things, there must have been hardship, though the only "austerity" they really complained of was the monks' vegetarian diet in the monasteries. But though they encountered many pilgrims – such as a man who kowtowed every second step, knocking his head against the stones, and a young man who was carrying his mother up and down a mountain to acquire merit – they themselves remained "travellers".

By contrast, the group Michael Wood joined in 1995, for a five-day journey to shrines in southern India on a "video-bus", most assuredly were pilgrims. His account in *The Smile of Murugan* is of an excursion and adventure, made all the more exciting by the fact that at the same time the pilgrims could view their favourite old movies – even the Brahmin priests on board were keen. But it was still a devotional journey. Not the distance, not the hardship, not even the goal, but only the intention behind the journey is what makes it sacred.

Lay pilgrims within traditional societies are nothing if not pragmatic: Bess Allen Donaldson wrote in *The Wild Rue* (1938) of pilgrims in Iran: "Since the coming of the automobile most pilgrims on the highways now travel by that means. Some claim that much of the merit is lost by covering the distance so rapidly; others argue

> "Suspense, suppressed excitement, the feeling of a profound experience soon to come, throbbed in every pilgrim heart as we neared Jeddah ... For the first time, as the white-garbed faithful lined the rails (of the boat), I heard the immemorial pilgrim chant, to be repeated again a thousand times during my stay there: "Labbayk, Alla humma, Labbayk!" ("We are here, O Lord, we are here!").
>
> *Idries Shah, "The Red Sea Journey"*
> *in* Caravan of Dreams *(1968)*

Awakening the hidden faith

My Mexican grandmother Josefa poured her Catholic faith into my mind and my bones until her beliefs became my own. The other side of my family, the Tarahumara Indian part, agreed with her on the essence of our religion: adoration of Our Lady of Guadalupe. Grandmother Josefa often urged me to make a pilgrimage to Our Lady, saying it would be the most special day of my life. At the age of fifty, after years in the United States, I fulfilled my grandmother's wish and travelled to Mexico City for the feast day at Our Lady of Guadalupe's shrine on 12 December. I had expected the pilgrimage to be wonderful, moving. But nothing had prepared me for being catapulted to a depth of faith as enriching as my grandmother's.

Guadalupe pilgrims seem to be of four kinds: tourists with cameras, Mexicans and *mestizos* (people of mixed blood like me), trained sacred participants, and Indians. What moved me was the sacrifice and trust of other believers, in particular the soul-baring devotion of the Indian pilgrims. They entrust their lives to the *mestizo* divinity who said: "I am the Mother of all of you who dwell in this land."

Grandmother often told me how Our Lady of Guadalupe appeared to the Indian Juan Diego on Tepeyac Hill in 1531, ten years after the Spaniards had devastated the Aztecs. The Lady spoke in Nahuatl, the Aztec language. Her message was not one of bloodshed but of love and compassion, the feminine face of God. Her image was miraculously imprinted on Juan's cloak, his *tilma*: her face is darkly *mestizo*, her garment is European, and she wears the Indian woman's sash to show that she is with child. Grandmother instilled in me that this healing, loving mother gave birth to a new race and a new church, merging Spaniards and Indians as no military force could.

All over Mexico people pray to her daily and promise that they will make the pilgrimage if she grants their pleas. They walk for days from tiny villages to the largest city on earth and on to Tepeyac. Holy banners, flowers, music, and hymns accompany the pilgrims. Many have no shoes. At night they clean cuts from family members' feet, oil and bind them with rags. Babies and food must be carried. I watched this holy host of countless thousands as they came from every direction, their footsteps echoed by drums.

All day I saw groups climbing the hill, some on their knees,

Mexico Distrito Federal
Tepeyac Hill, the site of the Basilica, is in the north of Mexico DF (the Mexican name for Mexico City).

Practicalities
There are always large crowds at the shrine, but particularly on the feast day, 12 December, the anniversary of the second apparition of Our Lady to Juan Diego. Hundreds of thousands come both in devoted pilgrimage and to celebrate with singing and dancing.

Visitors to the holy shrine should dress modestly, with arms and legs covered, or they may be denied entry to the Basilica. Altitude sickness may cause headaches: the city is 7000 feet above sea level. Also the high pollution levels may exacerbate respiratory conditions such as asthma.

Shared hopes and fears

Mike Nicholson's painting (below), inspired by his experiences at Assisi, conveys the pilgrims' shared ideal of healing ecological wounds.

The four routes to Assisi

Pilgrims travelled on foot, receiving food and lodging from volunteers along the way. In performances of dance, music, and drama they entertained their hosts and celebrated the diversity of their cultures.

St Francis of Assisi
In founding the Franciscan order, St Francis (1182–1226) aimed to return to Christ's own principles, rejecting the wealth and opulence of the medieval church. His friars lived in poverty with the ordinary people, preaching barefoot in the churches.
His creed of living simply and close to nature, and the legend of how he tamed a wolf which had been terrorizing a local town, led to St Francis becoming the patron saint of animals.

Nor is there a distinction between the spiritual and the material in Shinto, the national religion of Japan. This faith, without a founder or dogma, is transmitted not through scriptures but through annual observances and everyday customs. Japanese myths of the Creation say there was an original chaos which of its own indwelling power produced the *amatsu kami* or "deities of heaven". From the *kami* descended the islands of Japan, other spiritual beings, and the Japanese people. Thus human beings, the land, and nature are intimately related and consequently, the whole material world is seen to have a spiritual dimension as well.

Within this view of existence, there can be no distinction between the realm of God – the sacred – and the realm of humans – the profane. Not perceiving this, we may overlook things in sacred places that offer the possibility of spiritual growth, simply because we read them as "secular" – nothing to do with religion. In the context of Shinto, for example, the traditional Japanese garden is one of the main expressions of this faith. Water is an essential element, trickling, falling – the very word for gardener, *kawaracho*, means "he who makes the beds for streams". In a dry garden, such as the great meditation garden in the Tofukuji Temple in Kyoto, thoughts of water are evoked by raked sand or gravel.

The gardens of Islam also embody a religious ideal. The name "Paradise" comes from *pairidaeza*, Old Persian for a park or enclosure, and wherever Islam has held sway can be found enclosed, paradisal gardens. These ideal oases of a desert people have trees for shade, and water, revered as an elemental life force, for music and entrancement, and its ability to open the mind to inspiration. The gardens of the Alhambra in Spain, the Royal Gardens of Fin in Iran, the Garden of the Maids of Honour at Udaipur, India, are material expressions of Islam and convey more of the nature of matter and spirit than words can express.

> "Here at the Fountains sliding foot,
> Or at some Fruit-trees mossy root,
> Casting the Bodies vest aside,
> My soul into the boughs does glide:
> There like a Bird it sits, and sings,
> Then whets, and combs its silver Wings …"
>
> *Andrew Marvell (1621–78), "The Garden"*

RETREAT, CONTEMPLATION, AND DEDICATION

It is time for both inner and outer travellers now to retreat a little from the world, perhaps engaging in prayer or meditation. If these are already habitual to you, follow the methods you have learned. If you have never before done either, you may want to find somewhere to sit quietly – perhaps such a garden as we spoke of above – breathing gently and deeply, contemplating who you are, where you are and what your purpose is in coming. You may use imagery like that of Saint Teresa of Avila, who pictured the inner journey as one into a castle (the soul) with a series of rooms and corridors leading deeper and deeper within to where the "king" (God) sits enthroned.

Those who have made a long journey will need sleep. Others, whose pilgrimage begins here, may prefer to keep vigil. A vigil is a time when you stay awake (as in "vigilance"). Technically it was the evening service, often continuing through the night, that used to be held before a saint's feast day. (Since 1969, only the Easter vigil has been permitted in the Roman Catholic church.)

> "The way we set out on this pilgrimage of 'other-centredness' is to recite a short phrase, a word that is commonly called today a mantra. The mantra is simply a means of turning our attention beyond ourselves – a way of unhooking us from our own thoughts and concerns."
>
> *John Main OSB, Moment of Christ (1984)*

The vigil was a time of heightened expectation. Have you ever wondered why the most magical times in the European folk calendar are all "eves" – Christmas Eve, Midsummer's Eve, Hallowe'en? Each is the night before a Christian festival: Christmas; the feast of the birth of John the Baptist (24 June); All Hallow's (All Saints, 1 November). The

Knowing broadly what Buddhism is "about", Islam is "about", Hinduism is "about", does not provide with you with a blueprint for pilgrimage performance. Go to Sri Lanka, and you will find three major pilgrimage centers, all drawing large crowds: the Sacred City of Anuradhapura, the Temple of the Tooth at Kandy, and Kataragama. Anuradhapura, a Buddhist center which had been capital of the island from the fourth to the ninth century, had fallen into decay but was redeveloped as a regional capital under British colonial rule. After

religious behaviour is extrovert, physical, and ecstatic, involving among other things dance and loud rhythmic music, fire walking, and hanging from hooks. Kataragama used to be a place of pilgrimage for Tamil Hindus from Sri Lanka or southern India, but now the majority are Buddhist as at Kandy and Anuradhapura.

What a pilgrim does and what a pilgrim gets from each of these Sri Lankan pilgrimages is different. (And what the Hindus, Muslims, and Christians get who also attend the Kataragama festival is more or less subtly

"O world invisible, we view thee,

Independence, Christian, Muslim, and Tamil Hindu residents were expelled and their places of worship razed, to recreate Anuradhapura as a Buddhist national heartland, fulfilling a role similar to that of Jerusalem for Jews. At the Poson festival, which falls on the full moon in June, the city fills with Buddhist pilgrims who go to worship and make merit. The atmosphere is restrained and calm; there is no procession or spectacle.

By contrast, pilgrims, Buddhist again, come to the Temple of the Tooth in July/August to see the great annual pageant of the former kingdom of Kandy. It lasts a fortnight, with processions every night, getting ever bigger and better toward the end. Although the pilgrims make offerings in the town temples, they gather here mainly as onlookers, earning merit by simply watching the parade of the illustrious Buddhist past.

At Kataragama, the season of mass pilgrimage in July/August celebrates the union of the god Skanda with his mistress, Valli Amma. On each of fifteen successive evenings, Skanda's image is taken to her shrine. By contrast with Kandy, pilgrims are active participants: by contrast with Anuradhapura,

different again.) The substance of pilgrimage lies in the detail. For us to experience it we need knowledge and observation, but most of all a willingness to engage.

Pilgrimage is not about thinking, but about doing and feeling. We can learn from descriptions left by early Christian pilgrims to the Holy Land, who stress the experiential nature of the climax of their journey. Its essence often was and is a combination of ritual and physical, sensory experience. Many pilgrimages specify what the pilgrim must see, hear, touch, taste, smell.

This is not an accident but comes by contrivance: most pilgrimages and processions have been formulated by ritual specialists with long practice in this ancient craft that links Babylonian diviner with Persian mage and Christian priest. If we surrender to their art, give ourselves up to the process, like earlier pilgrims embracing what offers, we may encounter Otherness with their help.

The pilgrim who has arrived at a shrine has arrived at a trifork, a meeting of three ways on the Otherworld journey, where significant place and significant action meet with significant time.

"Prayer, the Church's banquet, Angels' age,
God's breath in man returning to his birth,
The soul in paraphrase, heart in pilgrimage, ...
A kind of tune, which all things hear and fear;

Softness, and peace, and joy, and love, and bliss, ...
The milky way, the bird of Paradise,
Church-bells beyond the stars heard, the soul's blood,
The land of spices; something understood."

George Herbert (1593–1633), "Prayer"

152

SIGNIFICANT PLACE

"Most of us have a sense of God in places of great natural beauty," writes Martin L Smith in *Nativities and Passions*. The natural, even raw, landscape acts almost too readily as a conduit for epiphany – the moment of manifestation of divinity – which comes as a sensory experience: I have known it in the desert as a feeling of immanence, a kind of great weight of air bearing down, as if something momentous were descending. After a desert journey we seem to understand why Moses heard

O world intangible, we touch thee,
O world unknowable, we know thee."

FRANCIS THOMPSON (1859–1907)
"THE KINGDOM OF GOD"

the voice of the Lord on Mount Sinai, why classic Arab music sounds like question and answer, one man's personal dialogue with God, and why the early Christian fathers were desert hermits.

Ecologists and conservationists in particular tend to seek God in the natural landscape, "but", Martin Smith continues, "the test of the practice of the presence of God lies in the settings that seem the most barren, anonymous and profane – the malls, the airports, the fast-food restaurants, the subway stations, the crowds..." Those crowds, in our case the crowds at great pilgrimage centers, are the milieu in which we must find our own particular epiphanies. How was and is it done?

Because it linked them directly to the figures of sacred history, early Christian pilgrims wanted to see the sites mentioned in the Bible for themselves. Thus in AD333, the anonymous Bordeaux pilgrim visited the place where Jacob wrestled with the angel (Genesis 33: 24–31), the tree Zaccheus climbed (Luke 19: 1–10), even the stone the builders rejected (Psalm 118: 22). The sites (whether traditional or manufactured to meet the needs of the pilgrim industry) bolstered faith by "proving" the scriptures to be true, and helped pilgrims visualize the events that took place there more vividly.

THE EXTERNSTEINE

GERMANY

Hannover

Hameln

Bad Pyrmont

Detmold

THE EXTERNSTEINE

Bad Meinberg

Horn

A temple in the forest

❮ A remarkable group of sandstone rocks in the forests of northern Germany, 30 miles southwest of Hannover, have been used as a place of worship since the time of Stonehenge. They rise out of the mountain range of the Teutoburger Forest and tower 125 feet above it. Weathered by the glaciers and fashioned further by both nature and humans, the rocks form a unique landscape temple known as the Externsteine (meaning Dragon Stones).

Since ancient times this has been a place to study the laws of the cosmos, and a place of transformation and healing. In pre-Christian rituals, initiates to the temple were lowered into the Rock Tomb, hewn out of the stone in the shape of a human body. For three days they lay in the suspended animation of "temple sleep" to experience the spiritual world.

Such a landscape temple is made up of intelligent energy flows, which reveal both Truth and the Holy Spirit. A landscape temple, according to Peter Dawkins, is a light center in which the energy flows are expressed in the landscape. Within this energy structure are seven chakras, which mirror the human chakras. This is the basis of sacred architecture and is shown very clearly at the Externsteine.

The Externsteine are part of a much larger landscape temple extending to Hermann's Monument, near Detmold, 5 miles to the northeast. Hermann united the old Germanic tribes for the first time and led them to victory over the Romans in a great battle in AD9. The monument portrays him as a huge St Michael figure with a winged head, waving his sword

Visiting the sacred site
This village of tents at Mina, near Mecca, accommodates up to three million Muslims. In the prescribed rituals of the Hajj, pilgrims repeat the sacred actions of the Prophet Mohammed.

ceremonial strategies. Those who could not go to the Church of the Holy Sepulchre in Jerusalem to cut their cross among the myriads cut into its walls by pilgrims, could instead visit an architectural copy. The circular eleventh-century Holy Sepulchre in the cathedral of Aquileia, in northern Italy, is a copy of the Anastasis Rotunda in the Jerusalem Holy Sepulchre, which marks the site of the Resurrection and contains Christ's tomb. The Aquileia copy contains a "tomb" with a removable lid and there on Good Friday a consecrated Host (communion bread), representing the body of Christ, and a crucifix were ceremonially "buried" to be "resurrected"

on Easter Morning. Another medieval Italian copy is the church of San Stefano, Bologna, where the distance between the copies of Christ's tomb, in the chapel of San Sepulcro, and Calvary in the central chapel, corresponds to the actual distance in Jerusalem.

Ordinary parish churches throughout Europe had "Easter Sepulchres": sometimes temporary wooden structures or niches, or else stone chest-tombs (containing burials) built against the north wall of the chancel. In England they were banned by the Protestants in 1548 and many destroyed. However, even in Puritan counties such as Norfolk some survive, notably at East Raynham, where Lady Townshend provided in her will for her tomb to be used as an Easter Sepulchre, thus conferring a blessing on her soul. The ceremonies performed on and around them dramatized the events of Easter; the body of Christ being represented, as at Aquileia, by a consecrated Host, and the women discovering the empty tomb on Easter morning played by veiled clergy.

At Chaource in Bourgogne, France, we can make a symbolic descent into an Easter Sepulchre, by going down into the semi-subterranean Sepulchre chapel of the church of St John the Baptist. Here the *Mise au Tombeau* (the placing in the tomb) recreates Christ's entombment with life-size and in some lights uncannily

Baroque Via Dolorosa (Stations of the Cross) created in the eighteenth century for parishioners who were too poor to go on pilgrimage abroad. In prayer and reflection at each of the 14 Stations, pilgrims experience the ritual actions of pilgrims in the Holy City, and in their own flesh recreate Christ's journey to Calvary.

SIGNIFICANT TIME

As well as movement through space on sacred journeys, there is movement through time. Some journeys are repeated within monthly, annual, seasonal, or periodic cycles. There are also particular times when the religious experience is more powerful or divinity more accessible

"So hallow'd and so gracious is the time."

WILLIAM SHAKESPEARE, HAMLET (1601)

lifelike figures. The Sepulchre, to which daylight is admitted only through two small windows, is guarded by three polychrome stone soldiers in the costume of 1515, when the *Mise au Tombeau* was created. Seven other figures, including the sorrowing Virgin and the Three Marys are gathered round the chest-tomb on which the dead Christ is being laid. The *Mise au Tombeau* is said to have been so designed that the first ray of sunlight on Easter morning strikes the fusion of altar and chest-tomb on which Christ's body lies.

Within the Hagia Sophia in Istanbul, Turkey, the whole landscape of the Holy Land was reproduced symbolically to provide a total experience. A more modern example is the "Holy Land in America" at the Franciscan monastery in Washington DC (dedicated in 1899), which contains copies of several significant Christian buildings, including a full-scale Tomb of Christ at the correct distance from the Calvary on the other side of the main church. At pilgrimage sites, both biblical scenes and ritual action may be imitated. The shrine of Bom Jesús, near Braga in Portugal, has a

than at others. The interplay of time and space is well illustrated by the Hindu pilgrimage to Pandharpur. Exactly four months and a fortnight after entering Pandharpur, some pilgrims make a second pilgrimage to the tomb of the saint Jnanesvar at Alandi. They may go directly from their homes to Alandi, or go first to Pandharpur, then make a fourteen-day journey symbolically retracing the steps of Jnanesvar as he returned from Pandharpur to Alandi after his own pilgrimage.

Pilgrims who make the double pilgrimage refer to their journey as *vari*, signifying the periodic appearance of a person at a particular place at a particular time. They themselves are known as *varkaris* – people who make pilgrimages. Some *varkaris* go once a year, some twice a year, some four times a year, some go every month. These latter are the *mahinemaha varkaris*, the most highly respected. They usually travel singly but often join a group after reaching the holy city, and can be relied on to appear to such an extent that, if a man has not joined his group by a certain day, the rest assume he must be dead and perform his obsequies.

Significant time has met with significant place at pilgrim-shrines from ancient times. In the Mediterranean world of 2000 years ago, the Mystery religions were pilgrim-initiation events correlated with the seasons. Crowds of pilgrims sought the Egyptian goddess Isis at her sanctuary at Philae, on the Upper Nile, at the full moon of the autumnal equinox. In the second century AD, the Latin satirist Apuleius joined the cult of Isis and described its rites. The pilgrims dipped themselves seven times in the sea and called on the goddess to appear in the sky – which she duly did, rising as its most brilliant star, the Dog Star, Sirius.

The secret Mysteries of Eleusis honouring Demeter, three days before the autumnal equinox, drew crowds of pilgrims, who bathed together in the sea outside Athens and then sprinkled their bodies with animal blood. Dressed in saffron robes with crowns of myrtle, they set out for the shrine, a day's walk from the city. There a mimesis or ritual re-enactment seems to have been stage-managed so that initiates witnessed some kind of metamorphosis, or forms in process of change. At the climax came a baby's cry, then the clash of cymbals and a bright light. Initiates from emperors down confessed themselves profoundly moved by the experience, though not one ever betrayed the exact details.

Christians nowadays participate in a cyclic mystery by entering a cave at Bethlehem. The Grotto of the Nativity, venerated as Christ's birthplace, is a true cave, not the above-ground stable of religious paintings. They make this ritual descent at Christmas, Christ's birthday, packing into the tiny space. By being there, at this time, they are mystically present, like Saint Jerome's friend Paula, at the Divine Birth.

Pilgrim journeys may also be related to cycles and movements of planetary bodies, especially the sun and moon. This may be a matter of timing – the Pandharpur pilgrimage is organized according to a lunar calendar; so is the Hajj to Mecca – but may also consciously link human movement through space in time with cosmic motion. The Yucatec Maya word *ximbal* is used to

THE WESTERN WALL

Connecting across time and space

My heart, my eye, my daughter, my mother, great mountain... Jerusalem is known by all these names and at least seventy more by Jewish people around the world. Jerusalem is the pupil of the Jewish eye, it is said; and on that pupil is etched for eternity the image of the holy temple. Solomon built the first temple in Jerusalem and its successor, erected by Herod, was destroyed by the Romans in AD70.

All that remained was the huge masonry platform on which the temple once stood and to which Jews made pilgrimage for centuries to lament its destruction. In the seventh century, Muslims built the Dome of the Rock on the platform, leaving the Western Wall as the only part of the temple area accessible for Jews. They come as they have always done to pray for the restoration of their temple, which will only rise again, they believe, with the coming of the Messiah and the dawn of world peace and harmony. Until that day, Orthodox Jews everywhere keep unpainted a portion of a wall in their house, to remind them that human existence will be marked by imperfection until the temple stands again.

To pray at the Western Wall is to nurture an image of hope that has held the Jewish people together through millenia of oppression and diaspora. It is to feel connected to Jews everywhere, through all time and across the globe. By extension, it is to feel part of humanity as a whole, for the Wall is a living symbol for the center of the world, where the earth receives the greatest influx of spiritual power from Heaven. "Jerusalem", one rabbi told me as he came away from his prayers at the wall, "is the Gate of Heaven through which prayers ascend and the spirit descends."

One Sabbath morning at the Western Wall I watched a group of young men dancing around a table piled with the holy books, dipping and bending and singing songs as they were led by their rabbi in joyous praise. They were American students, sons of modern Orthodox Jews who had sent them to the homeland for a year of study. Their rabbi, another American, had immigrated to Jerusalem some 20 years earlier. "The Sabbath is always a time of joy and celebration," he explained to me later. "Some sects dance after every prayer. 'All of my bones shall recite, O Lord,' it says in our psalms. Even if most people aren't quite as demonstrative as we are, they still move their bodies in prayer. Look at the people by the wall."

I turned to gaze at the scene behind me. It was true. The people lining the base of the Wall – sombre figures, all clad in black with hard black hats; young soldiers, their weapons slung over their arm; boys in jeans, grandfathers in suit and tie – all were vigorously leaning backwards and forwards, muttering earnest prayers, occasionally sticking petitionary notes in the cracks between the blocks of masonry.

"That rhythmic movement," the rabbi continued, "expresses a need to get closer, to feel physically connected to the temple. We are a soulful people, and the soul for us includes the body and extends to the whole community. We pray here as a community, not from a nostalgia for the past but out of a living vision of the future. That vision, I assure you," he smiled as he turned to rejoin his students, "will be realized. The temple will one day stand here again."

Roger Housden is a writer and photographer, the author of *Travels through Sacred India* and *Retreat*. He is a director of Open Gate Journeys, which leads groups on spiritual journeys to sacred sites.

Muslim quarter

Dome of the Rock

Christian quarter

Moor's quarter

Armenian quarter

Jewish quarter

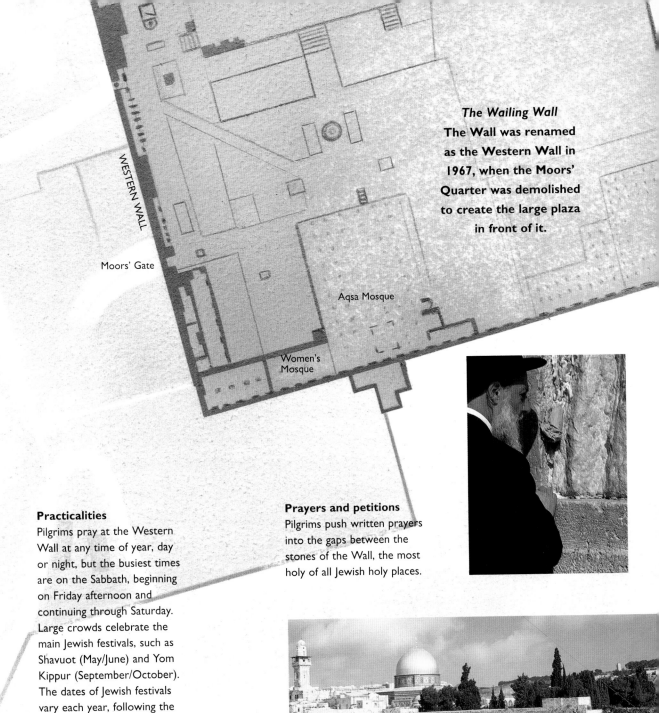

WESTERN WALL

Moors' Gate

Aqsa Mosque

Women's Mosque

The Wailing Wall
**The Wall was renamed
as the Western Wall in
1967, when the Moors'
Quarter was demolished
to create the large plaza
in front of it.**

Practicalities

Pilgrims pray at the Western Wall at any time of year, day or night, but the busiest times are on the Sabbath, beginning on Friday afternoon and continuing through Saturday. Large crowds celebrate the main Jewish festivals, such as Shavuot (May/June) and Yom Kippur (September/October). The dates of Jewish festivals vary each year, following the Hebrew lunar calendar. Following Orthodox Jewish tradition, men and women pray in separate enclosures. Pilgrims of both sexes should cover their legs and upper arms, and women should cover their heads.

Prayers and petitions

Pilgrims push written prayers into the gaps between the stones of the Wall, the most holy of all Jewish holy places.

describe both pilgrimage and the passage of the stars through the skies. Maya on pilgrimages today often avoid modern roads and follow old Mayan routes or trails through the bush, as if these were modern equivalents of the ancient *sacbe*, the elevated roadway that led to Mayan temples. The Maya still refer to the Milky Way as a celestial *sacbe* over which the deities pass. In medieval England the Milky Way was known as the Walsingham Way and regarded as a great sign across the sky pointing the way to the Holy House, in which the Holy Family had lived, miraculously transported from Nazareth to Norfolk. In France and Spain the Milky Way imaged the sacred pilgrim road to Santiago de Compostela. Thus the cosmic and earthly dimensions are linked, the pilgrims' movements replicating the celestial pilgrimage of the heavenly bodies.

Just as the circling of holy places and shrines is part of the sacred journey, so the same movement is part of pilgrim ritual on arrival at the sacred goal. Circumambulation (walking around) of the shrine is found in Hinduism, Tibetan Buddhism, and some Christian pilgrimages. In the sixth-century mosaic map of Roman Jerusalem in the church at Madaba, Jordan, Christ's cave-tomb has been totally separated from the hill out of which it was carved so that processions could walk all round it. Muslims on the Hajj perform the *tawaf*, circling the Ka'ba seven times; the very name Hajj probably derives from an old Semitic root meaning "to go around". As we saw in Chapter 4, the direction of circling is most often sunwise (clockwise). The *tawaf* is only performed anti-clockwise because Mohammed deliberately changed the direction, at the same time as he purged the Ka'ba of its idols, in order to dissociate it from the pagan ceremonial of pre-Islamic times.

The sun plays a more direct role in the Japanese Shinto pilgrimage to Mount Fuji, sacred mountain and home of the sun-goddess Amaterasu Omikami. In the nineteenth century worn-out straw sandals lined the routes to the top, cast off by the thousands of pilgrims who every summer climbed it. Like other natural shrines in Japan it was forbidden to women until 1868, but Fuji's summit was the goal of all devout followers of Shinto. Today, even for the foreign tourists and Japanese holidaymakers who have joined the pilgrims, the climax of the ascent remains the *goraiko*, watching the sunrise.

THE "MIRACLE OF THE SUN"

The *goraiko* on Mount Fuji is a natural epiphany – the rising of the goddess – but the first-ray effect observed in the Easter Sepulchre at Chaource is an ancient piece of ritual stagecraft used in temples and at pilgrim-shrines. Modern Druids gather at midsummer at Stonehenge, on Salisbury Plain, England, to watch the rising sun skim the top of the so-called Heel Stone. This stone cannot originally have been a midsummer sunrise marker, because of the change in the inclination of the earth's axis. But it has been argued that the axis of the trilithons (two upright stones with a third across the top) points to the first gleam of the midsummer sun in 2045BC, the best radiocarbon date for their construction.

Perhaps the most dramatic manipulation of light is in the Egyptian temple of Abu Simbel in what was formerly Nubia. This cave, cut into a cliff by order of Ramses II in the thirteenth century BC, was dedicated to the sun-gods Amon-Ra and Re-Harmakhis (the rising sun), and the deified Pharaoh Ramses himself. The vast chamber in the heart of the mountain is 59 feet long and 55 feet wide, supported on two rows of columns each 33 feet tall. In the central sacred precinct Ramses sits in the role of sun-god next to Amon-Ra, Harmakhis, and Ptah in his Osirian Underworld aspect.

"Thou living Aton, the beginning of life!
When thou art risen on the eastern horizon,
Thou has filled every land with thy beauty ...
Thy rays encompass the lands to the limit of all
that thou hast made. ...

When thou settest in the western horizon,
The land is in darkness, in the manner of death. ...
Darkness is a shroud, and the earth is in stillness,
For he who made them rests ...

Thou art in my heart ..."

*From "The Hymn to the Aton"
by Pharaoh Ahk-en-Aton (14th century BC)*

Nothing here was left to chance: the arrangement of the space was so precise that twice a year, around the vernal and autumnal equinoxes, the sun cast its rays through the entrance. A shaft of light moved down the hallway connecting the entrance to the sanctuary and gradually lit first the left shoulder of Amon-Ra, then a few moments later, after touching Ramses, fell on Harmakhis. After twenty minutes the light disappeared. It never touched Ptah, lord of the shadows.

This illumination of the statues takes place in February/March and October; on 20 February and 20 October the sun is exactly on the central axis of the temple. And 20 October was the date of Ramses' first jubilee, in the thirtieth year of his reign, and which probably led to the building of the temple. Perhaps just as remarkable as this ancient engineering is the fact that, when the temple at Abu Simbel was dismantled to save it from the rising waters of Lake Nasser in the 1960s, and recreated on higher land, the precise sacred geometry was preserved and the miracle of the sunlight repeated itself in February 1969.

THE POWER OF MYTH

For outsiders to a pilgrimage tradition, even being in the right place at the right time performing the right actions may not be enough to generate a transformative experience. But we may "get it" through myth. Understanding the mythological background unlocks hidden meanings that are part of the cultural heritage of the faithful – indeed permeate a whole society in often unsuspected ways. In the West we do not usually think of ourselves as having a mythology, but consider how a Christian myth can transfigure our experience of pilgrimage at

HOME DANCE OF THE HOPI

Bidding farewell to the spirits

The Great Painted Desert, Arizona – vast, serene, sere, overhung by an expanse of summer sky so bright that the dark storm dragging its tail over a strangely shaped distant butte only serves to accent the brilliance. A lonely Navajo hogan, one wisp of smoke, punctuates the red, vermilion, and gold sands stretching away.

Tomorrow is Niman, the Home Dance, when the Kachinas, I am told, go home to the San Francisco Peaks. This is an important dance; a chance to honour and say farewell to all the spirits that have served the people, the Hopi, during the past year. I sit on White Bear's front porch and watch the people arrive. They come from Flagstaff, Gallup, Winslow, even Phoenix. A long haul across the desert to honour the spirits and risk the thong of the Whipping Kachina or the mockery of the clowns. It's a tough journey. The road is dusty and hot. The seat across the width of each pick-up is jammed full of men, women, and children with long black hair.

So far, the Fords have it. Chevrolet is close behind, then Dodge. Great, solid, wind-blasted machines with big tyres. At dusk, their lights, one after the other, reach back into the blueness of the sands. A long, straight ribbon of equally spaced twin lights down-shifting as they reach Second Mesa and turn up the gradient by Prophecy Rock – sounding their horns as they pass by the house of a relative. Occasionally White Bear says, that's so-and-so, and describes his relationship to them – from way back and to the side, bloodlines reaching through the web of truck-lights and square, mesa-top homes.

This is a big pilgrimage. He's eighty-eight and he says he's never seen so many people come. He says there will be more Kachinas dancing tomorrow than ever. He doesn't talk to me. He just talks into the space across the desert. Now he talks of where the people came from. He says that the path of the people is a migration through the many worlds. A pick-up honks by on the hill. He waves, says it's the family of a niece. All I can see is blackness, the ribbon of lights, and now the stars.

The people, the Hopi, have come up through three previous worlds. When the last world was destroyed by flood they were shown the path into this, the fourth world.

Soon, White Bear says, it will be time to find the opening to the fifth. The Kachinas emerge from out of an opening on the top of the *kivas* (subterranean ceremonial chambers) to mark this progression. The path is shown by a line in the petroglyphs, the emergence points are spirals – together they mark the good road to follow in life. Every year this path is

The good road
The line in this petroglyph (rock-carving) shows the migration trail of the Hopi. The animals are symbols of the different clans and represent incidents in their journeys. The figure with one arm upheld is a Whipping Kachina.

retraced, redrawn in the corn pollen, told of in stories, in the dances, so the people know where they have come from and where they are going. If they did not dance, White Bear says, the rain would not come, the corn would not grow, the migration trail would not spiral up and on, the land and the people would die.

"Tomorrow," White Bear says, "the Kachinas go home." He indicates vaguely across the road.

I say, "I thought the Kachinas went to the San Francisco Peaks."

"Oh no. That's a story we tell the children. We come from over there."

His finger points upward, over the truck lights on the highway, over the silhouette of the houses on the mesas, into the night sky. I mull over what else is told to children and Anglos like myself. I can't help but wonder if the Hopi depict their migration path as a twin tyre-track now, after the advent of pick-ups, or whether the most popular transportation has Ford or Chevrolet or possibly HSA – the Hopi Space Agency – written on the side.'

Nicholas R Mann is the author of *The Isle of Avalon* and *Giants of Gaia*. He lives in New Mexico.

Kachinas

Mythical ancestors of the Hopi, the Kachinas are beneficent spirits who arrive at the Winter Solstice to revisit earth for half of each year. While on earth the Kachinas are impersonated by male dancers wearing masks. The Niman ceremony in July is the farewell dance before the Kachinas return to the spirit world and give their masks back to the spirits.

Hopi ceremonial dances

The masked Kachina dances are not open to visitors, but other "social dances", which can be witnessed, take place throughout the year.

Easter, to Jerusalem, and Christ's tomb. This is one of the most important descents I mentioned among patterns of pilgrimage: the re-enactment of the descent of Christ into death at his cave-tomb.

In the Western Church we sometimes underplay the Christ whose greatest festival was not Christmas but Easter, and we increasingly secularize Good Friday. "He descended into hell; The third day he rose again from

"I have come to set fire to the earth"

THE BIBLE, LUKE 12: 49

the dead, He ascended into heaven" says the Creed from the *Book of Common Prayer*, describing the interval between Crucifixion and Resurrection, between Good Friday and Easter Sunday. That lost day has been accounted for by the Church of Latter Day Saints by the belief that in that interval Christ preached in the Western hemisphere. Medieval Christians filled in that time with the Harrowing of Hell, a story of a power and grandeur to match any in world mythology.

According to the apocryphal Gospel of Nicodemus, compiled in the fifth century AD, Christ descended into Hell and harrowed (despoiled) it by releasing its captives. The souls of the dead were in the eternal night of the Underworld when at midnight there came a light brighter than the sun and a thundering voice demanded in the words of Psalm 24: "Lift up your heads, O ye gates, and be ye lift up, ye everlasting doors; and the King of glory shall come in." Hell (in the Anglo-Saxon version of the gospel much resembling Hél, queen-goddess of the Old Norse Underworld), skulking in the darkness, asked: "Who is this King of glory?" And the answer came: "The Lord ... mighty in battle." Then the gates of Hell are broken down, the dead loosed from their chains, and the victorious Christ, carrying the vexillum (the banner he holds in Christian art as a symbol of his Resurrection), strides into Hell, his radiance lighting up its farthest and darkest place. Trampling Death underfoot, he binds Satan and leads our fore-father Adam out of Hell, together with the righteous who had lived before his Incarnation, and into Paradise.

This tremendous myth dramatizes the doctrine that Christ died to redeem all humankind, from the very beginning of time to its end. It is the subtext of the Holy Fire ceremony enacted in the Holy Sepulchre in Jerusalem, part of the Orthodox Easter celebrations. Abbot Daniel, a Russian pilgrim who visited Jerusalem in the twelfth century, tells how "the grace of God comes down unseen from heaven and lights the lamps in the Sepulchre of the Lord". To this day, this mystery is played out at the tomb. One of the clergy goes alone into the empty tomb. Its door is sealed, and all lights in every part of the church put out. An hour or so later, hundreds of pilgrims waiting silently in the packed church see fire magically pass out from the tomb to kindle torches held by two deacons, who rush off with them to local churches. At the same time, fire leaps from candle to candle in the pilgrims' hands and suddenly the whole church is lit up into its farthest and darkest corners, just as in the myth.

In Orthodox churches Easter is generally celebrated with a ceremony of lights, in which the Holy Door (which in the Eastern Church closes off the sanctuary and altar, and represents both the Gate of Heaven and the Jaws of Death), is thrown open at the moment of Resurrection. After a candlelit procession outside the church, the priest burns incense at its doors, singing: "Christ is risen from the dead, trampling down death by death, and bestowing life upon those in the tomb ... We celebrate the death of death, the annihilation of Hades, the beginning of a life new and eternal."

In the medieval Church, a similar ceremony of lights began at midnight between Holy Saturday and Easter Sunday. By the time it ended, it would be close to dawn and the rising sun was greeted by the bells ringing out as the priest began the first Mass of Easter. These rites celebrating the light of Christ penetrating the tomb (Hell) and subduing Death, are entwined with the identification of Christ with the sun, encoded in the word-play between "risen sun" and "risen Son".

It is echoed, too, in the beautiful folk belief that on Easter Day the sun danced as it rose, in honour of the Resurrection. Though Sir Thomas Browne wrote in *Vulgar Errors* (1646): "We shall not, I hope, disparage the resurrection of our Redeemer, if we say that the sun does not dance on Easter-day ...", well into the nineteenth century people in England and Wales rose early in the morning on Easter Day in order to see it. Many believed they did see this natural epiphany. The Rector of Ross-on-Wye, England, the Rev R H Cobbold, wrote in 1879: "In the district called Hockley ... a woman whose maiden name was Evans, wife of Rowland Lloyd, a labourer, said she had heard of the thing but did not believe it true, 'till,' she said, 'on Easter morning last, I got up early, and then I saw the sun dance, and dance, and dance, three times, and I called to my husband and said, Rowland, Rowland, get up and see the sun dance!'"

> "Praise be to Thee, my Lord, with all Thy creatures,
> Especially to my worshipful brother sun,
> The which lights up the day,
> and through him dost Thou brightness give;
> And beautiful is he and radiant with splendour great ...
>
> Praised be my Lord for brother fire,
> By the which Thou lightest up the dark,
> And fair is he and gay and mighty and strong ... "
>
> *St Francis of Assisi (1181–1226), "The Canticle of the Sun"*

> "Can there be any day but this,
> Though many suns to shine endeavour?
> We count three hundred, but we miss:
> There is but one, and that one ever."
>
> *George Herbert (1593–1633), "Easter"*

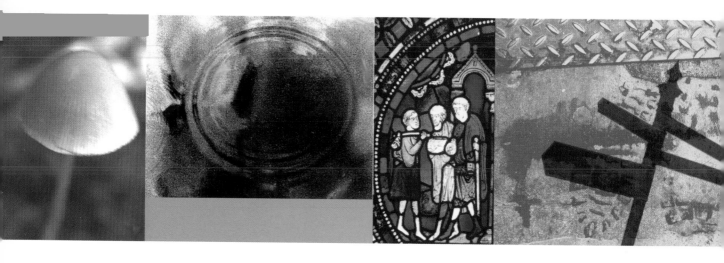

XI Reflection

CHAPTER 11

That was the journey *to*. There is still the journey *from*.

Whether you undertook your pilgrimage for its own sake, or as an act of devotion, or for a particular benefit, whether or not you encountered the divine in quite the way you had hoped, you have come far and now must go farther.

You may feel euphoric, or perhaps mentally and physically drained. Either way, this is a time for reflection. If you have kept a diary, do look it over. Do talk to other pilgrims. Do ask about the

and redirection

expectations they had and how the actuality matched up. Do listen if they try to describe their spiritual experience.

Don't go to sleep on your feet. Don't see this as the end of your journey, the aftermath, that frightful time for a child when Christmas is over and the next birthday a long way off.

There are more presents. They include a fuller understanding of where you have been and what you have seen. The most important part of the journey for you may be yet to come.

Sacred geography has great allure on paper and in the imagination, but when you finally arrived at your sacred site, and took part in or witnessed your sacred event, you may have experienced a great range of reactions.

DISTASTE, DISAPPOINTMENT, DISILLUSION

As I said in Chapter 7, pilgrimages often involve beliefs and observances that would be condemned as heretical if they appeared in your local mosque, synagogue, church, or temple. In particular they tend to be more tolerant of ecstatic experience. Watching the absorbed and remote faces of the Dervish Dancers of the Order of the Mevlevi, from Konya, Turkey, as they whirl on their own axes like celestial bodies is one thing. But if your sacred journey has taken you somewhere exotic, this may have been the first time you have seen sadomasochistic penances being performed in the streets, or witnessed people going into a trance or in the possession of a spirit, rolling their eyes, yapping, howling. You may have felt anything from terrified through appalled to embarassed or – like Margery Kempe's fellow-pilgrims every time she created a hysterical scene in the Holy Land – angry at being distracted from your own purposes.

There is often some distance between the idea we hold of a religion and the actuality we encounter. More than one person has gone to India hoping to find their own spiritual path in the contemplative disciplines taught in some ashram, only to turn tail on confronting the real-world experience of most Indians. They would agree with Shirley Park Lowry who writes in *Familiar Mysteries*: "Most members of 'contemplative' Eastern

"They set this idol [Juggernaut – Lord Jagannatha at Puri, India] with great reverence in a chariot ... and lead it about the city with great solemnity. In front of the chariot there go first in procession the maidens of that land, two by two; and then all the pilgrims that have come from far countries, some of whom out of great devotion to that idol fall down in front of the chariot and let it roll over them. And so some of them are slain, some have their arms and legs broken; and they believe that the more pain they suffer here for the love of that idol, the more joy they will have in the other world ..."

The Travels of Sir John Mandeville
(14th century)

societies are really too poor, sick and uneducated to know and enjoy the benefits of contemplation. These millions have no choice but to shuffle resignedly from day to day, their greatest hope not a better life but a final release from life."

Again, in Buddhist holy places, we may have seen pilgrims stopping during their circumambulation of the

commercialization kills the goose that laid the golden egg. In the 1970s a Catholic shrine in the small village of Devagama, India, suddenly became popular. Its decline after 1975 appeared to be because pilgrims were being put off by the degree of commercial exploitation. Sometimes we seem not to recognize it on our own doorstep – in Britain, Glastonbury has become a New

"Seen on close approach, the mountain of Fuji does not come up to expectations."

JAPANESE PROVERB

shrine to listen to monks telling stories from Buddhist history and legend. That Buddhists generally visit sacred sites for teaching as well as merit, being concerned more with hearing the sacred word and less with encountering the divine, fulfills Western expectations of the calm detachment of Buddhism. Yet if we have been to Sri Lanka and joined Buddhist pilgrims to Kataragama, we have seen them behave more like ecstatics, occupied not with knowledge but direct experience.

There is often also a distance between our idea of a place and what we find on the ground – in some cases literally. That nineteenth-century lover of Japan, Lafcadio Hearn, on close inspection found Mount Fuji to be "a frightful extinct heap of visible ashes and cinders and slaggy lava". The discrepancy between idea and reality nowadays has taken on a familiar twentieth-century form: though officially open for only two months of the year because of its snows, Fuji is now climbed by hundreds of thousands of people and the marks of their passing add a false note to the pilgrims' traditional chant of "Be pure ... O ye mountain!"

One of the worst shocks of pilgrimage comes from the commercialized, even downright materialistic nature of some sacred sites. It is a fine line for local populations and institutions to tread between reaping a just reward for providing support systems for pilgrims and going just too far. This can be a particular problem for developing countries with an emerging capitalism; sometimes

Age bazaar in my lifetime – but resent it in cultures we perceive as more "spiritual". In the BBC television "Rough Guide" travel series, several Westerners on the modern Indian "hippy trail" leading to a holy lake at Pushkar, Rajasthan, complained that they were charged to go down to the lake. Such public criticisms of how the local people run their *locus sanctus* could lead to the closing of this holy lake to all but Hindus.

Other shocks come from first encounters with relics. You can read differences in attitude toward them in the faces of visitors to the Basilica of St Claire in Assisi, Italy, as they file past her glass-sided coffin and view her body, turned to leather by time. Some look steadily with reverence, others quickly avert their gaze, evidently judging the display of mortal remains as morbid.

You may have seen some truly vulgar sights within and without the place of the holy: garish colours, crude painting and carving, idiot gods and simpering saints. Religious kitsch seems to abound in most cultures, even ones we judge to be highly aesthetic, such as the Japanese. Westerners are normally most offended by artefacts which do not have the glamour of exoticism or folk art, such as the mass-produced plastic souvenirs of Christian pilgrimage. You may well see objects even more tasteless than one I saw in France, at Les Saintes-Maries-de-la-Mer – Christ crucified on four clamshells.

WAR GRAVES OF THE SOMME

"They shall grow not old ..."

I was named Colin after Second Lieutenant Colin Graham Sutherland Shields, Royal Air Force. Had he lived he would have been my uncle. But he was posted "Missing, presumed dead" on 10 May 1918 while flying over the Somme. His body was identified after the Great War ended and he is buried in a British war cemetery at Cerisy–Gailly, halfway between Amiens and Peronne. He was nineteen.

Twenty-eight years later, at the end of the Second World War, I was a Captain and company commander in the Lovat Scouts, on active service in Greece. The Lovat Scouts recruit in the furthermost parts of the Highlands and Islands of Scotland, but I was even further from home than most of the men in my company, as my home was in Argentina. I was nineteen.

Years later, I inherited a few surviving mementoes: a cup Colin won for the 100 yards race at school, a framed picture of him as a cadet in London Scottish uniform, a dress version of his pilot's wings, and his last letter home – to his younger sister Barbara. Not much to show for a human life, even such a short one. He was an only son.

This reminder of my namesake's brief life led to my attending the annual Remembrance Day service at the war memorial in Beaconsfield, Buckinghamshire where he was born. C G S Shields is one of eighty names of those who died in the 1914–18 War, arranged neatly in groups of ten. An addition lists another sixty names of Beaconsfield men who died in the Second World War, 1939–45.

Second Lieutenant C G S Shields who was killed in action in 1918.

War cemeteries clustered in an area of the Somme Valley in Northern France.

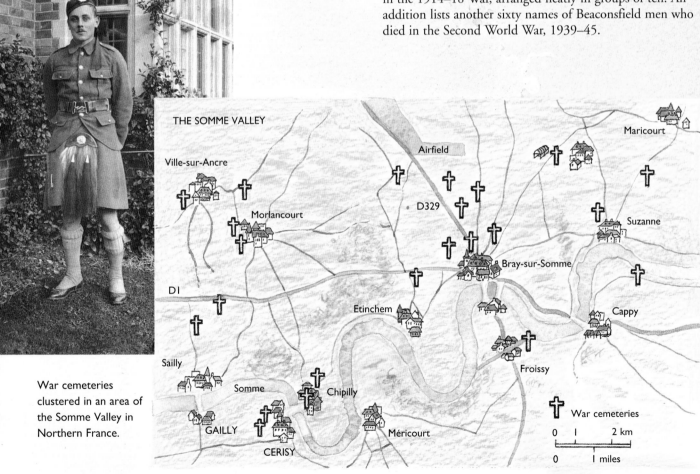

THE SOMME VALLEY

Maricourt

Airfield

Ville-sur-Ancre

D329

Suzanne

Morlancourt

Bray-sur-Somme

D1

Cappy

Etinchem

Sailly

Froissy

Somme

Chipilly

War cemeteries

GAILLY

0 1 2 km

Méricourt

0 1 miles

CERISY

Abbeville
Somme Amiens Peronne

After the battle
Troops leave the ruins of Ypres by
the Menin road in 1917. A monument to the missing now stands at
the Menin Gate.

It is now almost eighty years since the Great War ended –
at the eleventh hour of the eleventh month of 1918 – and
throughout Britain simple services of remembrance are still
held at war memorials in most villages and towns on the
nearest Sunday.

I became interested in war memorials and in what they
represent. I began studying them throughout the British Isles,
not only those on the village greens and in market squares, or
those on Scottish hillsides or in country churchyards, but also
the memorial plaques inside churches, on the walls of schools
and banks, in clubs and factories – anywhere where people
felt there was a need to remember those who lost their lives
serving their country in war.

Until very recently it was British practice to bury the
war-dead where they fell and not to repatriate the bodies. The
Commonwealth War Graves Commission is responsible for
over 23,000 burial grounds in 140 countries throughout the
world. The burial grounds house anything from a few bodies
in a foreign churchyard to vast CWGC cemeteries in the
places where major battles were fought: Ypres and the
Somme, the Dardanelles and Palestine for the Great War; and
Normandy and the Low Countries, Libya, Italy, Burma, and
the Pacific for the Second World War.

There are also those awe-inspiring monuments to the missing
listing all those with "no known grave": over 73,400 names at
Thiepval on the Somme and nearly 55,000 on the Menin
Gate at Ypres.

The thought of this kind of oblivion, of non-existence,
must haunt everybody from time to time. Coupled with it is
the guilt of the survivor, who is reminded regularly of those
who perished – be it on the battlefield, in an airline crash or a
sports stadium disaster – while he or she did not.

I resolved to make a pilgrimage to my uncle Colin's final
resting place at Cerisy–Gailly: Plot 2, row A, grave 2. A few
years ago I joined a summer battlefield tour with many others
who, like myself, had a relative or fellow-townsman who had
died in that First World War.

Laying a wreath of poppies, emblem of the battlefields of
Flanders, on Colin's grave was for me a most meaningful
moment. It was strangely cathartic, forgiving. As one of the
oldest pilgrims present I was later invited to stand by the
Cross of Sacrifice in another cemetery on the Somme and
read the words from Laurence Binyon's poem, in this instance
in remembrance of a soldier even younger than Colin:

> "They shall grow not old, as we that are left grow old:
> Age shall not weary them, nor the years condemn.
> At the going down of the sun and in the morning
> We will remember them."

Colin McIntyre is a freelance journalist and writer, the
author of *Monuments of War*. He lives in London.

Battlefield pilgrimages
Since the end of the First
World War many thousands
of pilgrims have joined tours
of the battlefields of France
and Flanders, or made personal pilgrimages to graves of
relatives or colleagues. Today
such pilgrimages embrace
both World Wars and many
other conflicts worldwide.

Some holy places dumbfound by the inappropriateness of what we see to the sacred history. When I first went to Assisi, I felt physically assaulted by what had been done there in the name of Saint Francis. The touching relics of the man himself – the coarse grey tunic and clumsy heel-less shoes preserved in his basilica – were eclipsed by things that seemed to me contrary to his spirit. Chief offender was that church of monstrous vulgarity, Santa Maria degli Angeli (Saint Mary of the Angels), built over the Porziuncola, the tiny chapel given to Saint Francis that became the birthplace of the Franciscan Order. How could someone build this florid thing on the spot where Francis himself, returning from the Crusades to find that his friars had replaced their normal shelters of branches with a tiny brick convent, tore its rooftiles off with his bare hands? This was not Francis' idea of how to imitate the life of Christ. And Santa Maria degli Angeli was not my idea of how to honour Saint Francis.

So you may find yourself not much liking the way your sacred place is conducted; and you may also find yourself not much liking its sacred personnel. At Rocamadour, in France, you will hear that a group of women who had changed their hair-colour by washing it in wine, had to cut it off before being allowed inside the church. They left their shorn tresses there as *ex votos*. One forced to do this finished her pilgrimage and was just leaving when she thought: "Holy Mary! My heart is sorrowful for my hair that I leave you, and I cannot well make my mind up to it." Immediately her tresses were restored. But the blindness of which she had been cured was restored to her also. Is this act of spite your notion of the Virgin Mary?

You may feel impatient (or guilty because you feel impatient) with the credulity and naivety of other sacred journeyers. During the great Mexican fiesta of the Three Kings at Tizimin in Yucatan, which lasts 18 days from

> "... how canst thou say to thy brother, Brother, let me pull out the mote that is in thine eye, when thou thyself beholdest not the beam that is in thine own eye?"
>
> The Bible, Luke 6: 42

176

December 31 to January 17, and when trainloads of pilgrims leave Merida Central Railroad Station at short intervals every day, motorists from as far away as Mexico City drive their cars to be blessed at the shrine. As far as they are concerned, the Three Kings who came from afar, themselves great travellers, would know the hazards of travel and therefore afford the best protection.

"Open thou my eyes, that I may behold wondrous things ..."

THE BIBLE, PSALM 119: 18

There is a moral in all of this. Iranian Muslims tell the story of Iskandr (Alexander the Great) and the Kaf. The Kaf is a mountain that encircles the earth, which is conceived of as a plane (like Terry Pratchett's *Discworld*). It is a mountain so high that a space equal only to the height of a man remains between its peaks and heaven. It is made of emerald, and the green of the land and blue of the sky are its reflections. There is another world on the far side of the Kaf: some say it is the home of the *jinns* and *peris* (demons and fairies), but others that there lives the race of Yájúj and Májúj (Gog and Magog in the New Testament of the Bible), who would have broken through to this side long ago if Iskandr had not built walls against them.

When Iskandr had conquered the world, he went to see the Kaf. He sent a slave up the mountain who, when he got to the top, saw another slave just like himself coming up the other side. So Iskandr sent a second slave, and a third, and a fourth, and every time another slave exactly like him came up from the other side. Finally Iskandr himself ascended the Kaf and looked over and, behold, another Iskandr looked back. Iskandr, who had thought he was master of all, now knew that there were other worlds and other conquerors, and died of disappointment.

But the Kaf is no less wonderful and mysterious and miraculous a place because Iskandr has come face to face with himself and lost his illusions.

ARUNACHALA

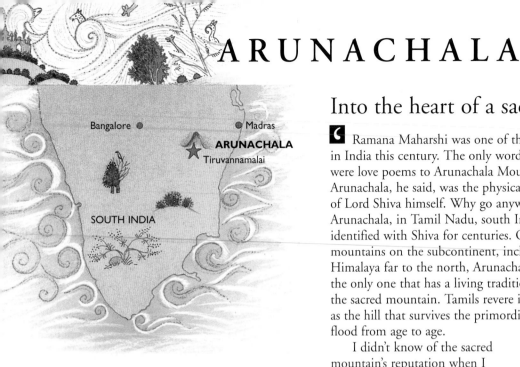

Bangalore
Madras
★ **ARUNACHALA**
Tiruvannamalai

SOUTH INDIA

When I came to realise who I am,
What else is this identity of mine?
But thee,
Oh thou who standest as the towering Aruna Hill?

Sri Ramana Maharshi – Stanzas to Arunachala

Deepam Festival
Hundreds of thousands of devotees celebrate this festival in November/December. A 10-day re-enactment of the story of Arunachala culminates in a climb to the top of the mountain, where a flame is lit to symbolize Shiva's manifestation at the mountain's creation.

Into the heart of a sacred mountain

Ramana Maharshi was one of the greatest saints in India this century. The only words he ever wrote were love poems to Arunachala Mountain. Arunachala, he said, was the physical embodiment of Lord Shiva himself. Why go anywhere else? Arunachala, in Tamil Nadu, south India, has been identified with Shiva for centuries. Of all the mountains on the subcontinent, including the Himalaya far to the north, Arunachala is the only one that has a living tradition of the sacred mountain. Tamils revere it as the hill that survives the primordial flood from age to age.

I didn't know of the sacred mountain's reputation when I first arrived in Tiruvannamalai, the town which spreads out at its base. I had come to visit the ashram of Ramana Maharshi. The mountain, though, was the first thing I saw as I drew near to the town. The surrounding area is a large flat plain, which extends through much of Tamil Nadu. Arunachala looms up from this plain, a solitary pyramid, some two and a half thousand feet high. It was purple and gold in the dusty light, and it drew me like a magnet.

I decided to explore the hill before I did anything else. I climbed up the path from the town and in twenty minutes I had arrived at Veerupaksha Cave, where Ramana Maharshi lived for sixteen years in silence and solitude. In the tranquil courtyard outside the cave entrance, a single breadfruit tree shaded a tiny lingam set in a circle of water. Someone had left a red rose on the lingam head and the petals of a yellow chrysanthemum were scattered round it in the water.

Three pairs of shoes were by the tree. I left my own shoes alongside them and passed through into the darkness. Three people were sitting motionless in front of a stone ledge. The air was hot and thick. What a relief to be in darkness after the glare of the sun. I was there for an hour or more when out of nowhere a voice suddenly rang through the quiet of my body. "Just rest," it said. "Just rest." I let the dark cave take me then, hold me; and in that moment it was as if the mountain moved through me. It was then that I felt Arunachala to be truly alive. It was as if the life of the mountain, the cave, and my own innermost being, were one and the same thing.

To climb the hill, to enter the hill through one of its caves, and to circle the hill are some of the ways of honouring the power of this ancient sacred place. The circular walk takes about three hours, and hundreds of people make the walk barefoot every day just before dawn. There have been many reports down through the years of visions of Lord Shiva and his consort, Parvati.

The shopkeeper who had served me tea the evening before showed me another way of revering the mountain. I was passing his house when he stepped in front of me and prostrated to a roadside figure of Ganesh, the Remover of Obstacles. Then he stood up and faced the mountain, his palms together in front of his heart, gazing with devotion. He turned in a circle on the spot, and facing Arunachala, bowed, and made off for his tea shop.'

Roger Housden is a writer and photographer, the author of *Travels through Sacred India* and *Retreat.* He is a director of Open Gate Journeys, which leads groups on spiritual journeys to sacred sites.

LOOKING WITH BETTER EYES

So our inbuilt expectations of our sacred journey may have been disappointed. Although unlike medieval pilgrims we have not been expected to sleep many people and both sexes to a bed, we have travelled here perhaps fairly uncomfortably, only to be pestered by touts, distressed by beggars, and oppressed by art and architecture that falls short of sublimity.

On top of all of this, we may feel we missed our moment of revelation. Look again. In the Bible the prophet Isaiah describes the day of the Lord's vengeance: "And thorns shall come up in her palaces, nettles and brambles in the fortress thereof: and it shall be an habitation for dragons, and a court for owls" (Isaiah 34: 13). When I was a child, I could never see why this was supposed to be a curse. Dragons and owls seemed infinitely desirable. It is a matter of perspective. In James Cameron's film about alien encounter *The Abyss* (1989) a character says "You have to look with better eyes than this." We sometimes need to look with better eyes to see what we have seen.

Reconsider your journey. The world is made up not only of ideas but of things – and the world of the sacred is a physical, sensual place, of landscapes, buildings, gardens, graveyards and cemeteries, paintings, sculptures, garments, and objects from bells to begging bowls. All these things have been your windows on the sacred.

In Japan, you have seen arches connecting nothing and in the middle of nowhere, standing in deep forests, beside great trees, on mountain peaks, on riverbanks and seashores. You now recognize them as Shinto *torii*, or shrine-gates, indicating that what lies beyond is holy ground. Near the *torii* you have seen the font where before entering the shrine visitors rinse their hands and mouths with water, in a symbolic purification of body and mind. You have learned much about Shinto already.

"Hey! What's this? I don't understand,' said Pigsy. 'You've just made the other two into Buddhas. Why aren't I a Buddha too?'

'Because,' said Buddha, 'your conversation and appearance still lack refinement, and your appetite is still too large. But ... it will be your job to clean up the altar everywhere and whenever there is a Buddhist ceremony and offerings are made. So you'll get plenty of pickings. I don't see what you've got to complain of."

Wu Ch'êng-ê n (c.1505-80), Monkey

Not far from Cuzco in Peru, you have fallen in with some of the remaining native speakers of Quechua, on pilgrimage to a distant shrine. They are going there to venerate not a statue in a cathedral, but a traditional image on a rock or crag. Though the rites will be Christian, conducted by a Christian priest, the image tells you that the shrine probably stands on a sacred site dedicated to one of the *apus*. These are the nature spirits who share this landscape, apparently on easy terms, with Christ and Mary, and the village patron saints. Whether nature spirit or Mary, the miraculous power these pilgrims seek is vested not in the shrine's relics, as in the European tradition, but in the image itself. You have learned something of how Peruvians view the operation of divinity.

All over the world, continuity of sacred place has built up layers of meaning. The Roman author Varro (116–27BC) recounts that before the temple of Jupiter, Juno, and Minerva was constructed on the Roman Capitol, the site had been occupied by the ancient deity Terminus, a boundary stone, who stolidly refused to make room for the new building and therefore had to be accommodated inside. At Daphne, near Antioch, the oracle of Apollo ceased to speak when on to its very site Christians introduced the cult of the martyr Babylas. At the conquest of the New World by Spain, Christian shrines were built on sites where pre-Columbian deities were worshipped. Sometimes practices seem to have carried over too, but now is a good time to abandon any notion of "survivals of paganism": the movement is not all one way. An observer at Zacaleu in Guatemala in 1976 saw Maya in ethnic dress and speaking the Maya language performing what appeared to be Christian devotions at the ancient Maya temple.

What we see at pilgrimage sites is creative religion: religion with some of the boundaries down answering the demands of human aspiration and human suffering. In India, Hindus are often among pilgrims at the shrines of *pirs* (Islamic Sufi saints), whether these be humble grave sites in small villages or great pilgrimage places such as Fateh Pur Sikri in Uttar Pradesh. The Muslim saints usually have high reputations for healing. Surinder Bhardwaj, writing in the *National Geographic Journal of India* in 1987, recalled that as a child, he had been taken to a living Muslim holy man for healing, and that in his mainly Hindu village there was a small grave site of a Muslim *pir* at which people generally used to light earthen lamps on Thursdays to pray for good health, and even success in school examinations.

On pilgrimage, the clue to what is happening in people's hearts and minds is often in what we see. That pilgrims offer artificial limbs made from silver or gold to Haji Malang for the relief of bodily pain is the explanation of why the timing of the Haja Malanga fair at Wadi in Kalyan Taluka, India, should be according to the Hindu calendar, though Haji Malang was a Muslim saint. It also explains why prayers at the shrine should be offered five times a day following Muslim practice, but the priest be Brahmin.

We learn from these offerings of golden arms and feet that the desire to end suffering can temporarily transcend religious difference.

REDIRECTION

Through our sacred journeying we have begun to reach beyond the urgency of our own desires to the wider dimension of the divine seen in the light of human history. We have touched hands across space with pilgrims on other roads, looking, like us, for their glimpse of the divine, and cast our gaze backward down the steps of time to see how those tens of thousands on our road before us went about their search.

> "We are always in the presence of mysticism when we find a human being ... feeling himself, while still externally amid the earthly and temporal, to belong to the super-earthly and eternal."
>
> Albert Schweitzer, The Mysticism of Paul the Apostle (1930)

Now when we see pilgrims in Asia or the Middle East or Europe, sleeping near to or touching the shrines of saints, we remember the Old Testament account of the grave of the prophet Elisha (II Kings 13: 21): "And ... when the man was let down, and touched the bones of Elisha, he revived, and stood up on his feet." When we see Muslims newly returned from the Hajj with snippets from the great cloth that covers the Ka'ba – necessarily renewed every year, as a gift from Egypt; when we see Christian pilgrims touching pieces of cloth to images and reliquaries; even when we see pieces of rag hung round holy wells in Britain and Eire, we remember the New Testament story of Saint Paul in Ephesus (Acts 19: 11–12): "And God wrought special miracles by the hands of Paul: So that from his body were brought unto the sick handkerchiefs or aprons, and the diseases departed from them, and the evil spirits went out of them."

What do I think now of that vast basilica at Assisi? Well, I see it as the result of several centuries of Italian Catholicism, during which the intention of honouring – and accessing the spiritual power of – Saint Francis has found different ways of expressing itself. I have learned not to fret about Santa Maria degli Angeli but instead to dwell on memories of Saint Francis' rock-hewn hermitage of the Carceri and Saint Claire's austere convent of San Damiano. I see the town as a whole as the living expression of dynamic faith, not as a time-frozen fossil.

We turn homeward, but the road home is not the road by which we came: it is a different road, for we are different. We have become pilgrims and we have been changed by our experiences. Never in our lives shall we be the same again. What we do with that new person is something to consider.

But still another step on our journey awaits us, and that is to begin to see what we do on pilgrimage in the light of eternity.

XII *Coming home*

CHAPTER 12

"If a man", says Sir John Mandeville, "set out from home on a journey and kept right on going, he would come back to his own front door."

Though no one would want this medieval pseudo-geographer as a guide, for pilgrimage this is not a bad model. It is when you get home, when you come full circle, that you perceive the "truth" of your journey. Though the sacred place is the source of spiritual power, it is at home that the effects of this power on you become visible. Your re-entry into everyday life is the test of your pilgrimage.

Will unpacking your mental baggage confirm that there has been transformation? That you are different? That your life has been changed?

How do the people at home see this new person, this pilgrim? Was your experience just for you, or will it enrich lives that touch your life?

And when they ask how this change came about, where will you say that you have been?

The pilgrim's return
In this Hajj painting, a stylized account of the pilgrimage to Mecca, a mother greets her daughter, who wears the plain white dress of a *hajji*.

Souvenirs of pilgrimage
Medieval pilgrims wore badges
or tokens (above and right)
from the shrines they had
visited, as proof that they had
reached their goal.

What is the "truth" of our journey? The British traveller Freya Stark (1893–1993) once said, that when she announced that she was setting out on one of her journeys, everyone asked her why. They had difficulty accepting that she simply wanted to go and look.

We have been to a sacred place to look, and we do not need to justify our journey or worry too much about how we should benefit from it. By the very fact of going on pilgrimage, we have exposed ourselves to the process of revelation and, if we let it, it will work out largely to its own ends.

Our journey toward the sacred has been awakening and humanizing, and has perhaps added a heroic dimension to our lives.

AWAKENING

If we have been abroad, we have experienced culture-shock, our removal to another setting bringing about shifts in perspective. We may have discovered how completely unfounded were our beliefs concerning other people, and gained a greater understanding of how they see life, the world, and God.

Coming home, like expatriates returning to the home country, we experience culture-shock in reverse. Because of the intensity of the pilgrimage experience, a shift in perceptions can take place after only quite a short exposure to a different world.

Descriptions of mystical experience, saints' legends, and folk traditions concerning fairies, all speak of the way in which, during encounters with the Other, time runs at a different speed. On the hillside above the ancient abbey of Lleyre in Spain is Saint Virilar's Spring. Legend says that Saint Virilar, hearing a nightingale, followed it up the slope to the spring, and stayed there spellbound until it had finished singing.

When he returned to the abbey, he found that the buildings had changed, and that the porter at the gate was a stranger. Three hundred years had passed by.

> *"This is my play's last scene,*
> *here heavens appoint*
> *My pilgrimage's last mile."*

JOHN DONNE (1572–1631), HOLY SONNETS NO I

This also describes quite well what happens on a sacred journey. Like Saint Virilar, when we return home we find that familiar scenes and faces look strange. We are seeing them with new eyes, receiving revelations about things we normally take for granted. The awakening may be wonderful or painful – it is always enlarging.

HUMANIZING

Many of us went to the holy place seeking salvation in one form or another – though not as explicitly, perhaps, as a Hindu journeying to Benares to avoid rebirth. Many will have sought some solution to an earthly problem, especially the three p's: powerlessness, poverty, pain. There we have seen others similarly engaged.

Paradoxically, one of the benefits we bring back from pilgrimage is more pain. We may return raw from the encounter with suffering humanity, our normal defences against others' unhappiness down. We have seen the search for salvation in individual faces, heard it in voices. We may have become aware that there is little or no direct action that we, as individuals, can take.

We heard earlier of the feelings experienced by an Indian pilgrim of the Brahmin caste at the realization that, back home, there could be little place in her life for the lower caste women she had travelled with. After the St Martin-in-the-Fields Pilgrimage for Homeless People from London to Canterbury, pilgrims with homes to go back to sometimes feel guilty at letting their homeless companions return to the streets.

If once we are back in the everyday, we want to keep our vision for ourselves, for humanity, or for our planet as clear and bright as it was during our journey, we must allow the humanizing memory of pain to work in and through us. Eventually it will bring about change.

THE HEROIC DIMENSION

Whether we want political equality, resources enough to feed the world, respect for other life forms, world peace, or planetary healing, the transformation of the world around us will be the result of personal transformation.

One of the terms the Koran uses for general sinfulness is *dalal*, aimless wandering, as opposed to the purposeful path of pilgrimage through life. As well as undertaking a pilgrimage which will subconsciously affect the rest of our lives, we can choose consciously to see the whole of our lives as a sacred journey.

I spoke earlier of King Alfred. His father, King Aethelwulf, had vowed to make a pilgrimage to Rome on behalf of his people. In the event, he sent as his substitute his youngest son, Alfred, then only four years old. The impact of the Eternal City, with its brick and stone buildings and gorgeous processions, on a child from what was by comparison a backwoods, must have been dazzling. There is little doubt that this visit to Rome, and another at age six, were formative experiences, colouring Alfred's whole life and giving him his guiding purpose of creating a Christian civilization in England.

SAINT WINIFRED'S WELL

A journey of healing and renewal

Over the past thirty years I have made the pilgrimage to St Winifred's Well many dozens of times – a benefit of having an ancient sanctuary virtually on one's doorstep. This familiarity has occasioned an ever-deepening awareness, not just of its intrinsic beauty, its extraordinary history, and the nuances of its sacred past, but of its present potency for renewal and restoration to physical and psychic wholeness. This numinous place, silent except for the murmurings of the water, is alive with power.

A constant current of whispered prayer activates, as it were, the 'mandala' of the star-shaped Well, and one senses what this place has meant to the thousands of pilgrims who have scratched or carved names or initials on to its walls and pillars over nearly five hundred years. Each name represents a cure or favour obtained, or at least devoutly hoped for.

But the Well is most alive, and the presence of its celestial patroness most easily accessible, during the stillness of a solitary pilgrimage, when its powerful present confronts and confirms its powerful past.

One of my pilgrimages requires a special telling. By 1982 I had been suffering from osteoarthritis for several years, unable to walk without a stick. That year, acting on impulse, I went to the Well on 3 November, the feast of St Winifred. Painfully, and very slowly, I walked the last mile. I don't remember praying, or even thinking: every bit of me was concentrated simply on making it to the Well. It took me about an hour and a half, and it was the longest distance I had walked in years.

There is a time-honoured ritual way of bathing at the holy Well. The present shrine, which was erected around 1505 under royal patronage, is two-storeyed: a large chapel over a crypt. Graceful pillars surround a star-shaped basin at

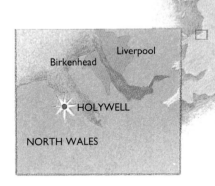

The pilgrim's road
St Winifred's shrine is in the town of Holywell (Treffynnon in Welsh), North Wales. The most evocative approach is on foot, up through the woods from the ruined Basingwerk Abbey one mile to the north at Greenfield: this follows the last stage of a medieval pilgrims' road.

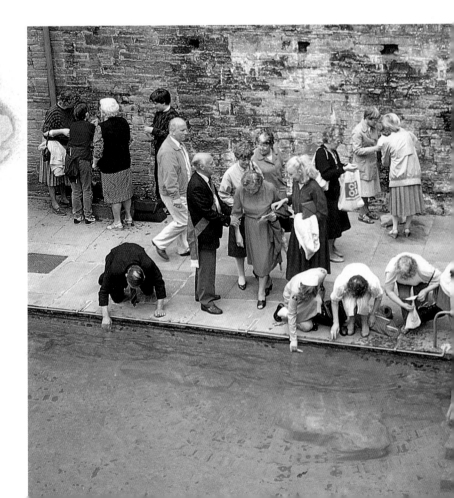

the center of the crypt, and from here the spring rises. Its stingingly cold water flows into an adjacent bath to a depth of about 4 feet. The pilgrim passes through the bath three times, and three times circles the source, saying a decade of the rosary and finishing the prayers kneeling on a stone in the larger pool outside the chapel. On that day I simply bathed, said a prayer, lit a candle, and went home. My pilgrimage had been an act of devotion rather than a specific plea for healing. Yet within two months I found myself cured, and permanently.

Nor was my cure simply physical: my inner, spiritual life was renewed. If I had not prayed as I bathed, I certainly prayed after my cure, and with certainty. St Winifred's Well appeared, according to legend, at the site of her martyrdom; at the same place she was brought back to life. These events have made the Well a place of continuous devotion and healing for thirteen centuries. In a sense, Winifred and I shared a common experience. My cure gave me a kind of jolt of recognition. From that time, Winifred became for me, not a dead saint – however prayerfully powerful – but a living woman. She and I, I feel, are friends.

Over the years I have taken many people to visit the shrine at St Winifred's Well. One of these, twelve years ago, was my partner; and he came to share my love and respect for the shrine, though he only came to understand it fully at the end. When he died last year, we buried him high on the hillside above the Well, and then went to the Well to light candles and to remember him. Home, they say, is where the heart is; and now that I too am dying of the same disease, I am very aware that I will follow and rejoin him soon, in like manner. And this, my last pilgrimage, will also be, in a real sense, a coming home.'

Tristan Gray Hulse is the editor of *Source – the Holy Wells journal* and an authority on holy wells.

The healing waters
Pilgrims collect water to take home from the pool outside the chapel (above). Bathing at the Well is by arrangement with the custodians.

Practicalities
This Catholic shrine is open all year round and welcomes pilgrims of any faith. Between Pentecost and 30 September a service including veneration of St Winifred's relic is held at the Well daily at 11.30am (Sundays 2.30pm). The Pilgrims' Hospice in Holywell is open throughout the year.

The Annual National Pilgrimage is on the Sunday following 22 June, when there is a procession through the town to Mass at the Well. There is also an annual Pan-Orthodox pilgrimage on the first Saturday in October.

Alfred saw himself as a pilgrim. He speaks of his life as a journey, hoping that God will "enlighten the eyes of my mind so that I can find out the straight road to the eternal home ..." He also tried to live as a hero, whose achievements would be remembered long after his death.

All pilgrims are heroes: pilgrimage is in itself an heroic act. The decision to find out the straight road through life is a noble decision.

WHO ARE WE?

When our families and friends welcome us home again, what do they see? In one sense, nothing special: just one among the millions who every year take to the road or the train or the airplane on a sacred journey. Pilgrims need a proper humility. The Japanese poet Basho, embarking on a pilgrimage in 1688, recorded in *The Records of a Travel-Worn Satchel* that his friends gave him a good send-off, providing him with necessities for his journey – the paper raincoat, the warm winter stockings – and also threw farewell parties and feasts. He says, with self-mockery: "I ... almost fell a victim to the illusion that a man of importance was leaving on a journey."

But in another sense, each pilgrim *is* very special indeed. We do not just "happen" to go on pilgrimage.

The Persian Sufi poet Rumi (1207–73) tells the story of a man who always prayed earnestly and most devoutly, late into the night. One night, when he was beginning to tire, Satan put into his mind the question: "For all your calling out 'O God!' have you ever heard God reply 'Here I am'?"

The man admitted he had never heard even a whisper. Then God sent a messenger to tell him that all the fear and love he had been pouring into his prayer had been God's gift to him in the first place. "Beneath every 'O Lord' of yours lies many a 'Here I am' from me."

In other words, no-one seeks God whom God is not calling. Pilgrims are people who have been evoked by someone or something to seek out the divine.

> "It is through the centre ... that the Holy Spirit enlightens the mind, fires the heart, makes firm the will. It is the focus of God's action, the sanctuary where he dwells."
>
> *C R Bryant SSJE,* The Psychology of Prayer

> "It is a great thing to know in our heart that God ... indwells our soul. Even greater is it to know that our soul ... dwells in the substance of God ... we are enfolded by him ... and he by us."
>
> *Mother Julian of Norwich,*
> Revelations of Divine Love *(c.1393)*

THE JOURNEY TO THE CENTER

Now we are home, we can look again at where we have been. The anthropologist's definition of pilgrimage as a sacred journey that begins in a familiar place and proceeds to a far place, fits many pilgrimage shrines, not least Mecca, fairly distant from most Islamic states. Yet Muslims regard Mecca as the center of their world.

That Jerusalem similarly stood at the center of the world was, according to the Anglo-Saxon historian Bede (c.673–735), scientifically proven, since on Midsummer Day a certain column in the city cast no shadow. The idea of the sacred place as the center of the earth and of the cosmos is embodied in Babylonian ziggurats, Chinese palaces, Indian cities, Borneo Dyak houses, Navajo shrines, and Buddhist *stupas*.

The center is the place of connection. It links Earth with Heaven (according to one tradition, Heaven was only 18 miles above Jerusalem) and also connects World and Underworld. Still today for Pueblo Indians, like the ancient Romans, the earth's center is a pit covered by a stone, which is removed on special occasions to give the ancestral spirits contact with the living. Similarly the ancient Greeks' earth center was a stone known as the Omphalos (navel), at Delphi. Through the image of the pit or navel, the center connects us with our human inheritance, with our genetic and cultural coding, who we are.

Through the cosmic center runs the Axis Mundi, the pole around which the cosmos turns. The Achilpas, one of the Australian Arandi tribes, carry their Axis Mundi around with them, represented by a sacred pole. They decide which direction to take according to which way the sacred pole leans: it both centers and orients them, so that they always know where they are and where to go. Their traditions say the pole was once broken and the people wandered for a time, and finally sat down and let themselves perish. Loss of orientation meant the end of their world.

What archaic and tribal mythology agree on is that we need the center to give us our bearings, without which we are aimless wanderers.

THE INNER JOURNEY

When Egyptian pilgrims return from the Hajj they sometimes have their houses decorated with a stylized pictorial record of their journey. A recurring image is the winged and human-faced creature, Buraq.

Buraq was the steed ridden by Mohammed on his traditional Night Journey to Jerusalem. According to some accounts, Buraq was left tied to the Rock of Jerusalem while the Angel Gabriel led the Prophet up a ladder to the very throne of God. Others say it was Buraq himself who bore Mohammed aloft. Sufi interpreters regarded the Night Journey not as a physical journey, but as an inward experience and a model for the spiritual path. Bayazid al-Bistami suggested that individuals are granted ascension (growth) on the "Buraq of self-forgetfulness", referring to the contemplative goal of loss of self in the absolute of God.

Cosmic imagery, the experience of Sufis and other mystics, and the practice of pilgrimage all seem to tell us the same thing: that there is a center that can give us meaning (connection) and purpose (direction). This center is the God described by Saint Bonaventure (1221–74) as a "circle whose centre is everywhere and whose circumference is nowhere".

The mystics' perception that God is both within and without is hard to understand. Saint Teresa of Avila asserts: "God visits the soul in a manner which prevents its doubting ... that it dwelt in Him, and ... He ... within it ..." For centuries, people have hoped to receive this assurance in a sacred place, or in the sacred place within: to stand for a moment at once fleeting and eternal before the very throne of God, in contemplation of Shekinah, the divine radiance.

"Let not your spirit be troubled
on account of the times;
For the Holy and Great One
has appointed days for all things ...
He will be gracious to the righteous
and give him eternal uprightness ...
And he shall walk in eternal light."

The Book of Enoch (1st century BC)
trans R H Charles

Part II

Guide to Sacred Places

JOURNEYS TO SACRED LANDSCAPES

Iona, Scotland

"Iona has cast its spell on the sons of men. In early times, it heard the sweet songs of God sung by Saint Columba and his followers. In later days, greater men than we have found there what they sought. This island set apart, this motherland of many dreams still yields its secret, but it is only as men seek they shall truly find".

This quote from an unknown author now graces the hallway of one of Iona's small hotels, and echoes the sense of enchantment that travellers to the island have experienced throughout the ages.

To reach Iona today, travellers must make the lengthy journey to Oban in the West Highlands of Scotland, and take the ferry to the Isle of Mull, before crossing the island to Fionnphort and boarding a smaller ferry to Iona. There the imposing abbey stands out facing the waves. St Columba's journey was more perilous: leaving Derry in Northern Ireland, he set sail on a "pilgrimage for Christ", and arrived on Iona in 563, where he founded the island's first monastery.

In more recent times, pilgrims have been drawn to Iona not only to visit the many places linked with the saint and the island's monastic tradition, but also to seek something more elusive: inner calm and spiritual renewal. Few tourists and day trippers venture further than the abbey and its nearby shops, but the west side of the island, overlooking the Atlantic Ocean, is more rugged, and alive with mysterious natural landmarks – the spouting cave, the healing pool, and the bay at the back of the ocean.

Iona lives at a leisurely pace: it is best to stay overnight to benefit from the island's relaxed rhythm. Accommodation should be booked in advance, as there are few hotels. Cars and camping are not generally permitted on Iona, but there are car parks and a camp site at Fionnphort on Mull. The island is exposed, and you will need rain-wear even in summer. Walkers will need good shoes and a large-scale map. The abbey now houses the Iona Community, who hold a Christian service on 15 June in honour of St Columba.

Lough Derg, Eire

To Catholic pilgrims the world over, the small island in the midst of Lough Derg (red lake), crowned by an octagonal basilica, is a place where they may spend three long, demanding days in prayer, vigil, and penitential retreat. According to tradition, St Patrick experienced a vision of purgatory on Lough Derg. His Welsh disciple Davog brought Christianity to the region and founded a monastery on nearby Saints' Island.

The island, known both as Station Island and St Patrick's Purgatory, has been a place of pilgrimage since the 12th century and today receives up to 30,000 pilgrims a year, with the largest numbers coming in June, July, and August. They make their way to the village of Pettigo and thence to the shores of the lough, from where they are ferried to the island. Each of them has fasted since midnight, and is prepared to eat nothing for the next three days save for one daily meal of black tea or coffee and dry bread.

Following a day's fast, pilgrims must complete three stations, which involves reciting prayers silently while walking barefoot over rocks and stones. Then they undertake a 24-hour vigil, during which they recite prayers at the last four stations in the basilica. Pilgrims support each other as they symbolically make themselves ready for the coming of Christ. On the morning of the third day they celebrate the Eucharist in a spirit of rejoicing and community after the rigours of their spiritual exercises.

The pilgrimage is organized by the office of St Patrick's Purgatory on Lough Derg, which stipulates that pilgrims must be over 15 years old, without ailment or disability, and able to walk and kneel unaided.

Cameras, radios, and musical instruments are forbidden. Pilgrims are provided with a bed at the hostel, and are advised to bring clothes to suit the weather, which can be either cold, windy, and wet, or hot and humid. Special one-day retreats are conducted in May, August, and September. These retreats, which must be reserved in advance, do not involve fasting or walking barefoot.

Mont-Saint-Michel, France

Pilgrims have made sacred journeys to Mont-St-Michel, a small island off the Normandy coast, since the 8th century. In 708, the Archangel Michael appeared to St Aubert, Bishop of Avranches, and ordered him to build a chapel on the summit. The abbey church was built from granite brought by boat from the nearby Chausey Islands and Brittany, and hauled up the steep sides of the hill by ropes.

The original building stood at the top of a cone-shaped hill. To enlarge the abbey over centuries, a huge substructure of stone and rubble had to be created. The feats of architectural ingenuity required are reflected in the name given to the buildings on the northern side – La Merveille. The abbey rises majestically from a clump of houses at its base and is crowned by a Gothic spire 540ft above sea level. The French author Maupassant called it "the most wonderful Gothic dwelling ever made for God on this earth". Once, according to Celtic myth, this small island was a sea-tomb where the souls of the dead were taken by boat.

Unusually among pilgrimage places, the cult of Mont-St-Michel is centered on the spirituality of the place itself, rather than on a saint or a sacred relic. At low tide you can walk to the mount, but go with a guide to avoid the treacherous quicksand. Since the building of the causeway in the 19th century, siltation has meant that the mount is only completely cut off from the mainland during the high tides of spring and autumn.

Two million pilgrims journey to Mont-St-Michel each year, crossing the causeway to enter the Porte de l'Avancée and walk up the Grande Rue to the abbey. The island is most crowded in summer, when the gates often close temporarily and admission is by guided tour only. The abbey is open every day except national holidays.

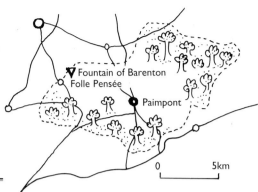

Brocéliande, France

The primordial woodland was an elemental force, both dangerous and miraculous. To early European civilizations it represented the threat of the untamed wild, home of Pan who could inspire terror and "panic". Forest deities required placatory worship, and early cults adopted the natural temples of groves and glades. But as humans began to dominate their habitat, cutting and burning the trees, so perceptions changed. The forest then came to represent freedom from authority, or the romance of Arthurian legend.

One such forest is the Breton Forest of Paimpont in France, which entered fable as Brocéliande, the wood where the wizard Merlin was bewitched by the nymph Viviane beside the miraculous Fountain of Barenton. High among the trees, the Fountain is reached from the village of Folle Pensée. A woodland track leads to the ancient spring – walled in moss and stone, set in the roots of a mighty tree, and filled with deliciously pure water. The medieval poet Chrétien de Troyes wrote:

"its water is colder than marble ... shaded by the most beautiful tree
That nature ever made."

After drinking from the spring, visitors can follow a 5th-century tradition: those who splash water on to Merlin's stone, the great slab in which the spirit of the wizard is still supposedly imprisoned, can test its power to call up storms and the vision of a black-clad horseman.

The forest lies 18 miles west of Rennes and is easily accessible by road. The village of Paimpont offers a range of accommodation. Although a forest fire in 1990 caused some damage, the country-side remains idyllically unspoilt, rich in associations with an age of chivalry. Here, according to the poets of the Middle Ages, Lancelot du Lac spent his childhood, stolen by magic from his parents.

Each landmark conjures echoes from a legendary past – from the Rocher des Faux Amants, where Morgan le Fay tempted young men to their doom in the evocatively named Valley of No Return, to the beautiful Château at Comper, the birthplace of the enchantress Viviane. It is said that near the fateful spring where she first encountered Merlin, still further in the depths of the forest, lies the Fountain of Eternal Youth, hidden from all but the pure in heart.

Lalibela, Ethiopia

Ethiopia follows the Julian calendar and consequently is seven years and eight months behind the Christian world. During the celebration of Timkat (Epiphany), the time lag seems far greater. In Lalibela, a high mountain town which boasts eleven ancient churches hewn out of rock, Timkat is observed much as it has been for the past 800 years.

In contrast to the other countries of sub-Saharan Africa, where European missionaries introduced Christianity, Ethiopia has its own indigenous variation of the religion. The Ethiopian Orthodox Church was founded in the 4th century and incorporates aspects of Judaism. In the 12th century King Lalibela ordered the construction (or, more precisely, excavation) of the town which bears his name. He envisaged a new Jerusalem.

Timkat, which is celebrated throughout the country, is the most important annual event for Ethiopia's Orthodox Christians, and takes place on 19 January, twelve days after the Ethiopian Christmas. Pilgrims descend on all of the major religious centers. Those converging on Lalibela from the surrounding countryside travel by mule or on foot (often without shoes), and journey for days. Tourists arrive by airplane, to a rough airstrip.

On the eve of Timkat, the *tabotat* (replicas of the tablets on which the Ten Commandments were inscribed) are removed from the Holy of Holies within each church and paraded, wrapped in damask, to the banks of the River Jordan, which flows through Lalibela. The pilgrims and priests hold vigil over the *tabotat* throughout the night,

when temperatures can fall close to freezing. At daybreak, the priests bless the pilgrims with holy water and the processions return to their respective churches.

Timkat processions in Lalibela are dusty, colourful, noisy affairs. People dance, chant, and ululate; drums beat and horns blare. Amid the throng, ceremonial umbrellas emroidered in gold provide shade for the lucky few. The priests are resplendent in their brightest robes and carry processional crosses, whilst the pilgrims predominantly wear the traditional white shawls and turbans.

Armanath Cave, Kashmir

A pillar of ice at the heart of a yawning cave is the climax of an annual pilgrimage that draws thousands of Hindus from all walks of life. Perched high in the Himalaya north of Srinagar in Kashmir, the cave is believed to be where Shiva and his consort, Parvati, spent their wedding night. Shiva melted himself and then solidified into the pillar, a giant *linga* that became Parvati's object of adoration. Created from seeping spring water under unusual temperature and pressure conditions, the pillar waxes and wanes with the moon, and may grow as tall as 10 feet.

Known as a *yatra*, this ancient pilgrimage is timed to coincide with the full moon in July/August, when

weather conditions permit the arduous but rewarding trek through a glacial landscape of sheer escarpments, glorious lakes, and precipitous trails. Despite the disruptions caused by political conflict (would-be pilgrims are advised to check with the authorities before setting out), the *yatra* is very well organized. Pilgrims, or *yatris*, must register at the main starting point at Pahalgam and then move off together for the four-day, 30-mile journey. Pilgrims are recommended to take a tent, sleeping bag, waterproof shoes, warm clothing, a torch, and a walking stick to use in crossing the snow and ice fields.

Raw, cold, and often wet, the *yatris* arrive at Armanath Cave at dawn on the day of the full moon. Here they wash away their sins in the sacred river Amaravati, where Shiva conferred immortality on the other Hindu gods. After taking off their shoes they ascend a stone platform and enter the cave. Once inside and past two sadhus – one holding a holy book, one collecting cash offerings – they ring a large bell. Behind an iron grille is the pillar – milky yellow, scattered with rose petals, scarves, and tinsel. Pilgrims have little time to dwell on the experience before they receive the *tilaka*, a red mark on the forehead that symbolizes a devout Hindu, and are ushered out of the cave. The pillar of ice is considered to be the *darshan*, or glimpsing of god – to worship here frees a pilgrim from the fear of death.

Hemkund, India

"And now my own story I tell, how from rigorous austerities I was summoned by God; called from the heights of Hemkund, where seven peaks so grandly pierce the sky ... the place where the Pandava king practised yogic rites."

Thus the tenth Sikh Guru, Govind Singh, describes meditating at Hemkund before his incarnation. The Almighty told him,

"Preach the way of truth and purge them of every evil way."

Hemkund is regarded as a very holy place by Sikhs, who seek to be immersed in bliss as they immerse themselves in the blue-green waters of the lake, which lies at a height of 15,000ft surrounded by seven Himalayan peaks. Nearby is the Valley of the Flowers, where more than 200 species of flower (some unique) bloom during the summer.

In the 1930s, Pandit Tara Singh Narottam discovered the site and a Gurdwara (Sikh temple) was built in 1936. Nearby is a shrine where Lakshmana, brother of the Hindu deity Rama, meditated. Hemkund is 190 miles northeast of Rishikesh in the Garhwal region of Uttarakhand (Northern Uttar Pradesh).

Uttarakhand is a sacred landscape with many *yatras* (traditional Hindu pilgrimages) to a number of sites associated with important Hindu deities, sages, and heroes. The sacred rivers, Ganga (Ganges) and Jamuna, rise here. The landscape is host to ancient Buddhist sites, too. Between May and October many thousands of pilgrims journey to the Char Dhams (four temples) at Gangotri, Kedarnath, and Badrinath, sources of tributaries of the Ganga, and at Yumnotri, source of the Jamuna. These temples are also the homes of Vishnu and Shiva.

Pilgrims usually travel the first part of the journey by bus but walk the last 13 miles from Govind Ghat or 4 miles from Ghangaria. A visit to these sites has to be completed in a day as there is nowhere to stay or camp beyond Ghangaria. Journeys can also be undertaken by hired car, tourist taxi, or trekking. Permission is needed to camp in national parks. You will need warm clothing and rainwear, mineral water, and insect repellent.

Sri Pada, Sri Lanka

There is a holy mountain in Sri Lanka in the hill country south of Kandy that Buddhists call Sri Pada. 'Pada' means footprint and 'Sri' is a term of respect. Near the peak is a great boulder impressed with a footprint that is venerated as the first place Buddha stood on Earth. On tourist maps the mountain is called Adam's Peak. According to both Christian and Muslim legend the giant footprint is the place of Adam's penance, where he was forced to stand on one leg for a thousand years after he had been thrown out of the Garden of Eden.

Few tourists climb the mountain but thousands of locals make the pilgrimage annually, climbing at night in family groups that include children and grandmothers. There are steps cut into the mountainside for most of the climb. The idea is to reach the summit at dawn when the triangular shadow of the peak is projected on to the mists over the awakening countryside. In some weather conditions you may see your own shadow floating on skeins of mist looped with a rainbow.

Most pilgrims take a bus or taxi from Ratnapura to one of two starting points, from which it is either a four- or seven-mile climb up stone steps to the peak. As the pilgrimage is not a normal tourist activity you will need to seek out local knowledge. You can make the journey between December and April before the monsoon, when torrential rains make the paths dangerous. Training shoes are more suitable than boots but take plenty of warm clothing, including rainwear, and a bag to carry your clothes for the hot climb down. Stalls sell food and hot drinks but many pilgrims prefer not to eat on the way up but to wait for the dawn, symbol of enlightenment, before breaking their fast.

An ancient name for Sri Lanka is Serendip, from which comes "serendipity", meaning to find something important while searching for something else. This is an appropriate theme for a pilgrimage up a holy mountain to a footprint symbolizing a great teacher.

Fuji-san, Japan

On a very clear day you can see the symmetrical cone of Fuji-san from Tokyo. Especially in winter, when the peak is capped with snow, this is a sight of awe-inspiring beauty. But Fuji-san hides a silent, volcanic power. The last time the volcano erupted, in 1707, the streets of Tokyo, 60 miles away, were covered in ash.

Traditionally women were only allowed to climb the mountain on one special day every 60 years, because the female mountain *kami* was believed to be jealous of other women. (The Shinto concept of *kami* means something powerful and awe-inspiring.) Nowadays there are no such restrictions.

The pilgrimage season is in July and August when large crowds of people of all ages, from children to grandparents, follow the clearly marked mountain paths to the summit. Pilgrims should not attempt to climb Fuji-san out of season unless they are experienced climbers. At 12,400ft this is a serious mountain. The weather conditions can change suddenly and even in midsummer the temperature at the top is close to freezing. Climbers should wear boots and take several layers of warm clothing, hat, gloves, rainwear and sun cream, and a torch for night climbing. Meals and hot drinks can be bought in the mountain huts en route.

The climb is divided into ten stages, but most pilgrims travel by bus to the fifth station. The idea is to time your climb so that you arrive at the top by dawn. Though freezing cold and windy on the summit, this is the time when the mountain is least likely to be shrouded by cloud and where the sunrise is spectacular. As the first rays of sunlight appear, thousands of pilgrims all over the mountain throw up their arms and shout "Bonsai!", which is like sharing a huge "Hurrah!".

Morning frost,
Mount Fuji
brushed lightly.

Haiku written by TANTAN 1674–1761

Plaine du Nord, Haiti

The Church of St James commands the center of Plaine du Nord, a fertile farming area where slave uprisings commenced the Haitian revolution in 1791. Running past the church is a dirt track marked by a series of potholes which fill in during summer rains to become small ponds. Should the rains fail, townspeople will come with pails of water to ensure plenty of mud. For them, these are not potholes but terrestrial emergence points for Ogou, an Iwa (deity) who is the commander in chief of the Vodou pantheon. These mud pits are his most important shrine in Haiti.

For three days prior to the canonical feast of St James (25 July) pilgrims descend on the town wearing blue suits and red scarves, or the multi-striped garb of a penitent. They have come to fulfill vows, or to seek blessings. Pregnant women and tubercular children line up for a bath and a blessing from itinerant herbalists. Bony bulls with red ribbons around their necks, and candles stuck on

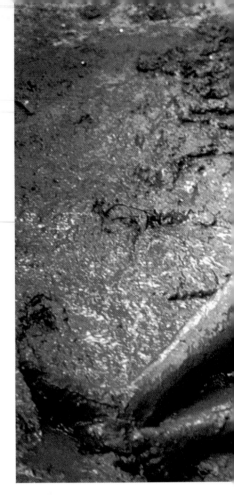

their horns, become lumbering sacrifices for Ogou. After the muddy tauracide, the bulls' blood will be used to anoint the pilgrims.

Other pilgrims fall face down in the sludge, not visibly breathing. When they arise they look like primal creatures, flinging their mud-covered torsos in ecstasy. Groups of drummers play sacred rhythms at crosspoints around the mud pits. The music never stops until the morning of 25 July, by which time most pilgrims have departed for other festivals nearby.

Throughout the pilgrimage, crowds gather on the steps of the church, which they cannot enter. Iron gratings bar the doors and windows. So they shout prayers

Paying homage to Ogou
Pilgrims at the mud pit shrines to Ogou
writhe in the mud to sacred drum rhythms.

and hurl candles, pennies, or rum bottles through the gratings. They aim their missiles at an empty niche that used to contain an image of St James. Catholic clergy have removed the image, noting that the church is being used to honour a Vodou deity. For indeed, in Haiti everyone knows St James is Ogou, senior brother of a lineage of divine warriors. Through a long process of appropriation, Haitians have refigured an important Catholic festival in order to honour their own African god.

Señor de Qoyllor Rit'i, Peru

Amid the bleak immensity of the southern Peruvian Andes, three great glacial tongues reach down to the desolate Sinakara valley. A stone chapel houses a figure of Christ crucified – the miraculous Señor de Qoyllor Rit'i (Lord of the Snow Star) – painted on a rock outcrop. Each year, between the Christian feasts of the Ascension and Corpus Christi, 25,000 pilgrims (predominantly Quechua-speaking highlanders) converge on the chapel in an explosion of pagan colour, noise, and ritual movement.

In 1783, it is said, a shepherd-boy, Mariano, was befriended in Sinakara by Manuel, a pale-skinned stranger. Church representatives travelled from Cuzco (55 miles away) to see Manuel but instead, on 23 June, found Christ's agonized body hanging in a *tayanka* bush. Mysteriously, the body disappeared, leaving only a tree shaped like a crucifix. In the meantime Mariano died and was buried beneath the adjacent crag.

Later embellished with a painted Christ figure, this crag today forms the focal point of devotion. Pilgrims firmly identify the Señor de Qoyllor Rit'i, or *taytacha* (little father), with the most powerful mountain deity – the 20,000ft Ausankati in whose shadow the fiesta unravels. They believe that as weather creator he has the power to blight crops or bestow health and fertility.

Pilgrims travel by road to Mawallani village and then trek the five miles to Sinakara. Colourfully robed dancers dominate the scene. Through formalized choreography, village dance groups, or *comparsas*, pay homage to the *taytacha* on behalf of their home communities. Scattered among them, the *ukukus*, or bear men, sport woollen masks and whips to maintain order. Always speaking in falsetto tones, they protect the pilgrims yet are themselves disorderly.

The central day of the pilgrimage is Trinity Sunday (May/June). The dancing hardly stops all day while an image of the *taytacha* is paraded up and down the valley. Then, in the early hours, maned ranks of *ukukus* ascend the glaciers where they plant candles, retrieve a cross placed there a few days earlier, and return to the valley. Many carry blocks of ice which, when melted down, provide a supply of holy water for the following year.

JOURNEYS TO SACRED TEMPLES

Westminster Abbey, England

The Abbey's mystique is inseparable from its role as the site of the coronations of the kings and queens of England. The presence within the abbey of two supreme totems, the tomb of Edward the Confessor and the Coronation Chair, make it the heart from which the blood of royalty springs. Here the Celtic, Anglo-Saxon, and Norman roots of Britain meet.

In the 11th century, when King Edward the Confessor built his new church on the site of a small monastery, the Isle of Thorns – as the Saxons knew Westminster – already had royal associations with both King Offa and King Canute. After the Confessor's death in 1066 the Saxon Bishop Wulfstan, threatened with dispossession, struck his staff into the king's tomb. Like King Arthur's Excalibur, it could be withdrawn by none but Wulfstan himself. Other miracles followed, and in 1161 Edward was canonized. His shrine has remained the paramount place of pilgrimage in Britain, with the exception of Canterbury, although modern pilgrims can find private meditation interrupted by the programme of hourly prayers.

William of Normandy claimed to be Edward's rightful heir. Thus Edward was the link between the Norman succession and the older Anglo-Saxon tradition in which the vitality of a people depended upon the *mana* (luck) of its monarch. Edward's tomb represents a bridge between Anglo-Saxon and Norman royalty. Beside the tomb stands a far more ancient talisman, the Stone of Scone.

Seized from the Scots in 1296 by Edward I (Longshanks) and housed in the Coronation Chair, the Stone was traditionally thought to be Jacob's stony pillow from the Bible story. Later it was identified with the Irish *Lia-Fail*, the Stone of Destiny which revealed the royal line. The founder of the Scottish monarchy, Fergus Mor MacEirc, may have taken it to Argyll in the 5th century. Certainly by AD840, when Kenneth II brought it to Scone in Scotland, it was such a potent symbol of Scottish identity that over a thousand years later, in 1950, the Stone's "capture" by Scottish nationalists caused a furore throughout Britain. According to legend, wherever the Scots find the Stone they will rule – a prophecy fulfilled when James VI of Scotland was crowned James I of England. In July 1996 the British government announced that the Stone would be returned to Scotland, but would be brought back to Westminster Abbey for coronation ceremonies.

Stonehenge, England

Stonehenge is probably the best known prehistoric monument in Britain and ranks as one of the most powerful spiritual sites in Europe. Although crowds and competing interests are a perennial problem for the pilgrim, the great stones of Salisbury Plain, massive and brooding like a council of giants, have not lost their magic.

Stonehenge was not built as a single construction. A series of earth, timber, and stone works were revised and remodelled over a period of more than 2000 years, from about 3200 to 1100BC. Many of the original stones are missing or have fallen. The sarsen stones come from the Marlborough Downs 20 miles away, while the bluestones were transported over 200 miles to the site from the Preseli Mountains in southwest Wales.

This awe-inspiring monument was probably a temple, or a neolithic observatory for predicting solstices and eclipses. However, the Earth has tilted further on its axis since Stonehenge was built, and so the alignments of the stones with the sun have changed.

Salisbury Plain is dotted with tumuli and sites of neolithic encampments. Ley lines link Stonehenge with places further afield, such as Salisbury Cathedral, which may have been built on a pre-Christian site, and the Iron Age earthworks of Old Sarum.

In recent years the site has been fenced to prevent damage to the stones. Even this restriction and the large crowds of visitors cannot destroy the powerful atmosphere of this place. Those who wish to get closer to the stones can arrange with English Heritage (who manage the site) to visit outside the daily opening times.

The monument is near the A303 road, easily accessible by car or bus. A more evocative approach is on foot from Salisbury, following the route believed to have been used in transporting the bluestones from Wales. The 10-mile walk follows the river Avon northwest to the villages of Middle and Upper Woodford and then through woods to the edge of Salisbury Plain.

Chartres Cathedral, France

The world's most complete and glorious example of Gothic art and architecture soars above the town it guards from a hilltop which has been sacred for over 2000 years. In ancient times a rough stone dolmen covered a point where invigorating energy was believed to flow from the earth; beside it was a well.

The Druids later had a college here. They carved a statue of a child-bearing virgin seen in a vision and placed it beside the well. In the 3rd century Christians worshipped her as the "Black Virgin", or the "Virgin about to bring forth" and built a church dedicated to Mary around her. That church, and four after it, burnt down between 743 and 1194.

The most treasured relic, the Virgin's "sacred tunic", escaped the last devastating fire. This was taken as a sign that Our Lady wished an even finer church to be built on the site. The result, today's mighty cathedral, is an extraordinary blend of the supreme in architecture, sculpture, and stained glass.

A legend tells how, during the Crusades to the Holy Land, the Knights Templar brought back the secrets of divine Number, Weight, and Measure from Solomon's Temple and that these were used in building the cathedral. Its interior proportions and symbolism are so powerful that they are said to affect the consciousness, by provoking a realignment of the spine.

Traditionally, the pilgrim approaches on foot, and ideally, barefoot. The cathedral's energizing effects can be felt upon entering the Western door. The interior is flooded with intensely coloured light shining through the great rose window and other windows of vivid jewel-coloured stained glass, such as the "Notre-Dame de la Belle Verrière", a masterpiece of early Gothic art.

An oddly angled flagstone by the entrance has a "solar nail" which catches the sun's rays at noon on Midsummer Day.

Eleven circles in blue and white stones around a six-petalled rose (see pattern, left) form "The Path to Jerusalem", a labyrinth at the center of the nave. This represents the pilgrim's path to salvation. Esoterically, it is believed, when trodden correctly, to indicate the point where the Druids' thought-converging currents of cosmic power were focussed.

Chartres lies beside the river Eure, 25 miles southwest of Paris. To see the stained glass at its best, visit in the bright light of spring or summer. Ideally choose a festival of the Virgin – either 25 March (the Annunciation) or 15 August (the Assumption). A more cosmic moment would be to coincide with Midsummer Day.

Aachen, Germany

Long before the Emperor Charlemagne built his imperial palace at Aachen, the site was sacred to the Celts because of the hot springs that rise here. The Celts dedicated the waters to their god of healing, Granus. Later the Romans built bath complexes and shrines, and called the place Aquis Grani.

Charlemagne chose the site for his palace because of the springs. He enjoyed bathing in the hot waters but the spiritual significance of the area was not lost on him either. His aim was to Christianize the pagan holy places and accordingly he built his eight-sided royal chapel, spiritual heart of his palace, directly over the Roman baths.

Charlemagne, the first Holy Roman Emperor after the title was revived, was crowned in Rome as protector of the Christian faith. All his successors were crowned in Aachen's octagon chapel. In the 14th century a choir was added to the chapel to create Aachen Cathedral, all that now remains of the imperial palace.

The cathedral houses many holy relics collected by Charlemagne throughout his life, such as the swaddling clothes of the infant Jesus and the loincloth Christ wore on the cross. Charlemagne's remains were enshrined here on his death in 814, and 400 years later were moved to a golden shrine in the east end of the cathedral. His marble throne in the gallery looks down on the altar below. Through-out the Middle Ages the throne, shrine, and holy relics made Aachen one of the key centers of European pilgrimage. Nowadays visitors who wish to see the throne must join a guided tour of the cathedral.

Aachen is in western Germany, close to the Dutch and Belgian borders. The city is also known as Aix-la-Chapelle because of the eight-sided chapel, still the spiritual heart of the city.

Nidarosdomen, Norway

Nidaros Cathedral (Nidarosdomen in Norwegian) stands on the banks of the River Nidelven in Trondheim, the former capital city of Norway and meeting place of the early Norse parliament. For almost a thousand years pilgrims have paid homage here to Olav Haraldsson, Norway's legendary Christian king and saint.

Olav was killed in battle in 1030 at Stikelsad by King Canute's armies, and his body was buried near the river. From his grave springs of water began to flow, reputedly with healing properties, and there were reports of miracles. One year after his death, Olav's body was disinterred and was found to be undecayed, an indication of his sanctity. His body was then removed to the town's only church.

Norway declared Olav a saint and martyr, and in 1070 his nephew Olav Kyrre started building a vast stone church on the site of his first burial place. The oldest parts of this church to survive date from the 12th century and form part of Nidarosdomen, which was granted cathedral status in 1152. In the Middle Ages countless pilgrims made the journey on foot to Trondheim, from Sweden in the north and from Oslo in the South. A chain of pilgrim hostels marked the southern route to the shrine.

The Reformation in 16th-century Europe destroyed the tradition of public pilgrimage, along with other Roman Catholic forms of worship. However, Nidarosdomen is still the traditional burial place of the Norwegian monarchs, and

Trondheim's finest building. Visitors may admire its Gothic architecture, the magnificent rose window, and the Norwegian Crown Jewels. Modern Norway's first king and queen were crowned here in 1906 and the current king and queen, Harald and Sonja, were formally blessed here in 1992.

The best time to visit is in the late afternoon, when the tour groups have departed. Trondheim is warmest in summer, though the winters are not strikingly severe. On 29 July, the official anniversary of St Olav's death in 1030, carloads of modern pilgrims return to the ancient battlefield of Stikelsad, near Trondheim, to see a re-enactment of Olav's last battle in his fight for the evangelization of Norway.

St Peter's Basilica, Italy

The basilica of St Peter's is the principal shrine of the Catholic Church and the curving colonnades around St Peter's Square symbolize the protecting arms of the Catholic Church, inviting all who come here into its embrace.

Since the Middle Ages, Rome has been a center of pilgrimage, largely because of the tombs of the many martyrs who were put to death here by the Romans. The obelisk believed to have marked the spot where St Peter was executed in Nero's Circus was moved in 1586 to St Peter's Square. In the 4th century the Emperor Constantine erected a basilica with the saint's grave, encased in a huge cube of marble, as its focal point. The present basilica, a 16th-century building on a far grander scale than the original church, contains works

by many prominent artists from the Italian Renaissance.

A 13th-century bronze statue of St Peter has one silver foot, polished by the kisses of pilgrims over generations. At the base of the main altar, which is built over the saint's tomb, oil lamps burn continuously by an open crypt where pilgrims pray.

The Pope holds public audiences every Wednesday in a hall off St Peter's Square. Admission is by ticket only, available in advance from the Prefettura della Casa Pontificia, also in the Square. On Sundays at noon the Pope says the Angelus and blesses the crowd from the balcony of the Vatican Offices overlooking the square.

The basilica is open daily and attracts large crowds, especially for the major Christian festivals. Rome in midsummer is hot and oppressive, so the best time to visit is in spring or autumn. Visitors should dress modestly, with their upper arms covered. Those in unsuitable clothing, such as shorts and miniskirts, are refused entry.

Hagia Sophia, Turkey

The glory of Christendom rose up in Constantinople, the city which Constantine made the center of the Eastern Roman Empire. The Emperor Justinian employed two of the last mathematicians of the Athenian Academy to design a church combining the rectangular basilica of Roman civic centres with the soaring spirituality of the great dome. They succeeded so well that the people thought the dome must be suspended from heaven by a golden chain. And Justinian, on entering his basilica for the first time in AD548, declared: "Oh, Solomon! I have surpassed you!"

Hagia Sophia became a focus of pilgrimage for Christians from Asia and Russia, and was famous for its golden mosaics depicting the life of the Holy Family. Many of its treasures and relics were looted during the Crusades. When the Turks took Constantinople in 1453, Hagia Sophia was converted to a mosque and the interior white-washed. Thus it remained until 1933, when Kemal Ataturk turned it into a museum and began to restore the mosaics. The museum is open daily, except Mondays.

Pilgrims can fly to Istanbul but there is a more interesting route. Those with time on their hands can take a train (perhaps even the historic Orient Express) from Paris to Venice, and thence travel by boat via Piraeus through the Dardanelles to Istanbul. This gives a first view of the city of domes and minarets over the Sea of Marmora.

Turkey is popular with tourists and holiday-makers, and it is best to avoid the summer months which are crowded and hot. April to mid-June, or September/October are preferable. Clothing needs to be lightweight but modest, since Turkey is a mainly Muslim country.

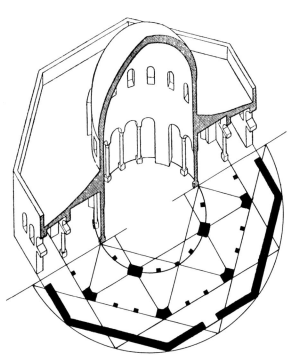

The Dome of the Rock
The design of this 7th-century mosque is based on intricate mathematical detail. The gold-plated aluminium dome rises majestically from the octagonal lower storey.

The Dome of the Rock, Jerusalem

The magnificent golden dome of Jerusalem's most celebrated Muslim shrine dominates the entire old city in order to announce both the might and beauty of Islam and the miracle and sanctity of a cave. At the heart of the dome, protected by a fine wooden screen, stands the great Holy Rock, which is also sacred to Jews and Christians. Muslims believe that the dome stands at the center of the world, for it is said that the waters of Paradise flow beneath the cave.

Stairs lead the pilgrim down below the rock into a large cave which, according to legend, is where Abraham offered his son Isaac in sacrifice to God. There, too, Muslims believe, the Prophet Mohammed began his miraculous night journey to heaven on his legendary steed, Buraq. Near the entrance to the cave a shrine contains relics of the Prophet, including a hair from his head.

The Qubbat al-Sakhra, as the dome is known, was built by the fifth Umayyad Caliph, 'Abd-al-Malik, and was completed in AD691–2. It stands on the masonry platform that was the original foundation for Herod's temple, which in turn was built on the site of the Temple of Solomon. Thus the Muslim shrine looms over the platform's Western Wall, now the focal point for Jewish pilgrimage.

Islam's third holiest place after the Ka'ba in Mecca and the Prophet's mosque in Medina, the dome is second in importance only to Mecca as a place of pilgrimage. Tourists and pilgrims alike flock there throughout the year, though one of the best times to visit is in April when the crowds are not at their heaviest and the temperature is pleasantly warm. Anyone can visit the dome and its cave, as long as they are modestly dressed. The building, which is a shrine in honour of the prophet and not a mosque or a place of formal worship, is free of ceremony and ritual. It is a place of pilgrimage and personal prayer.

Haifa and Acre, Israel

Bahá'ís all over the world aim to make the sacred journey at least once in their lifetime to the World Center of their Faith, at the shrines of the Báb and Bahá'u'lláh in the cities of Haifa and Acre in Israel.

Bahá'u'lláh (1817–92), founder of the Bahá'í Faith, endured forty years of imprisonment and exile for teaching the unity of humankind and the oneness of religions. To several million Bahá'ís worldwide, his resting place in Acre is the holiest place on earth. The Báb (1817–50) was a Divine Messenger who was executed for heralding the mission of Bahá'u'lláh in his native Persia. The Shrine of the Báb on the slopes of Mount Carmel in Haifa is popularly known as the 'Queen of Carmel', and is one of the most distinctive sights in the Holy Land.

The shrines and their surrounding gardens are open to visitors, of which there are currently a quarter of a million annually. These are places of reflection, contemplation, and prayer. The Bahá'í Faith has no fixed devotional rituals, and as long as they do not disturb others anyone may pray or meditate here as they see fit, or simply enjoy the peace and beauty of the gardens. Visitors should dress and behave modestly, in a manner befitting a holy place.

Haifa, a busy port and Israel's third largest city, is accessible from other parts of Israel by road and rail. Regular buses make the short trip from Haifa to Acre, or you can travel inexpensively by *sherut* (taxi). The Shrine of the Báb, which is clearly visible on approaching Haifa, is open each morning. The gardens

Shrine of the Báb, Haifa
Bahá'is believe that they come into closer contact with the Creator at this shrine to His Divine Messenger, the Báb.

are open for most of the day and in the evenings the shrine is brilliantly illuminated.

The Shrine of Bahá'u'lláh is open in the morning from Friday to Monday; its gardens, too, are open for most of the day. Both shrines and gardens are closed for short periods between July and September and public access is also limited on nine Bahá'í holy days. Tour guide agencies in Israel are informed of the exact dates of closure each year.

Mashad, Iran

From Tehran, pilgrims may fly to Mashad or take the train, but the adventurous will go on the "Golden Road to Samarkand", all 600 dreary miles of it, skirting the edge of the desert. Mashad is Iran's paramount holy city, visited by more than 14 million pilgrims each year. It contains probably the greatest concentration of religious buildings anywhere in the world – a shrine, several sanctuaries, two mosques, five theological schools, libraries, and a museum.

The city grew up on the site of the village of Sanabad, where, in AD817, the Eighth Imam, Ali Reza, died after eating grapes. Reza's father had prophesied his murder, and most Shi'ites believe that he was poisoned by his father-in-law, Caliph Ma'mun. Nevertheless, Ma'mun built a mausoleum over Reza's grave, close to that of his own father, the famous Harun al-Rashid. Sanabad soon grew into a place of pilgrimage, under a new name, "Mashad", meaning "place of the martyr". A pilgrimage to Imam Reza's tomb was said to equal

70,000 visits to Mecca and pilgrims now come to Mashad from all parts of the Muslim world.

Mongols sacked the holy city in AD1230 and most of the oldest part dates from the 14th century. The jewel in Mashad's crown was the gift of a remarkable woman, Gohar Shad, the wife of Shah Rokh. Between 1405 and 1418, she and her architect Qavam od-din of Shiraz created the mosque which now bears her name and which some art historians call the most beautiful building in Islam.

A golden dome covers Imam Reza's shrine and his sarcophagus is protected by a silver grille. Entry into the shrine is not permitted for non-Muslims. Attached to the sacred precinct, through a garden at the side of the Gowhar Shad Mosque, is the Qods-e Razari Museum, where visitors can see many of the treasures that have been given to the shrine.

Throughout Iran, women must observe the Islamic dress code. This means a scarf to cover the head and neck, long sleeves, long skirts or trousers, and a dark calf-length coat. Feet should also be covered, and jewellery and make-up kept to a minimum.

Non-Muslims are granted only limited access to the sacred area at Mashad. It is best to avoid major pilgrimages and festivals – 10th and 11th Moharram, 20th and 28th Safar, and Ramadan in particular. Bear in mind that the climate is changeable and harsh, and in winter it is bitterly cold.

All travellers to Iran require a visa, and for most nationalities only a 5-day transit visa is available. The easiest way to visit Mashad is on an organized group tour.

Amritsar, India

"I would bathe at the place of pilgrimage, if that would please God, but without his blessing, nothing is obtained," said Guru Nanak (1469–1539), the founder of Sikhism. One of his followers later observed that "if bathing at pilgrimages does any good, frogs are assured salvation!"

The Guru's teaching emphasized the importance of interior religion and was opposed to mindless ritual. The only pilgrimage which matters is inside your own heart. As the "one beyond time" is everywhere, all of space is equally sacred. Sikhs believe that the teaching spirit which passed through the Gurus is now lodged in the Guru Granth Sahib, the Sikh holy book. A copy of this is kept in every Sikh Gurdwara (temple).

The most famous Sikh Gurdwara is the Harmandir Sahib or God's Temple, known in the west as the Golden Temple, at Amritsar. This city in the Punjab, northern India, was founded in 1577. The main feature of the original site was the pool constructed by the fourth Guru, where Sikhs still bathe. Many stories recount how pilgrims have been healed there. The original Gurdwara was constructed by the fifth Guru, but several temples were demolished and rebuilt on the site. The present building, which dates from the 18th and 19th centuries, was mainly built under the direction of Maharaja Ranjit Singh, who ruled Punjab from 1799 to 1839. A long bridge leads across the sacred pool to the temple, with its inlaid marble walls and golden dome.

Festivals associated with Amritsar are Baisakhi in mid-April, and Diwali, which is in October/November.

Baisakhi was originally a spring fair, a traditional meeting time, but it is also the anniversary of a massacre which occurred in 1919, when soldiers fired on civilians in a garden called Jallianwala Bagh. During Diwali, the festival of light which Sikhs associate with the release from prison of the sixth Guru, the Golden Temple is illuminated.

The best time to go to Amritsar is between October and March, when the weather is coolest. The nights can be cold, so warm clothes are advisable. Wear a scarf or other suitable head-covering, and remove shoes and socks before entering a Gurdwara.

Wangdi Phodrang, Bhutan

Bhutan is a secretive kingdom in the eastern Himalaya, without television and largely roadless. Nonetheless the indigenous form of Tantric Buddhism permeates every remote valley, every isolated homestead. Monasteries and roaming monks relay the message throughout this mountainous country and, once a year, rural people converge on their district dzong – an imposing cross between a fortress and a monastery – to attend the Tshechu festival. One such dzong stands on a cacti-covered spur above the Puna Tsang River in the town of Wangdi Phodrang, a two-hour drive east from the capital, Thimpu.

Tshechus are dedicated to Guru Rinpoche, who converted Bhutan to Buddhism in the 8th century, and take place on the 10th day of the month. The precise definition of the 10th day is determined by the abbot

of the dzong, and sometimes the festival begins a day or two later than originally scheduled. It lasts between three and five days.

By law, the Bhutanese must always wear traditional dress in public. On the October day of the Wangdi Phodrang Tshechu, the men add to their gho (a garment resembling a rugged dressing-gown) a decorative sash denoting in colour their social status – sashes range from white for a commoner to saffron for the king. Women wear a kira (dress) and their best brooches.

Approaching the dzong, a journey which can take several days on foot for those from the farthest-flung reaches of the district, pilgrims pass numerous water-driven prayer wheels, and prayer flags. After the hardship of the trek, the Tshechu is a joyous and often raucous occasion, a mixture of the social and the spiritual. The focal points of the festivities in the courtyard of the dzong are the dances, performed by monks and laymen in elaborate masks and costumes. These dances often last over an hour each and involve athletic leaping and spinning. Between the dances clowns provide entertainment. On the final day, with the unveiling of a thangka, a giant embroidered banner depicting Guru Rinpoche, solemnity returns to the proceedings as the pilgrims are reconfirmed in their religion.

Bhutan restricts tourism to 2500 visitors each year. The government publishes a list of festival dates each year and some organized tours are timed to coincide with the Tshechus in the major dzongs, such as Paro, Thimpu, and Wangdi Phodrang. For the Bhutanese, the Tshechu is an annual event. For an outsider, it is the experience of a lifetime.

Shwe Dagon, Myanmar

From an aircraft descending out of dark monsoon rain clouds toward the brown parched paddy fields surrounding Rangoon, the Shwe Dagon glistens golden in the sunlight. This most venerated pagoda is a wonder of Asia, if not the world, and one of the largest of its type.

Revered as a pilgrimage center by Burmese Buddhists, it resonates with their joyous devotion. It was built 2500 years ago to enshrine the eight sacred hair-relics given personally by the Buddha to two Burmese devotees. The relics' enshrinement is celebrated at the full-moon harvest festival of Htaname in February. The Shwe Dagon has been enlarged over the centuries to a height of 330ft, its apex adorned with 5000 diamonds and semi-precious stones.

Easily reached by taxi from the center of Rangoon, the Shwe Dagon is best entered from the southern entrance, where you climb up steps past friendly traders' stalls. Their wares are not tourist trinkets; fragrant lotus blossoms, incense, candles, bells, and multi-coloured flower garlands are essential ritual offerings for pilgrims.

Intricate carvings, mosaics, and symbolic statues adorn more than 82 shrines around the many levels encompassing the immense central stupa, the shrine built to house the relics of the Buddha. Some shrines shelter vast reclining Buddhas, while others contain small "spirit" or "Nat" houses, where you can offer incense, food, flowers, and prayers as personal tributes. You might enter the Prayer Pavilion with the

28 incarnations of Buddha, sit still on the floor, and hear a Buddhist monk talk in English of health through meditation, clearing the mind, and of finding paths to peace and happiness.

Pilgrims should show respect with their manner and dress modestly, removing shoes and socks before entering the pavilion. The Burmese visit in their hundreds in everyday clothes – both men and women wear colourfully woven sarongs. Children play as their elders sit in prayer and meditation; young couples kneel close to each other, press their foreheads to the marble floor, then rise to give thanks and offer praise to Buddha.

Those who wish to ignore the political realities of Myanmar in the mid-1990s, and the requests of the elected leader to boycott the country, should first contact their respective embassies. Tourists are advised not to stray beyond the limits of the officially designated areas for visitors.

Angkor Wat, Cambodia

"Suddenly, and as if by enchantment, [the traveller] seems to be transported from barbarism to civilisation, from profound darkness to light ..."

So wrote Henri Mouhot (1860), a French naturalist who stumbled across the magnificent ruins of Angkor Wat – the largest and one of the most spectacular religious monuments in the world. Angkor itself was once the capital of a powerful Khmer kingdom, whose 12th-century ruler, the god-king

Suryavarman, personified the Hindu god Vishnu to whom the temple was dedicated.

Created as Suryavarman's tomb, Angkor forms an architectural allegory that depicts in stone the epic tales of Hindu mythology. As a result, Angkor Wat is a colossal, terraced structure covering almost one square mile and crowned by five towers, each in the shape of a huge lotus bud.

Early pilgrims paid homage to the god-king. In later centuries, with Buddhism the predominant form of worship, pilgrims revered the 1000 statues of the Buddha.

The progression from darkness to light which Mouhot expressed is an image of particular resonance to Angkor Wat. Created in the midst of jungle, it became the spiritual and cultural heart of the kingdom until the Thai invasion of 1431. Eventually abandoned, it then became overgrown and lay undisturbed for 400 years.

This period of darkness, more recently compounded by war and devastation, appears to be ending and Angkor's designation as a World Heritage Site should ensure that it once more becomes a place of inspiration. Since the 1991 ceasefire, visitors – up to 1000 a day – have returned to Angkor.

Travellers approach the western gate of Angkor Wat along a causeway lined with carvings of sacred snakes, representing the bridge between heaven and earth. They then cross the broad moat. Inside, behind a platform guarded by stone lions, the outer gallery contains the 1000 statues of the Buddha.

The best time to travel to the temple complex is between November and January when the

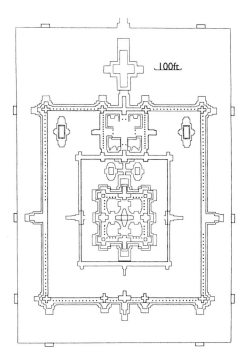

Plan of Angkor Wat
The Cruciform Platform leads into the Gallery of a 1000 Buddhas, with two libraries at either side. The main Sanctuary is at the heart of the complex.

monsoon is over and before the hottest weather arrives. However hot and humid it is, visitors to the temple should dress modestly.

The security situation in Cambodia is difficult and travel is carefully controlled. Public transport is not recommended. Some travel agents can book internal flights in Cambodia. You will also need to purchase a visa on arrival in the country, for which you will need several passport photographs. Pilgrims are advised to hire a car and driver in Phnom Penh, or to fly into Siem Reap, the nearest town, and take a minibus or car tour. You should allow three days to explore Angkor fully.

Wong Tai Sin Temple, Hong Kong

He lived among the mists on a mountain in China, seeking eternal life. Now, immortal, he floats above this magnificent Taoist temple built for him 1500 years later in Hong Kong, listening to the endless petitions of worshippers. He is Great Immortal Wong: "Wong Tai Sin". During the 20th century his temples in China were destroyed. He found refuge in Hong Kong: his image was brought to the city by two believers in 1915. Now his believers are innumerable, and have spread from Hong Kong around the world. Many Hong Kong people living overseas return to his temple to worship and seek his help.

Wong Tai Sin's original speciality in China was healing. A clinic next to the Hong Kong temple offers free Chinese herbal medicines. (Prescriptions from the god can be obtained by divination.) But most worshippers now consult him for advice about careers, marriage, business, or emigration. Once, he spoke to worshippers through spirit-writing: a Taoist in a trance wrote his words on a table. Now, most devotees receive his messages by shaking a bamboo cup containing 100 numbered sticks. When one falls out, the number on the stick tells the worshipper which of 100 fortune-poems contains the god's answer. Fortune-tellers in booths next to the temple interpret these poems for those who do not understand the god's message. His advice and predictions are so much sought that this temple contains the largest concentration of fortune-tellers in Asia.

To visit the temple, take the MTR (subway) to the Wong Tai Sin Station. The temple is open daily from 7am to 5pm, but is most busy on Sundays. There are large crowds at the Chinese New Year (January or February), for Wong Tai Sin's birthday on the 23rd day of the 8th lunar month, and throughout the 7th lunar month.

Once a tranquil religious retreat set among empty fields, this shrine is now surrounded by the metropolis. But the city fades as the visitor walks among offerings of food, clouds of incense, and throngs of worshippers seeking help, advice, or peace of mind. Donations at the gate, and inside the complex, go to hospitals, schools, and homes for the elderly.

Borobudur, Java

One of the finest monuments in the Southern hemisphere, Borobudur in Java was constructed around AD800, during the reigns of the kings of the Cailendra dynasty. It is believed to have taken 10,000 men 100 years to build, depleting the population of central Java and exhausting five generations.

For around 150 years this Mahayana–Buddhist monument was the spiritual center of Buddhism in Java. But with the fall of the king-dom of Mataram in about AD919 it was neglected and suffered wide-spread decay. Interest in it was revived at the beginning of the 18th century, since when the slow process of restoration has been taking place.

Borobudur sits on top of a hill and is built in the form of a step-pyramid, comprising six rectangular storeys, three circular terraces, and a central *stupa*, or dome, which forms the summit. Together, these different elements resemble a single *stupa*, representing the highest symbol of Buddhism, and also replicating the universe.

To visit Borobudur, and to climb it, is truly to experience something magical, but it is important to plan carefully to benefit from this. Go very early in the morning to avoid the heat of the day and the large crowds, and avoid public holidays. Carry drinking water and protect yourself from the sun. Allow at least two hours to climb the stepped monument. There are ten terraces from the base to the main *stupa* at the top, each signifying the stages toward perfection in life.

The walk takes you round the temple nine times, past the many pictorial and ornamental relief panels which tell stories from the Buddha's life and take in the entire Buddhist cosmos. In this way the lower terraces are richly adorned for the senses, while the top ter-races are for the soul. The higher you climb, the more heavenly the themes become. The terraces near the top represent the stage in the striving for enlightenment where desire is eliminated, though the devotee is still tied to the realm of the senses. Perfection is finally reached at the top, where all suffering ends.

Plan of Borobudur

Six rectangular galleries are surmounted by three circular terraces of small *stupas*, rising to the central *stupa*, making this the largest Buddhist monumnet in the world.

Journeys to Sacred Shrines

Walsingham, England

England's "Nazareth" is an Anglican, Catholic, and Christian Orthodox pilgrimage site around the village of Walsingham, inland from Wells on the north Norfolk coast. According to legend, Lady Richeldis, widow of the lord of the manor, had three visions in 1061. The Holy Mother took her in spirit to the house in Nazareth where the Angel Gabriel had appeared to the Virgin Mary at the Annunciation. Richeldis was told to note the dimensions of the Holy House and to build a replica in Walsingham. As she engaged builders, a heavy fall of dew one night left dry two similarly-sized spaces in a meadow. From this "sign" she chose for the house the dry site closest to twin wells.

An Augustinian Priory was built in 1169 to guard the shrine, with a separate Lady Chapel enclosing the Holy House. England's Reformation destroyed the shrine and the priory in 1538, though the wells were still used as wishing wells, where people drank, then wished.

Walsingham's status as a place of pilgrimage was revived by Catholics in 1897. Today, there are separate shrines for Catholics, Anglicans and Orthodox Christians.

Of these, the Anglican shrine now exists as a small windowless room lit by candles inside a larger church. Known as a center for the Holy Family, the site holds the Church of England's largest collection of relics including several fragments of the True Cross. Twin staircases lead from the shrine to the well below.

In the surrounding gardens, the fourteen Stations of the Cross serve as a symbolic journey of contemplation for pilgrims. In an unbroken tradition, each evening at 6pm pilgrims may join a gathering for Shrine Prayers. The Rosary is said, and those in need can request the Virgin's intercession. Every afternoon a Sprinkling ceremony offers a blessing, and gives an opportunity to touch and drink the holy water of Walsingham.

Throughout the year the shrine hosts a number of important events. One of the most widely known of these is the Anglican National Pilgrimage, held on the last weekend in May. This celebration ends with a procession encircling the village. Other special days in the shrine's calendar are devoted to youth and the sick, and a day in May sees MPs asking blessings on their responsibilities in government.

Knock, Eire

In 1878 the little church in the remote and windswept village of Knock in the west of Eire was battered by gales in a great storm. The slate roof and windows were damaged and some statues were smashed. The following year, on the wet evening of 21 August, a group of women saw figures standing outside the church and assumed they were new statues. Returning later, they noticed that the figures were moving, and ran to fetch family and friends to witness this miracle. These fourteen people claimed to have seen the Virgin Mary, dressed in white wearing a golden crown, accompanied by St Joseph and St John.

Word of the apparition spread, and soon pilgrims began to arrive on foot from all over Ireland. The sick and disabled came or were brought to the shrine and many claimed miraculous healings. At first the Church discouraged such stories and stood aloof, leaving the pilgrims to create their own rituals. They reverted to traditional Gaelic forms of worship, making circuits of the church grounds and chanting the Rosary and the Liturgy out loud.

Knock draws thousands of pilgrims annually, many making their journey in organized church groups. The majority fly to the airport ten miles away and arrive at the shrine by coach. Knock boasts a basilica which can accommodate 12,000 people, and a folk museum which houses craft tools and costumes from the time of the apparition, as well as detailing the miraculous apparition and cures attributed to attendance at the shrine.

One recent visitor observed that what most impressed her was the prayerful attitude of the people. Young families were circling the grounds together, praying aloud as they followed the rituals developed by the early pilgrims. She remarked that even the youngest children seemed totally engrossed in what they were doing. "The place", she said, "is stark rather than beautiful but has the authentic feeling of spiritual power."

Noyal-Pontivy, France

A traditional Breton prayer runs: "Ste Noyale preserve us, especially from sin; so that not one person from Noyal will be missing, O our Patroness, from Paradise". Legend tells how, in the 6th century, an Irishwoman sailed to Brittany on a leaf, and settled as a hermit at Ste-Noyale, a scatter of farms and a church just north of Noyal-Pontivy. Pestered by a local tyrant, she fled south for some 18 miles to Bezo, where her pursuer found her and beheaded her. Undismayed, the saint picked up her head, and walked home to Ste-Noyale, where she was buried.

Noyal-Pontivy, which lies east of Pontivy in the Morbihan, enshrines the memory of its patron saint Noyale. The ancient parish observes two Pardons (processions to a sacred location associated with the saint, and a conventional patronal festival) in her honour. On the Sunday nearest 24 June, the only day when the church is open (it is otherwise closed to protect its frescoes of the saint's life), cars and tractors file slowly past the church in procession after High Mass.

The major Pardon takes place two Sundays later. After morning Masses in the large medieval parish church in Noyal-Pontivy, where Noyale's legend is told in the choir windows, the villagers bear an image of the saint carrying her head and trace one section of her last strange journey. They process from the church through the fields to Les Trois Fontaines, a mysterious site in a wooded valley where three springs rise in a large sunken court-yard. A small Calvary stands in the trees above the fountains. Close by are two other stones, the saint's "bed" and "prie-dieu", which bears Noyale's knee-prints. Water from the three wells flows into a large shallow pool near the shrine, and is so pure that local women still come here to rinse their linen. By a stream some 150 feet away is a large stone, Ste Noyale's "Chair".

Ste Noyale's shrine
Three sacred springs rise in this courtyard, set in a wooded valley midway between the towns of Noyal–Pontivy and Ste-Noyale.

According to legend, this was the saint's last stop before she reached the village of Ste-Noyale. Here, while the saint rested on her chair, three drops of blood fell from her severed head, causing three springs to well up. It is said that the three drops are still to be seen in the depths of the well-basins – but only by the pure in heart.

On the afternoon of the Pardon, parishioners become pilgrims, bathe their faces and hands in the wells, drink the sacred water, and bottle it to carry home. After Vespers at 3pm, the procession returns to the town to light the "feu-de-joie", or ceremonial bonfire, stuffed with fireworks, and dance around it.

Rocamadour, France

The mountains curve spectacularly; a medieval French castle and churches cling perilously to a cliff above the Alzou River. Nearby, a cave harbours 20,000-year-old paintings. A Black Virgin, just over two feet high, nearly nine centuries old, is carried through the village in procession. Pilgrims on their knees mount the stone stairs cut into the cliff. A blind beggar asks "Has *she* passed yet?" Intense human and divine energy merge in religious climax at Rocamadour.

Rocamadour is located near Souillac, east of Bordeaux, in the Dordogne. The name comes from the Langue d'Oc expression *roc amator*, "He who likes the rock", and from St Amadour, who in folk tradition was the servant of the Mother of God. According to legend his body was found buried, perfectly preserved beneath the threshold of the Chapel of the Virgin, and was later burned and hacked to pieces. Cathars, a sect which denounced the church's material wealth, were brought here from Provence to renounce their "heresy" in front of the statue.

Only 800 people now live in Rocamadour, but on 8 September, Our Lady's birthday, thousands surge into the narrow street, barely leaving space for the Black Virgin to pass. A wash of candles glows, each person lighting the next as Notre Dame comes closer. Prayers and murmurs hush. She passes. An ever-lengthening column of pilgrims follows the statue. The 223 stairs are unbelievably rugged and steep. Pilgrims mount skyward, some on their knees, some old, crippled, and hurting. They crowd into the basilica and the Virgin's Chapel, having completed the Pilgrim's Way, the passage to forgiveness.

The annual pilgrimage takes place in the week of 8 September. The town is particularly busy in July and August, the French holiday season.

Taizé, France

"Ah, Taizé, that little springtime!" These affectionate words spoken by Pope John XXIII in 1960 express the hope and the lightness of being emanating from the simplicity of the Taizé experience, which since 1957 has attracted increasing numbers of young people from around the world. They come to discover, or to be nourished by, the sources of the Christian faith.

Situated on a hill amidst the colourful fields and slopes of the Bourgogne countryside in France, the Taizé community is the home of 90 monks. Living rooted in prayer, contemplation, and an alertness to news arriving from every continent, their daily aspiration is to enable the young to become creators of trust and reconciliation.

All year the pilgrimage of young people continues, numbering up to 8000 visitors at Easter and in summer, the community's busiest times. Visitors share in a daily routine of prayers and multi-national meetings with the community's monks. Accommodation is allocated each Sunday afternoon. Families stay at Olinda, a 15-minute walk away, and the over 30s are set slightly apart from the central site. It is advisable to bring a tent, a sleeping bag, warm clothing, and to register in advance, particularly for family accommodation.

On arrival you are confronted with what appears to be a sprawling campsite. The slightly disconcerting impression is of coaches arriving or departing, fields full of tents, and a few inauspicious buildings. There are few visible signs that this is a place of religious significance. Ubiquitous rucksacks and a calm sense of youthful anticipation dominate the scene.

To visit Taizé is to experience communion; sharing space, time, thoughts, and routine tasks with others in small groups. Three times a day everyone files quietly into the Church of Reconciliation. The silence is astonishing as the crowd sits, enveloped by the soft amber glow of candlelight, waiting. Then the singing begins – the hallmark of Taizé. Simple chanted psalms, sung over and over again, immersing all in a powerful tide of worship. The songs of Taizé are known throughout the world. They are a special gift from Taizé – an aid to prayer, which continues to reconcile, to heal, and nourish the inner journey.

Lourdes, France

Lourdes, Mary, and pilgrimage – the connection is axiomatic, even for those for whom Mary is no more than a name or a distant memory. Lourdes 150 years ago was little more than a backward village – not even worth connecting with the French national railway – in the foothills of the Pyrénées. Then, in February 1858, Lourdes was wrenched from obscurity to ceaseless celebrity by the startling appearance of Mary, Mother of God to an illiterate asthmatic child called Bernadette Soubirous.

Guadalupe, Spain

The small town of Guadalupe, on the slopes of the Guadalupe Mountains in western Spain, has long been the heart of Christian worship in Extremadura and the goal of countless pilgrims from all over the Spanish-speaking world. Both the Caribbean island of Guadeloupe and the Mexican shrine Guadalupe owe their names to this Extremaduran town whose fame far exceeds its size.

Guadalupe's reputation rests on a relic – the Virgin of Guadalupe – the patron saint of the region. This small black statue, which now stands in the town's cathedral, was reputedly carved by St Luke. Pope Gregory the Great presented it to Bishop Leander of Sevilla in 580. When the Moors invaded southern Spain in 711, the Christians fled north, taking the statue with them. They buried it in a cave near the Guadalupe River, where, in the ensuing centuries of strife, it lay forgotten until the 14th century, when the Virgin Mary appeared to a cowherd and ordered him to assemble the townsfolk and clergy and dig until they found her statue.

The statue was unearthed and the King of Spain ordered a chapel to be built on the spot, which soon became a shrine. Reports of cures and healings followed and wealthy aristocrats donated clothing and a jewelled head-dress to the statue. Ferdinand and Isabella, the first monarchs of modern Spain, met Christopher Columbus here in 1490, prior to his first voyage. Columbus' arrival in the Americas is still celebrated here, with all the Spanish-American flags flying from the monastery on 12 October.

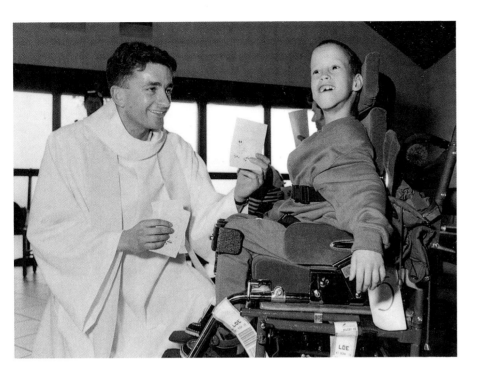

True to her uniquely individual "style", the Virgin Mary chose to make her appearance to Bernadette in the Massabielle grotto on the banks of the River Gave, which was then little more than the municipal rubbish tip. With breathtaking audacity in bourgeois France, and thus proclaiming that nothing was beneath her compassion, the Queen of Heaven stood in the dump and proclaimed herself as the Immaculate Conception.

Radiant among the rubbish, and already performing miracles of healing as she went, Mary indicated a hitherto unsuspected perennial spring of water to the bewildered but trusting child. This spring has ever since flowed to the "healing of the nations". Mary also requested processions and pilgrims to seek her in that unlikely spot.

At Lourdes, Mary's victory – and thus the victory of compassion and the human spirit – is confirmed.

The healing of the nations
Pilgrims from all over the world make the pilgrimage to Lourdes.

Bernadette became a nun, and her enclosed life made of her a great saint, though she never returned to the grotto. But in her place, from all over the world, millions have gone, and still more go, to bathe in the waters, and visit the sacred places on the banks of the Gave.

The nightly candlelit procession around the shrine's domain is an unforgettable experience. But even more impressive is the midnight flicker of candles in the darkness at the grotto, which has been open for prayer continuously since 1858.

Over 6 million pilgrims visit Lourdes each year, mainly between Easter and mid-October. Most pilgrimages are organized by local groups, churches, or societies for the sick, but individual pilgrims are always welcome.

For over five hundred years the medieval monastery was home to Hieronomite monks, who founded a celebrated faculty of medicine and performed surgery within its walls. The monastery is now occupied by Franciscans, and modern pilgrims must join a compulsory guided tour. Although not included in the official tour, it is worth requesting to see the Gothic cloisters. As well as the rich Mudejar architecture, the monastery houses eight paintings by the artist Zurbarán, who lends his name to the Parador opposite, once a pilgrim's hospital.

Accommodation is easy to find, except during Easter Week, on the Virgin's feast day on 8 September, and 20 October. At other times Guadalupe remains an ordinary white-walled town, save for the clamouring bells of the monastery.

Fátima, Portugal

The sun spun and danced in the sky, flashing every colour of the spectrum, and then plummeted toward the earth and the terrified crowd before whirling back into the heavens. On 13 October 1917, around 70,000 people witnessed this Miracle of the Sun at Fátima, a small village in the wooded hills of central Portugal. The Virgin Mary had promised the miracle to Lucia, Francisco, and Jacinta, three peasant children to whom she had appeared each month since 13 May that year.

In the six visitations the Virgin revealed three secrets. The first was a vision of hell; the second a prophecy that unless Russia was converted, that country's errors would spread throughout the world, provoking war. This has been interpreted as a prediction of the spread of Communism and also of World War II. The third secret, which is believed to foretell the end of the world, was later written down by Lucia and given to the Pope. He has judged it too terrible to be revealed.

Two major festivals are held each year at Fátima on 12–13 May and 12–13 October. Around 100,000 pilgrims set up camp around the village. A candlelit procession leads to the vast square in front of the basilica, where Mass is celebrated at 5pm on the 12th. Singing continues throughout the night until a second Mass later in the morning of the 13th. The celebration ends at 12 noon when all the women in the crowd wave white handkerchieves.

Pilgrims dress respectfully, with covered legs and shoulders. They walk on their knees along the path to the Chapel of the Apparition at the Cova da Iria, and follow the Stations of the Cross along the white marble *via sacra*, which leads to the Loca do Cabeço. It was here that the three children saw an Angel of Peace in the year before the Miracle. The basilica contains the tombs of Francisco and Jacinta, who died in 1919 and 1920 respectively, fulfilling the Virgins's promise that they would soon go to heaven. The Portuguese say that "Fátima has nothing to satisfy mere curiosity. What matters here is the heart."

Hostyn, Czech Republic

From Tesák the path winds through a forest, past the Machova Studánka Well with its carved Madonna, to emerge on Mount Hostyn, the most popular pilgrimage place in Moravia. A vast baroque cathedral, a healing spring, and a host of pilgrim hostels now stand on the hill where the Virgin Mary is said to have sent a terrible storm, to save the near-defeated Moravians from the siege of the Tatars in 1241.

Her portrait depicts her as Protectrix of Moravia, shielding the Christians with her cloak, while from the safety of her arms the infant Jesus hurls lightning at the tents of the Mongols. Whatever the reasons for the sudden retreat of the Tatars from Moravia in the 13th century, Hostyn has long since attracted pilgrims to worship the Virgin on its wooded slopes.

In earlier times, around 2000BC, Mount Hostyn was the fortress of the Lusatian people, and later it lay close to the ancient amber route from the Mediterranean to the Baltic Sea. The Slavic saints, Cyril and Methodius, brought Christianity to Moravia, and according to legend persuaded the people to part with their dedication to their pagan god Radost in return for a painting of the Blessed Mother Mary.

Over the centuries Moravians have kept faith in Mary as both their mother and protector, despite disapproval from the authorities, Nazi occupation, and the expulsion of the Jesuits from their monastery on Mount Hostyn. The settlement on the hill has grown and now, as well as the cathedral, encompasses the monastery, a healing spring and a "water chapel", the Stations of the Cross created by the famous Slovak architect Jurkovic, a small cemetery, and a lookout tower offering panoramic views over the surrounding countryside.

Pilgrims to Hostyn in the spring and summer can walk on the trails through the woods and along the Hostyn ridgeway from Tesák and Rusava. In winter it is wiser to approach by road, leaving the car at the town of Bystrice pod Hostynem. Pilgrims' hostels on the hill provide accommodation. On the Saturday nearest 15 August, the feast of Mary's Assumption draws pilgrims from all over Moravia.

Czestochowa, Poland

The industrial town of Czestochowa in southwest Poland attracts over 100,000 pilgrims a year. They come to worship at the shrine of the icon of the Black Madonna ("Matka Bozka Czestochowska"), Our Lady of Czestochowa. The most famous of the Madonnas in Poland, the icon's exact origin is unknown, but it probably dates from the 5th century, and originates from the Middle East. In 1655 the icon hung outside the town hall, and the citizens believed it helped them withstand a prolonged siege by invading Swedes. The icon became the focus of a successful campaign to drive out the invaders.

Pilgrimages to Czestochowa began shortly afterward. The biggest and oldest pilgrimage starts in Warsaw at dawn on 6 August, arriving at Czestochowa 180 miles and 9 days later, on the eve of the Assumption, the most important feast of Mary in the liturgical year. This pilgrimage has taken place without fail for over 200 years, surviving partition, Nazi atrocities, and decades of official disapproval.

Pilgrims register in the crypt of Pauline Church in Warsaw, where they are divided into 15 groups of about 1000 people who walk as one straggly column. Academics walk side by side with coal miners, teachers with peasant farmers, infants are carried by mothers, elderly women hobble along in torn plimsolls. Most are Polish and active Catholics. They sing and recite the rosary, the rhythm of their prayers keeping pace with their walking. At night, pilgrims sleep in groups of up to 100 on straw in barns. Along the route local people wait, offering gifts of cake, bread, water, fruit, and flowers. Each town and village on the route is adorned with flowers and decorations.

The journey ends in anticlimax at the fortified medieval monastery on a "shining mountain" at the center of Czestochowa. Pilgrims enter the chapel of the Black Madonna and once inside, walk briskly past the icon before dispersing. Although their devotion to the icon would lead most of them to deny it, their behaviour on this pilgrimage is in the spirit of the Japanese saying "the path is the goal in itself".

Medjugorje, Bosnia

The Hollywood actor Michael York said that he had been "spiritually moved" by the peacefulness of Medjugorje when he visited the Bosnian shrine in 1994. He had "felt totally energised" by the experience during the filming of *Gospa*, a film based on the events at Medjugorje.

The actor is just one of millions of pilgrims who have been to this small village in Bosnia, where six young people claim to have seen apparitions of the Gospa (Virgin Mary) daily since 24 June 1981. The Gospa has given them messages for all humankind, and has inspired a more peaceful way of life in the village. Tired from the hustle and bustle of their daily lives and hungry for a deeper relationship with God, many pilgrims respond whole-heartedly to the Gospa's call to repentance, conversion, prayer, penance, and fasting.

In recent years, Medjugorje has been an oasis of peace for people of all nationalities and religions throughout the civil war which engulfed most of the former Yugoslavia. (Rockets and bombs aimed at the church at Medjugorje mysteriously failed to explode.) Most people travel to Medjugorje during the busy summer months when high-factor sun cream, insect repellent, and a hat are all needed.

Many begin their spiritual journey by climbing Podbrdo, known today as the Hill of Apparitions, where the Gospa is said to have appeared to the teenagers for the first time. Most pilgrims also make the steep ascent of Mount Krizevac, which boasts a large cement cross, built by local people in 1933 and where many have reported seeing the sun "dance" and other mysterious light effects. Some make the journey barefoot in the heat of the day, as an act of penance and to meditate on the crucifixion.

The overall experience of Medjugorje, however, is centered on the parish Church of St James where the priests and visionaries encourage people to attend Mass and join in a collective offering of the Rosary. Pilgrims also speak of miracles at the shrine and of the "Medjugorje effect" – a state of euphoria, which follows an initial hostility to believing in the events at the shrine.

Kataragama, Sri Lanka

Hindus, Buddhists, Muslims, and Christians all make their sacred journey to Kataragama, the holiest place in Sri Lanka. Kataragama is associated with the Hindu war deity Skanda (called Murugan in South India). Buddhists come to visit a *dagoba* (mound) on a site where Buddha meditated. Muslims come to pray at a local mosque. Yet all gravitate to the Kataragama Devala, the principal shrine. In times gone by, the pilgrimage was a dangerous trek through the jungle; now many travel by public transport.

The biggest crowds gather in July/August for a festival celebrating the union of Skanda with his mistress, Valli Amma. This comes shortly after the Perahera, the enormous procession at the Temple of the Tooth in Kandy, where the Buddha's tooth is kept. Visitors approach through the Menik Ganga (Jewel River). They bathe in the river and buy offerings – lotuses and other flowers – from the near-by stalls. The principal shrine is a white stone building. It is said to contain Skanda's lance, but only priests may see this.

Whatever their religion, people who face difficulties, who have lost something or someone, often make vows. These vows are honoured during the festival, which lasts a fortnight. Some pilgrims skewer their tongues, cheeks, and other parts of their bodies. A few are hung up on hooks, which pierce their bodies. A demonstration of faith at Kataragama is shown in fire walking when devotees – old and young, male and female – walk across hot embers with no visible ill-effect. The crowds provide noisy accompaniment by blowing conch shells and beating drums.

At other times of the year most people simply worship, give alms, and circle the great *dagoba*. The festival finishes with a procession, ending in a water-cutting ceremony. A sacred sword is used to part the water with a circular sweep and clay pots are filled with water from this circle, to ensure a supply of water for the coming year.

Chimayó, United States

The name Chimayó comes from the Tewa Pueblo Indian *tsi mayoh*, meaning "obsidian chief". Chimayó valley, 30 miles north of Santa Fe, New Mexico, is watered by small rivers and springs. Prehistoric Indians chose to live in such valleys for their alluvial soil, trees, and water supply. Legend says that in the Tewa village in Chimayó there was a pool whose mud had healing properties. This pool dried to dampness when an obsidian chief (a giant volcano) was destroyed, spewing smoke and fire. The nearby sacred hill was believed to be an entrance to the underworld.

The Indians left the valley around 1400, and Spanish settlers arrived in 1692. They constructed several chapels in the valley, one on the site of the healing mud. This adobe church with its old painted wooden saints and altar carvings, is called El Santuario de Chimayó, and is the site of a major pilgrimage by Hispanics and Indians during Easter Holy Week.

Pilgrims walk from a hundred or more miles away across mountain and desert, although it is possible to drive. Some carry tall crosses, some photos of sick relatives, some nothing but water. On Good Friday, about two thousand pilgrims gather here. The rarely seen Penitentes, or Brotherhood of Jesus Christ, similar to fraternities in Sevilla, Spain, meet in private to suffer for Christ. A century ago, Penitente novices had to kiss the *santa tierra*, the "blessed earth" of Chimayó, as part of their initiation.

From underworld entrance to volcano to mud, Chimayó's history tells of power in the earth and of rebirth. Today, that power is accessed through the earth at the sacred spot in the church. From the sacristy a narrow, low door leads to a tiny room, with a dry earth "well" in the middle of

Miracles of healing
Small images of body parts hang at the shrine. Called *milagros* (miracles), each represents a prayer for healing of that part.

the floor. Pilgrims take away bags of soil from this hole, or rub the soil directly on their bodies. The priest is on hand to replenish the soil, whose healing powers are attested to by the crutches hanging nearby, the votive offerings, photographs, flowers, candles, and touching stories written in Spanish. The Holy Week penitents leave at Easter, the busiest time in the sanctuary's calendar, but other pilgrims visit Chimayó every day of the year to experience the healing, holy earth.

Resources

The general bibliography is followed by a chapter-by-chapter list of books cited in the text, plus addresses and recommended further reading for the sacred journeys featured in Part 1 (pp. 216–18).

For Part 2, addresses and further reading are given for the sacred places featured (pp. 218–20). Addresses of specialist pilgrimage and travel organizations follow (pp. 220–1), plus health and safety advice for travellers (p. 221). Addresses of specialist journals are given in the final section (p. 221).

All telephone/fax numbers are the international numbers, as dialled from the UK.

All addresses were correct at the time of going to press.

General bibliography

Abram, D et al *The Rough Guide to India* Rough Guides Ltd, London 1994

Adair, J *The Pilgrims' Way, Saints and Shrines in Britain and Ireland* BCA, London 1978

The Apocrypha from The Bible, New Revised Standard Version, OUP, Oxford 1995

Attar, Farid ud-din (trans Darbandi and Davis) *The Conference of the Birds* Penguin, London 1984

Barber, R *Pilgrimages* The Boydell Press, Suffolk 1991
— *The Penguin Guide to Mediaeval Europe* Penguin, London 1984

Baring-Gould, S and Fisher, J *The Lives of the British Saints* Honourable Society of Cymmrodorion, London 1913

Basho, Matsuo (trans Nobuyuki Yuasa) *The Narrow Road to the Deep North* Penguin, London 1966

Bhardwaj, S and Rinschede, G (eds) *Pilgrimage in World Religions* Dietrich Reimer Verlag, Berlin 1988

Blake, William (ed Stevenson W H) *Complete Poems* Longman, Harlow 1989

Brandenburger, C (ed) *The Traveller's Handbook* Wexas, London 1994

Brooke, R and P *Popular Religion in the Middle Ages* Thames & Hudson, London 1984

Buckley, J (ed) *Europe The Rough Guide* Rough Guides Ltd, London 1994

Bunyan, John *The Pilgrim's Progress* Penguin, London 1965

Carmichael, A (coll) *Carmina Gadelica* Vols 2 and 3, Floris Books, Edinburgh 1992

Chaucer, Geoffrey (trans Coghill, N) *The Canterbury Tales* Penguin, London 1977 (revised)

Cole, W O *Six Religions in the Twentieth Century* Stanley Thornes, Cheltenham 1984

Coleman, S and Elsner, J *Pilgrimage Past and Present* British Museum, London 1995

Collinson, C and Miller, C *Pilgrimages: Journeys from a Multi-Faith Community* Hodder & Stoughton, London 1990

Crumrine, N R and Morinis, A *Pilgrimage in Latin America* Greenwood Press, Westport, Connecticut and London 1991

Delaney, J J *A Woman Clothed with the Sun* Image Books, New York 1961

Donaldson, B A *The Wild Rue* Luzac & Co, London 1938

Durham, M S *Miracles of Mary* HarperCollins, London 1995

Eade, J and Sallnow, M (eds) *Contesting the Sacred* Routledge, London 1991

Fabri, Felix *The Book of the Wanderings of Felix Fabri* (2 vols) AMS, New York 1971

Farmer, D *The Oxford Dictionary of Saints* OUP, Oxford 1978

Fiennes, J *On Pilgrimage* Sinclair-Stevenson, London 1991

Finucane, R C *Miracles and Pilgrims* Dent, London 1977

Gardner, H (ed) *The Metaphysical Poets* Penguin, London 1976

Gascoigne, Bamber *The Christians* BCA, London 1977

Gurdjieff, G I *All and Everything 1st series: Beelzebub's Tales to his Grandson* Viking, London 1992

Harpur, James *The Atlas of Sacred Places* Marshall Editions, London 1994

Hearn, Lafcadio "Glimpses of Unfamiliar Japan" from *Writings from Japan* ed Francis King, Penguin, London 1984

Hilton, Walter (trans Sherley-Price, Leo) *The Ladder of Perfection* Penguin, London 1957

Housden, Roger *Retreat* Labyrinth, 1995
— *Travels through Sacred India* Thorsons, London 1996

Kumar, Satish *No Destination* Green Books, Bideford 1992

Moseley, C W R D (trans) *The Travels of Sir John Mandeville* Penguin, London 1983

Mother Julian of Norwich (trans Wolters, C) *Revelations of Divine Love* Penguin, London 1966

Karve, Irawati "On the Road: A Maharashtrian Pilgrimage" *Asian Studies* 1962, 30:1

Marsden, John *Sea-Road of the Saints: Celtic Holy Men in the Hebrides* Floris Books, Edinburgh 1995

Melrod, G (ed) *Destination: Israel* APA Publications, Hong Kong 1990

Palmer, Martin *Travels through Sacred China* Thorsons, London 1996

Punja, S *Great Monuments of India, Bhutan, Nepal, Pakistan and Sri Lanka* The Guidebook Company, Hong Kong 1994

Purcell, William *Pilgrim's England* Longman, Harlow 1981

St Vincent, David *Iran: a Travel Survival Kit* Lonely Planet, London & Sydney 1992

Seward, Desmond *The Dancing Sun* Fount/HarperCollins, London 1994

Shakespeare, W (ed Alexander, P) *The Complete Works of William Shakespeare* HarperCollins, New York and London 1994

Smart, Ninian *The World's Religions* CUP, Cambridge 1989

Sumption, Jonathan *Pilgrimage: an Image of Mediaeval Religion* Faber & Faber, London 1975

Teresa of Avila, *The Interior Castle* Fount Paperbacks, London 1995

Toibin, C *The Sign of the Cross* Jonathan Cape, London 1994

Toulson, S *The Celtic Year* Element, Shaftesbury 1993

Triggs, Tony D (trans) *The Book of Margery Kempe* Burns & Oates, Tunbridge Wells 1995

Walsh, A (ed) *Nothing Ventured: Disabled People Travel the World* Harrap Columbus, London 1991

Warner, Marina *Alone of all her Sex* Weidenfeld and Nicolson, London 1976

Watts, A *Myth and Ritual in Christianity* Thames & Hudson, London 1983

Westwood, Jennifer (ed) *The Atlas of Mysterious Places* Marshall Editions, London 1987

Wolters, Clifton (trans) *The Cloud of Unknowing* Penguin, London 1961

PART I: The Pilgrim's Path

CHAPTER 1

Gonzalez Balado, J L *The Story of Taizé* Mowbray, London 1994

Menuhin, Yehudi in Hobsbawm, Eric *The Age of Extremes: The Short Twentieth Century 1914–1991* Abacus, London 1995

Morinis, Alan *Sacred Journeys: The Anthropology of Pilgrimage* Greenwood Press, London 1993

MECCA pp. 22–3
Muslim World League
46 Goodge Street
London W1P 1SJ
Tel: 0171 636 7568/2080
Fax: 0171 637 5034

CANTERBURY pp. 26–7
Canterbury Tourist Information
34 St Margaret's Street
Canterbury, Kent CT1 2TG
Tel: 01227 766567

Director of Visits
Cathedral House,
11 The Precinct
Canterbury, Kent CT1 2EH
Tel: 01227 762862

Fax: 01227 762897
Group pilgrimages should be organized in advance.

du Boulay, Shirley *The Road to Canterbury: A Modern Pilgrimage* HarperCollins, London 1995

BENARES pp. 34–5
India Tourist Office
7 Cork St
London W1X 1BP
Tel: 0171 437 3677
Fax: 0171 494 1048

Open Gate Journeys *see Specialist Travel (p. 221)*

CHAPTER 2

Torkington, Sir R *Oldest Diary of English Travel* W J Loftie, 1833

GLASTONBURY pp. 42–3
West of England Pilgrimage Association
37 Devonshire Buildings, Bath
North Somerset BA2 4SU
Tel: 01225 446670
Summer pre-pilgrimage retreat, Christian pilgrimage, Orthodox service at Glastonbury Abbey.

Isle of Avalon Foundation
The Courtyard
2–4 High St, Glastonbury
Somerset BA6 9DU
Tel: 01458 833933
Fax: 01458 831324
Welcoming service for pilgrims of all beliefs.

Ashe, Geoffrey *The Glastonbury Tor Maze* Gothic Image, Glastonbury 1979

George, Jamie *Glastonbury, Maker of Myths* Gothic Image, Glastonbury 1982

CAMARGUE pp. 46–7
Office du Tourisme
BP 34-13732
Les Saintes-Maries-de-la-Mer
Provence, France
Tel: 00 33 490 97 82 55
Fax: 00 33 490 97 71 15

CHAPTER 3

Doughty, C *Passages from Arabia Deserta* Penguin, London 1956

O'Flaherty, W D (trans) *The Rig Veda: an Anthology* Penguin, London 1981

van Gennep, A *The Rites of Passage* Chicago and London 1960

Stokes, W *The Book of Lismore* Llanerch Publishers, Wales 1995

BLESSED KATERI TEKAKWITHA pp. 54–5
Shrine of North American Martyrs
Auriesville
NY 12016, USA

Fonda National Shrine of
Blessed Kateri Tekakwitha
Box 627, Fonda
NY 12068, USA

St Francis Xavier Mission
PO Box 70, Kahnawake
Quebec J0L 1B0, Canada
Tel: 001 514 632 6030
Fax: 001 514 632 5116

MOUNT ATHOS pp. 62–3
The Mount Athos Society
Ironstone Farmhouse
Milton, Banbury
Oxon OX15 4HH
Publishes Pilgrim's Guide to Mount Athos. Information on permits to visit Mount Athos.

CHAPTER 4

Campbell, J *The Masks of God* Penguin, London 1992

Hitching, F *The World Atlas of Mysteries* BCA, London 1978

Khayyam, O (trans Fitzgerald, E) *Rubaiyat* E Dobby, Orpington 1994

Perowne, S *Roman Mythology* Hamlyn, Middx 1969

Purce, J *The Mystic Spiral* Thames & Hudson, London 1974

SANTIAGO DE COMPOSTELA pp. 70–1
Confraternity of Saint James
First Floor, Talbot Yard
87 Borough High St
London SE1 1NH
Tel: 0171 403 4500
Fax: 0171 620 4356
Promotes the pilgrim routes through Europe and organizes lectures, walks, conferences.

Coelho, Paulo *The Pilgrimage* HarperCollins, New York and London 1995

MOUNT KAILASH pp. 78–9
Tibet Foundation
10 Bloomsbury Way
London WC1A 2SH
Tel: 0171 404 2889
Fax: 0171 404 2366
e-mail: getza@gn.apc.org
website: www.gn.apc.org/tibetgetza
Refers pilgrimage enquiries to people who have been to Mount Kailash.

Allen, Charles *A Mountain in Tibet* Futura, London 1983

Ramanujan, A K (trans) *Speaking of Siva* Penguin, London 1973

Schmidt, Jeremy *Himalayan Passage* The Mountaineers, Seattle 1991

Swift, Hugh *Trekking in Nepal, West Tibet and Bhutan* Hodder and Stoughton, London 1989

Taylor, Chris *Tibet Travel Survival Kit* 3rd edition Lonely Planet, London 1995

SHIKOKU pp. 82–3
Shikoku Reijjôkai
Anraku-ji, Hikino 26
Kamiita-chô
Tokushima-ken, Japan 771
Association of Pilgrimage Temples

Statler, Oliver *Japanese Pilgrimage* Picador, London 1984

CHAPTER 5

Aldersey, Laurence, *Trip to Jerusalem* 1581, Hakluyt's Voyages, Hakluyt Society, London

Cable, M and French, F *The Gobi Desert* Hodder & Stoughton, London 1942

Man, Myth and Magic (part work) Purnell, London 1970–1

Rt Rev Peter Nott *Bishop Peter's Pilgrimage* Canterbury Press, Norwich 1996

Somerville, C "A Canterbury Tale of Blisters and Bonhomie" *Daily Telegraph* 11.5.96

CROAGH PATRICK
pp. 90–1
Bord Fáilte
The Mall, Westport
County Mayo, Eire
Tel: 00353 9825711
Fax: 00353 9826709
Tourist information office

Eliot, T S "Burnt Norton" *Four Quartets* Faber, London 1996

Gallico, Paul *The Steadfast Man* Michael Joseph, London 1958

Harpur, James *The Monk's Dream* Anvil, London 1996

Hughes, Harry *Croagh Patrick* H Hughes, Westport, Eire 1991

ATOMIC MIRROR
pp. 98–9
Pamela Meidell (Director)
The Atomic Mirror
PO Box 220, Port Hueneme
CA 93044, USA

del Tredici, Robert *At Work in the Fields of the Bomb* Harper and Row, New York 1987

Gerzon, Joseph *With Hiroshima Eyes: Atomic War, Nuclear*

Extortion and Moral Imagination, New Society Publishers, Philadelphia, USA 1995

Poison Fire, Sacred Earth: Testimonies, Lectures, Conclusions World Uranium Hearing, Salzburg 1992

CHAPTER 6

Ballard, James *One and Two Halves to K2* Penguin, London 1996

Cohen, I *A Jewish Pilgrimage* Valentine Mitchell, London 1956

Dey, M *My Pilgrimage to Ajanta and Bagh* Thornton Butterworth, London 1925

Gallwey, W Timothy, *The Inner Game of Tennis* Pan Books, London 1986

Newby, Eric *A Short Walk in the Hindu Kush* Pan, London 1981

MOTHER MEERA
pp. 110 –11
Adilakshmi
General Information
Oberdorf 4a
65599 Dornburg–Thalheim
Germany
Tel: 0049 6436 91050
Information about Mother Meera from her secretary, travel advice, bookings.

Harvey, Andrew *Hidden Journey* Rider, London 1991

CHAPTER 7

Barker, Eileen *New Religious Movements* HMSO, London 1989

Bhardwaj, S M *Hindu Places of Pilgrimage in India* University of California Press, Berkeley 1973

Castaneda, C *The Teachings of Don Juan* Penguin, London 1990

Hobbes, Thomas (ed Gaskin J C A) *Leviathan* OUP, Oxford 1996

CHACO CANYON
pp. 118–19
New Mexico Dept of Tourism
491 Old Santa Fe Trail
Santa Fe, NM 87503, USA
Tel: 00 1 800 545 2070
Fax: 00 1 505 827 7402

SAINT CATHERINE'S MONASTERY pp. 122–3
Egyptian State Tourist Office
Egyptian House
170 Piccadilly
London W1V 9DD
Tel: 0171 493 5282
Fax: 0171 408 0295

Praill, David *Return to the Desert* Fount Paperbacks, London 1995

Wayne, S and Simonis, D *Egypt and the Sudan Travel Survival Kit* Lonely Planet, London 1994

CHAPTER 8

Aziz, Barbara Nimri "Personal Dimensions on the Sacred Journey: What Pilgrims Say" *Religious Studies* 1987, 23

Dowse, Ivor *The Pilgrim Shrines of England* Faith Press, London 1963
— *The Pilgrim Shrines of Scotland* Faith Press, London 1965

Mullikin, M A and Hotchkis, A *The Nine Sacred Mountains of China* Vetch & Lee Ltd, Hong Kong 1973

Turnbull, C "A Pilgrimage to India" *Natural History* 90:7

Turner, Victor "The Center Out There" *History of Religions*, 1973 12:3

Wood, Michael *The Smile of Murugan* Penguin, London 1996

X, Malcolm (ed Haley, A) *Autobiography of Malcolm X* Penguin, London 1970

SODO pp. 130–1
Office National de Tourisme
34 Avenue Marie-Jeanne
Port-au-Prince, Haiti
Tel: 00 509 230723

OUR LADY OF GUADALUPE pp. 134–5
Basilica de Nuestra Señora de Guadalupe
Plaza Hidalgo No 1
Colonia Gustavo Madero
Delegación Gustavo Madero
07050 México DF
Republica de Mexico
Tel: 00 52 5 577 6022

Elizondo, Virgilio *La Morenita: Evangeliser of the Americas* MACC Publications, San Antonio, Texas 1974

Fisher, John *Mexico: The Rough Guide* Harrap-Columbus, London 1989

Sylvest, Edwin *Nuestra Señora de Guadalupe: Mother of God, Mother of The Americas* Bridwell Library (Southern Methodist University), Dallas 1992

CHAPTER 9

Durkheim, E (trans Fields, K E) *Elementary Forms of the Religious Life* Free Press, US 1995

SAINTE ANNE DE BEAUPRÉ pp. 142–3
The Secretariat of the Basilica
Sainte-Anne-de-Beaupré
Quebec,
Canada G0A 3C0
Tel: 001 418 827 3781
Fax: 001 418 827 8227

ASSISI pp. 146–7
Basilica San Francesco
Piazza San Francesco
06081 Assisi, Umbria, Italy
Tel: 00 39 75 81 9001

Palmer, M, Nash, A & Hattingh, I *Faith and Nature* Century Hutchinson, London 1985

CHAPTER 10

Abbot Daniel, *The Pilgrimage of the Russian Abbot Daniel in the Holy Land 1106-1107* Eastern Orthodox

Browne, Thomas (ed Robbins, R) *Vulgar Errors* 1981

The Canon of the Easter Liturgy *Service Book of the Holy Orthodox Catholic Apostolic Church* (trans Hapgood, I) New York 1922

Rev Cobbold in Burne, C S and Jackson, G F *Shropshire Folk-Lore* London 1883

Smith, M *Nativities and Passions: Words for Transformation* Dartman, Longman and Todd, London 1996

THE EXTERNSTEINE
pp. 154–5
Haus der Begegnung
Muhlenstraße 2
31812 Bad Pyrmont, Germany
Tel: 00 49 5281 3240
Fax: 0049 5281 607499
Organizes pilgrimages

Dawkins, Peter *Zoence* Wigmore, London 1995

THE WESTERN WALL
pp. 162–3
Council of Christians and Jews
Drayton House
30 Gordon St
London WC1H 0AN
Tel: 0171 388 3322
Fax: 0171 388 3305
Organizes study tours to Israel.

Israel Tourist Office
18 Great Marlborough St
London W1V 1AF
Tel: 0171 434 3651
Fax: 0171 437 0527

Prag, Kay *Blue Guide Jerusalem* A&C Black, London 1989

HOME DANCE OF THE HOPI pp. 166–7
Hopi Cultural Center
PO Box 67
Second Mesa
AZ 86043, USA
Tel: 00 1 520 734 2401

CHAPTER 11

Bhardwaj, S M "Single Religion Shrines, Multireligion Pilgrimages" *National Geographic Journal of India* 33: 4 1987

Park Lowry, S *Familiar Mysteries: The Truth in Myth* OUP, Oxford 1982

Pratchett, T *Discworld* Corgi, London 1995

Schweitzer, A *The Mysticism of Paul the Apostle* (trans Montgomery, W) A & C Black 1931

Wu Ch'eng-ên *Monkey* (trans Waley, A) Unwin, London 1985

WAR GRAVES OF THE SOMME pp. 174–5
The Pilgrimage Department
Royal British Legion Village
Aylesford, Kent ME20 7NK
Tel: 01622 716 729/716182
Fax: 01622 715768
Organizes pilgrimages to war graves of British forces worldwide for adults and children.

Commonwealth War Graves Commission
Head Office, 2 Marlow Rd
Maidenhead, Berkshire SL6 7D
Tel: 01628 34221
Fax: 01628 771208
Maintains and records the graves and monuments to the missing of all Commonwealth casualties of both World Wars.

Binyon, Lawrence "For the Fallen" *Collected Poems* MacMillan, London 1931

McIntyre, Colin *Monuments of War* Robert Hale, London 1990

Only available from the author at 47 Smith St, London SW3 4EP.

Middlebrook, Martin & Mary *The Somme Battlefields* Penguin, London 1994

ARUNACHALA pp. 178–9
Indian Tourist Board
(*see Benares – Chapter 1*)

CHAPTER 12

Basho, M "The Records of a Travel-Worn Satchel" in Basho, M *The Narrow Road to the Deep North* (see General bibliography)

Brooke, C *From Alfred to Henry II 871–1272* Thomas Nelson, London 1967

Renard, J *In the Footsteps of Muhammad: understanding the Islamic experience* Paulist Press, Mahwah NJ 1992

Spencer, B and Gillen, F J *The Arunta* (2 vols) London 1926

SAINT WINIFRED'S WELL pp. 186–7
The Custodian
St Winifred's Well
New Rd, Holywell
Flintshire, Wales CH8 7PN
Tel: 01352 713054
Arranges bathing in the well.

Metcalf, Philip *The Life of Saint Winefride* Catholic Truth Society, London 1917

PART II:
Guide to Sacred Places

JOURNEYS TO SACRED LANDSCAPES

Iona, Scotland
West Highlands and Islands of Argyll Tourist Board Ltd
Albany St, Oban
Argyll PA34 4AR
Tel: 01631 63122
Fax: 01631 64273

Iona Community
The Abbey, Isle of Iona
Argyll PA76 6SN
Tel: 01681 700 404
Fax: 01681 700 460

Sheldrake, Philip *Living Between Worlds, Place and Journey in Celtic Spirituality* Darton, Longman and Todd, London 1995

Lough Derg, Eire
The Prior
St Patrick's Purgatory
Lough Derg, Pettigo
County Donegal
Tel: 00 353 726 1518
Organizes a programme of short retreats and pilgrimages.

Heaney, Seamus *Station Island* Faber & Faber, London 1984

Purcell, Deirde *On Lough Derg* Veritas, Dublin 1988

Mont-Saint-Michel, France
Office de Tourisme du Mont-St-Michel
BP4, 50116 Le Mont-St-Michel
Tel: 00 33 233 60 14 30
Fax: 00 33 233 60 06 75

Brocéliande, France
Syndicat d'Initiative à Paimpont
Abbey de Paimpont
35380 Paimpont
Tel: 00 33 299 07 84 23

Markale, Jean *Brocéliande* Berger-Lerrault, Paris 1984

Ovazza, Maud *Brocéliande* Editions Ouest-France 1994

Saunders, Corinne *The Forest of Medieval Romance* D S Brewer, Cambridge 1993

Ward, Greg *Brittany & Normandy Rough Guide* Rough Guides Ltd, London 1992

Lalibela, Ethiopia
Ethiopian Travel Agency
211B Clapham Rd
London SW9 0QH
Tel: 0171 738 3197
Fax: 0171 737 2345

Armanath Cave, Kashmir
For travel and safety information,
contact your travel agent.

Alexander, Caroline *The Way to
Xanadu* Phoenix, London 1994

Hemkund, India
Indian Tourist Board
(see Benares – Chapter 1)

Sri Pada, Sri Lanka
Sri Lanka Tourist Board
22 Regent St
London SW1Y 4QD
Tel: 0171 930 2627

Plaine du Nord, Haiti
Office National de Tourisme
34 Avenue Marie-Jeanne
Port-au-Prince
Tel: 00 509 230723

Señor de Qoyllor Rit'i, Peru
Peruvian Embassy
52 Sloane Street
London SW1X 9SP
Tel: 0171 235 6867

Sallnow, Michael J *Pilgrims of the
Andes: Regional Cults in Cusco*
Smithsonian Institute Press,
Washington DC 1987

JOURNEYS TO
SACRED TEMPLES

Westminster Abbey, England
Chapter Office
Westminster Abbey
20 Deans Yard
London SW1P 3PA
Tel: 0171 222 5152

Abbot, D, Betjeman, John et al
Westminster Abbey, Weidenfeld
and Nicolson, London 1972

Carpenter, E & Gentleman, D
Westminster Abbey Weidenfeld &
Nicholson, London 1987

Dean and Chapter of
Westminster *Westminster Abbey
Official Guide* Jarrold & Sons,
Norwich 1993

Gerber, Pat *The Search for the
Stone of Destiny* Canongate
Press, Edinburgh 1992

Stonehenge, England
English Heritage
Stonehenge, Nr Amesbury
Wilts SP4 7DE
Tel: 01980 625368
*For walkers: Ordnance Survey
Landranger Map, sheet 184*

Chartres Cathedral, France
Office de Tourisme
Place de la Cathédrale
28000 Chartres
Tel: 00 33 237 21 50 00
Fax: 00 33 237 21 51 91

Aachen, Germany
Tourist Office
Atrium Elisenbrunnen
Friedrich Wilhelm Platz, Aachen
Tel: 00 49 241 180 2960

Nidarosdomen, Norway
Tourist Information, Trondheim
Tel: 00 47 739 29400

St Peter's Basilica, Italy
Italian State Tourist Office
1 Princes St, London W1R 8AY
Tel: 0171 408 1254

Hagia Sophia, Turkey
Turkish Tourist and Information
Office
170 Piccadilly,
London W1V 9DD
Tel: 0171 629 7771
Fax: 0171491 0773

**The Dome of the Rock,
Jerusalem**
Israel Tourist Office
18 Great Marlborough St
London W1V 1AF
Tel: 0171 434 3651
Fax: 0171 437 0527

Landay, Jerry M *Dome of the
Rock: Three Faiths of Jerusalem*
Reader's Digest, London 1972

Haifa and Acre, Israel
The Bahá'í Faith Centre
27 Rutland Gate
London SW7 1DP
Tel: 0171 584 2566
Fax: 0171 584 9402
e-mail: nsa uk & cix. compulink.
co.uk

Mashad, Iran
2nd Floor, Mashad Ministry of
Culture and Islamic Guidance
Eslâmi Rd, Khiâbân-e-Bahâr,
Mashad

Loveday, H *Odyssey Illustrated
Guide to Iran* The Guidebook
Co Ltd, Hong Kong 1994

Amritsar, India
Indian Tourist Board
(see Benares – Chapter 1)

Dhanjal, Beryl *Amritsar*, Evans
Brothers Ltd, London 1994

Shwe Dagon, Myanmar
Nicholas Greenwood
36C Sisters Avenue
London SW11 5SQ
Tel/Fax: 0171 223 8987
*Organizer of small group tours for
those specifically interested in
Buddhism or Burmese Culture.*

Greenwood, N *Burma Then and
Now* Bradt Publications,
Chalfont St Peter 1995

Mahon, Yvette, *Burma: The
Alternative Guide* Burma Action
Group, London 1996

Angkor Wat, Cambodia
Dagens, Bruno *Angkor – Heart
of an Asian Empire* Thames and
Hudson, London 1995

**Wong Tai Sin Temple,
Hong Kong**
Lang, Graeme and Ragvald, Lars
*The Rise of a Refugee God: Hong
Kong's Wong Tai Sin* OUP, Hong
Kong 1993

Borobudur, Java
Embassy of the Republic of
Indonesia

Education and Culture Section
38 Grosvenor Square
London W1X 9AD
Tel: 0171 355 3866

JOURNEYS TO
SACRED SHRINES

Walsingham, England
Tourist Information Centre
Shirehall Museum
Common Place
Little Walsingham, Norfolk
Tel: 01328 820510

Knock, Eire
Our Lady's Shrine
Knock
County Mayo
Tel: 00 353 948 8100

Noyal-Pontivy, France
Office de Tourisme
61 Rue Général de Gaulle
56306 Pontivy, Morbihan
Tel: 00 33 297 25 04 10
Fax: 00 33 297 27 87 09

Rocamadour, France
Office de Tourisme de
     Rocamadour
46500 Rocamadour
Tel: 00 33 565 33 62 59
Fax: 00 33 565 33 74 14

Taizé, France
The Taizé Community
71250 Taizé, Cluny
Tel: 00 33 385 50 30 00
Fax: 00 33 385 50 30 16
*Publishes letters from Taizé, in
nine languages, bi-monthly.*

Lourdes, France
e-mail: nddlourdesámail.edi.fr

Handicapped Children's
     Pilgrimage Trust and Hosanna
     House Trust (HCPT)
100a High St, Banstead
Surrey SM7 2RB
Tel: 01737 353311
Fax: 01737 353008
*Holiday pilgrimages to Lourdes for
children and adults with disabilities
and special needs.*

Society of Our Lady of Lourdes
21A Soho Square
London W1V 6NR
Tel: 0171 434 9966
Fax: 0171 434 9965
Organizes the annual English National Pilgrimage for the Sick. Financial and other assistance to pilgrims from England and Wales who could not otherwise afford to go to Lourdes.

Lourdes Magazine
1 Avenue Monseigneur Theas
65100 Lourdes, France
Tel: 00 33 562 42 79 41
Monthly magazine, produced in English, French, Spanish, and Italian. Comprehensive information for pilgrims to Lourdes.

Marnham, Patrick *Lourdes A Modern Pilgrimage* Heinemann, London 1980

Guadalupe, Spain
Turismo
Plaza Mayor s/n 10140
Cáceres
Tel: 00 34 27 15 4128

Neillands, Rob *Walking through Spain* MacDonald/Queen Anne Press, London 1991

Sánchez, Maria Angeles *Itineraries Through Spain: Castile – La Mancha, Estremadura* Turespaña, Spain 1990

Fátima, Portugal
Catholic Friends of Fátima
37 Larches Road
Kidderminster
Worcs DY11 7AB
Tel: 01562 68886

Czestochowa, Poland
Center Czestochowa
al. NMP 65
Czestochowa
Tel: 00 48 34 24 13 60
Fax: 00 48 34 24 34 12

Medjugorje, Bosnia
Medjugorje Network
The Centre for Peace
The Cardinal Heenan Centre

326 High Rd, Ilford
Essex IG1 1QP
Tel: 0181 478 3068
Expert advice for pilgrims on safe travel to Medjugorje.

Kataragama, Sri Lanka
Sri Lanka Tourist Board (see *Sri Pada*, p. 219)

Wirz, P *Kataragama: The Holiest Place in Ceylon* Lake House, Colombo, Sri Lanka 1966

Chimayó, United States
(see *Chaco Canyon* – Chapter 7)

Kay, Elizabeth *Chimayó Valley Traditions* Ancient City Press, Santa Fe 1987

Specialist pilgrimage organizers

Worldwide, many groups organize pilgrimages around particular themes. To find out about such groups ask your local religious leader or organization, or read the specialist journals.

The following groups attract participants from many countries and faiths.

Across Trust
Bridge House
70/72 Bridge Rd
East Molesey, Surrey KT8 9HF
Tel: 0181 783 1355
Fax: 0181 783 1622
Organizes accompanied holidays for the disabled by "jumbulance" to destinations including Lourdes, Rome, and Knock.

Anglo–Israel Association
9 Bentinck St
London W1M 5RP
Tel: 0171 486 2300/935 9505
Fax: 0171 935 4690
Promotes understanding of Israel to the non-Jewish population in the UK. Organizes study tours to Israel.

The Fourth Order of Saint Francis, c/o Dr Trevor Riches
St Luke's Cottage,
57 Northend, Batheaston
Bath BA1 7EG
Tel: 01225 858883
Ecumenical Franciscan sanctuary. Organizes sacred journeys to UK, Eire, France, and Canada.

ICOREC
Manchester Metropolitan University
799 Wilmslow Rd
Manchester M20 2RR
Tel: 0161 434 0828
Fax: 0161 434 8374
Religious advisers to Alliance of Religions and Conservation, and WWF (UK). The Sacred Land project revives old pilgrimage routes in the UK.

Living Stones
c/o Dr Michael Prior, CM
St Mary's College
Strawberry Hill
Middlesex TW1 4SX
Tel: 0181 240 4000
Fax: 0181 240 4255
Promotes understanding between Christians in Britain and the Holy Land. Advises organizers of pilgrimages; runs its own pilgrimage programme.

Oikoten Community
175 Lipsestraat
3150 Tildonk, Belgium
Tel: 00 32 16 20 21 93
Fax: 00 32 16 20 19 57
Organizes pilgrimages; provides alternatives for Belgians in special youth care.

Pilgrim Adventure
120 Bromley Heath Rd
Downend, Bristol BS16 6JJ
Tel: 0117 958 6525
Ecumenical Christian organization that takes small groups on guided pilgrimages to remote parts of the UK and Eire.

The Pilgrims of Saint Francis
Mrs Pam Foster
49 Haughton Rd, Shifnal
Shropshire TF11 8DF

Tel: 01952 460694
Organizes annual international and national pilgrimages for groups of 20–25 people committed to sharing a 10-day journey on foot. Send a SAE with enquiries.

Pilgrims Way 1997
Andrew Davies, Administrator
12 The Close
Norwich NR1 4DH
Tel: 01603 219483
Fax: 01603 766032
Ecumenical Christian pilgrimage project honouring the traditions of St Columba and St Augustine. Promotes greater unity between churches. In 1997, pilgrims, some starting from Rome, walk along various UK routes to converge in Derry, Northern Ireland.

Vision Quest
The Sacred Trust
PO Box 603, Bath BA1 2ZU
Tel: 01225 852615
Fax: 01225 858961
Mystical and practical journeys of self knowledge.

Westminster Interfaith
82 The Avenue, Ealing
London W13 8LB
Tel: 0181 997 2858
Roman Catholic organizers of the annual London Pilgrimage of Faith for Peace, involving participants from Bahá'í, Buddhist, Christian, Hindu, Jain, Jewish, Muslim, Sikh, Unitarian, and Zoroastrian faiths.

Worldwide Fund for Nature (WWF) UK
Panda House, Weyside Park
Godalming, Surrey GU7 1XR
Tel: 01483 426444
Fax: 01483 426409
e-mail: http : //wwfed.king.ac.uk/
Works with religious organizations and schools in the UK.

Specialist travel

Cox & Kings Travel Ltd
4th Floor, Gordon House
10 Greencoat Place

London SW1P 1PH
Tel: 0171 873 5000
Fax: 0171 630 6038
Organizes tailor-made journeys for small groups/individuals to India, Bhutan, Tibet, Sri Lanka, and other destinations worldwide.

Gatekeeper Trust
The Secretary
Flat 3, Birdsall House
Birdsall, Malton
North Yorkshire YO17 9NR
Tel: 01994 768338
Organizes UK and international foot pilgrimages, with the aim of healing the earth and ourselves. Publishes Gatekeeper News *annually.*

Open Gate Journeys
PO Box 1892
Bath BA1 9YY
Tel: 01225 428557
Small parties twice yearly to sacred places in India.

Orientours Pilgrimages
Sovereign House
11/19 Ballards Lane, Finchley
London N3 1UX
Tel: 0181 346 9144
Fax: 0181 343 0579
Specializes in pilgrimages to St Catherine's Monastery and other destinations worldwide.

Pettitts Ltd
14 Lonsdale Gardens
Tunbridge Wells
Kent TN1 1NU
Tel: 01892 515966
Organizes tailor-made journeys to the Indian subcontinent for small parties. Provides information on personal safety.

Health and safety

When planning foreign travel always check the safety of the current political situation. In the UK, contact the Foreign Office; in other countries call the External Affairs department for travel advice.

Your doctor will advise you about necessary medications and vaccinations. National airlines may also operate travel clinics – ask your travel agent for details.

The Foreign Office Travel Advice Unit
Teletext: BBC 2
Ceefax: pages 546 upwards
e-mail: http://www.fco.gov.uk
Automated line: 0374 500 900
Individual help: 0171 238 4503
Latest information about political conditions and safety advice for over 120 countries.

British Airways Travel Clinics
Call 0171 439 9584 to find your local British Airways Travel Clinic, open to all travellers. Advice, immunization, emergency needle packs, water purifiers, mosquito protection.

Medical Advisory Service for Travellers (MASTA)
Tel: 0891 224100
Advises on health and immunization.

Specialist Journals

Caerdroia
The Journal of Mazes and Labyrinths
53 Thundersley Grove
Thundersley, Essex SS7 3EB
Tel: 01286 751915
Labyrinths/mazes in churches and cathedrals worldwide.

Herald House
The Christian Media Centre
Herald House
96 Dominion Rd, Worthing
West Sussex BN14 8JP
Tel: 01903 821082
Fax: 01903 821081

Pilgrim's Herald
The Rosses, Henbrook Lane
Brailes, Banbury
Oxon OX15 5BA
Tel: 01608 685 625
Earth energies, sacred sites, and pilgrimage.

Planet Talk
Lonely Planet Publications
The Barley Mow Centre
10 Barley Mow Passage
London W4 4PH
Tel: 0181 742 3161
Fax: 0181 742 2772
Free newsletter and latest information from returned travellers.

Resurgence
Ford House, Hartland
Bideford, Devon EX39 6EE
Tel: 01237 441293
Fax: 01273 441203
Subscriptions 01208 851304
International forum for ecological and spiritual thinking.

Source — the Holy Wells journal
Pen-y-Bont
Bont Newydd, St Asaph
Denbighshire LL17 0HH
Wales
Tel: 01745 584 814
Holy wells in the British Isles and overseas.

YogaLife
The Sivananda Yoga Centre
51 Felsham Rd
London SW15 1AZ
Tel: 0181 780 0160
Organizes the annual Sivananda Himalayan Yatra.

Photographic Credits
p. 2 Trip, A. Tovy; p. 9 Associated Press, Pavel Rahman; p. 11 Trip, J. Wakelin; p. 12 Lincoln Potter; p. 13 Magnum, S. Franklin; p. 15 Colorific, Wang Zhipang; p. 16 Images of India, Jan Knapik; p. 23 Magnum, Abbas; p. 27 Woodmansterne; p. 31 Dan Burn-Forti; p. 35 Robert Harding, Ross Greetham; p. 39 Christine Osborne; pp. 42–3 Janet & Colin Bord/ Fortean Picture Library; p. 45 Colorific, Raghubir Singh; p. 46 Derek Davies; p. 55 Dr James Preston; p. 59 Ann Parker; p. 63 Ancient Art & Architecture, Chris Hellier; p. 67 Tibet Image Bank, Robert Beer; p. 70 (top) Walter Lombaert (bottom) Magnum, Bruno Barbey; p. 74 Link Picture Library/India Images, Chandra Kishore Prasad; p. 78 Tibet Image Bank, Robert Beer; p. 82 Lincoln Potter; pp. 90–1 James Harpur; p. 93 Lincoln Potter; p. 95 Fitzwilliam Museum, Cambridge, UK; p. 99 Pamela Meidell; p. 107 Ann Parker; p. 110 Mother Meera; p. 117 Magnum, Josef Kondelka; p. 119 (left) Robert Harding (right) Charles Fletcher; pp. 122–3 Ancient Art & Architecture, Ronald Sheridan; p. 127 Trip, F. Good; pp. 130–1 Hutchison, J. Henderson; pp. 134–5 Hutchison, Libba Taylor; p.139 Trip, A. Bloomfield; p. 151 Magnum, H. Kubota; pp. 154–5 Images; p. 157 Robert Harding; p. 159 Magnum, Abbas; p. 162 (top) Roger Housden (bottom) Ancient Art & Architecture; p. 167 Camera Press, Ken Lambert; p. 175 Imperial War Museum, London, UK; pp. 178–9 Roger Housden; p. 183 Ann Parker; pp. 184–5 Topham Picture Point; pp. 186–7 Janet & Colin Bord/ Fortean Picture Library; p. 190 Trip, H. Rogers; pp. 196–7 John Martin; p. 209 Tristan Gray Hulse; p. 211 Simon Archer.

All artwork by Ann Savage except pp. 146–7 Mike Nicholson, and photo collages on pp. 18–19, 50–1, 86–7, 102–3, 114–15, and pp. 170–1 by James Mealing.

Index

ALSO PUBLISHED BY GAIA

For a complete list of titles published by Gaia Books, write to Gaia Books, 20 High Street, Stroud, Gloucestershire, GL5 1AS or telephone 01453 752985 Fax: 01453 752987
e mail: gaiabook@star.co.uk or www.bookshop.co.uk/gaiabooks

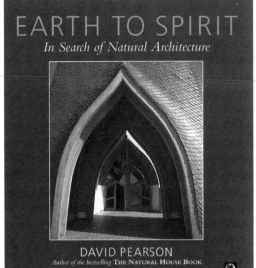

EARTH TO SPIRIT

In search of natural architecture

David Pearson

£11.99

ISBN 1 85675 046 9

Explores new architecture that
honours old traditions yet uplifts
them with current ideas.

ECOYOGA

Practice and meditations for
walking in beauty on the Earth

Henryk Skolimowski
£10.99 hardback

ISBN 1 85675 071 X

Learn how to be at peace with
yourself and with the world today
through simple exercises and
meditation techniques.

THE FENG SHUI HANDBOOK

How to create a healthier living
and working environment

Master Lam Kam Chuen
£12.99

ISBN 1 85675 047 7

Practical steps to improve the energy
flow in your home and work, and
harmonize with the life forces
around you.

BEYOND THE FOREST GARDEN

Robert A de J Hart
£8.99

ISBN 1 85675 037 X

Inspired by the insights of scientists,
artists, philosophers, and healers,
this work explains the significance
of Robert Hart's well known
Forest Garden.